This non-fictional, autobiographical,
account is dedicated to the loving memory of
Mrs. Doris Jeanette Kelley-Wessel
who has
our unending deepest respect and admiration.

Shopping Cart Filled with
LOVE

Laurel & Nick Salupo

Library of Congress Control Number:		2012905769
ISBN:	Hardcover	978-1-4691-9190-4
	Softcover	978-1-4691-9189-8
	Ebook	978-1-4691-9191-1

This book was printed in the United States of America.

To order additional copies of this book, contact:
Xlibris Corporation
1-888-795-4274
www.Xlibris.com
Orders@Xlibris.com
111782

CONTENTS

Reviews

There were times while I was reading this book that I had to stop and wipe the tears from my glasses that fell from my eyes so that I could continue reading.
— Ken Cash, CEO, Seekers Publishing, Inc.

This is a really good book and a heartwarming read.
— Joe Eschelman, Inter-office Communications Engineer.

I really admired Laurel's father in the book. He was a real inspiration to me because he had the courage to make drastic life style altering changes in his life against some pretty tough odds.
— Jim Hedrick, Student, Tri-C West.

I fall in love all over again every time I read and re-read this book.
— N. Salupo-Teacher, Author, Editor.

This book is a story of courageous triumph over adversity.
— Gerry Nemeth, Executive Sessions Director, Tri-C Metro.

This book tells an emotionally driven story that is easily relatable. The book draws you in and gives readers a sense of attachment to the characters. At times I felt like the people in the book were part of my own family.
— Jim Henderson, Tri-C Student.

This literary venture covered the whole gamut of my emotional arsenal. There are chapters in the book that I found to be sad, happy, and laugh out loud hilarious. The two main characters are very lucky to have each other in their lives.
— Dave Coulter, International Entrepreneur.

Acknowledgments

This work is a combination of hard work, grit, creative inspiration, and a lot of help from friends and relatives who have encouraged, motivated, and kept inspiring us to forge ahead at the most difficult times in the process. This book is essentially a tribute to a special lady who touched many lives. It is also meant to be a special recognition piece to all the mothers raising children and sacrificing every day to see that their children are safe, well nurtured, and moving along well on the difficult road of maturity. It is also a special homage to a wonderful woman and her daughter, who together weathered all of the hardships through childhood, young adulthood, and the adult years of a life filled with turmoil and sometimes chaos. Mrs. Doris Wessel had eight children that she loved and cared for to the best of her ability. This novel is a focused glimpse of her life through the eyes of one of her children.

The book is a close look at the problems that young girls, young women, and grown women go through day in and day out throughout the journey of life and the many bumps in the road women face at the different stages of their lives.

Also, a special thanks to Mr. Ken Cash, our dear friend and colleague, whose support, encouragement, helpful advice, and keen editorial eye helped us bring this project to completion. On many occasions throughout the book, the writers and editors have intentionally compromised some of the basic rules of grammar in order to tell a more entertaining story.

Laurel Salupo also sends out a special vote of thanks to her husband who spent many hours fighting the fatigue of the daily routine of earning a living and then coming home to negotiate through the writing process with his wife to make this book happen. Finally, to all the daughters and sons who have had a special relationship with their mom, like ours, and find them to be their best friends, our blessings go out to you. We would love to hear from our readers. Please e-mail us at n.salupo2@sbcglobal.net. May God bless all who venture through these pages and a special spiritual thanks to Saint Jude for being our guardian angel throughout this process.

Chapter 1

Womanhood and Recess

I grew up in the "South Side," as we called it, in Cleveland. You may have heard of this neighborhood by its original name—Tremont where they filmed the "Deer Hunter" and the "Christmas Story," the movies that had the famous leg lamp, which is now a neighborhood landmark that shines brightly every year throughout the holiday season. I can remember as a family how we watched them film the "Deer Hunter." I recall how the streets were blocked off and there were lots of film crews crowding up our city streets with lights, cameras, and movie trailers all over our neighborhood.

Remembering back to my childhood, at that time, it felt like "Hollywood" became a part of the "South Side," if only for a short time. I can also recall how the film crew would rope off certain parts of the streets. There were crowds of people bunched together near the ropes as they watched how Robert De Niro walked up and down Starkweather and finally into a phone booth. It seemed like it was twenty times before the director said they got the scene right.

I watched the people from the neighborhood get excited as they watched a film being made and how all the women were "Star-Struck" over Robert De Niro. This helped to put the neighborhood on the map. Looking back now, I can see how growing up in a blue-collar, working-class, mostly poor, neighborhood, was something special.

It is easy to get to downtown Cleveland and it is accessible to the freeways that can get you to the West or East side of town. Also, the "South Side," as we called it, had a church of every kind of denomination one could think of on just about every corner. I found the sounds of ringing church bells very comforting. We also had people of different races and nationalities who spoke many different languages. There were also people of many different faiths in our neighborhood, but the best part of our neighborhood, as far as the kids were concerned, was Lincoln Park on West Fourteenth Street. It is named after our most famous president and was used by the Northern troops to camp out and rest while on their way to the battle of Gettysburg. The park had plenty of room for us kids to play on the playground and there was a big swimming pool in the middle of the park to go and cool off from the hot summer heat.

Many young teenagers had gotten a small round dot tattooed on their hand to show a sign that you grew up on the "South Side." I had never gotten one on my hand.

It was very true that the many surrounding areas around Cleveland never knew where our dot on the map was. People would often confuse us with "Ohio City," which is also a near Westside neighborhood similar to ours.

The "South Side," as we knew it, is now trendy "Tremont" after the yuppies took it over. It is a good thing because the "South Side" had moved in a good direction and away from all the really bad problems we once had, and now no one needs a tattoo on their hand to show where they came from. There are now fine dining, art galleries, and coffee houses throughout the neighborhood. To watch the transformation happen has been a thrill for all of us original "South Siders," and at times of special events one could get a free show like when the air show came to town, we could hear the roar of the planes hovering over our neighborhood. And when a sporting event happened downtown, one could get to see a free fireworks display that would light up the skies.

It was a warm September day in Tremont and all of the second graders were out running and playing during recess. While the children cut loose, there were the sounds of laughter filling up the school yard.

But there was always someone in a class who thought she knew everything about everything and I was hoping to set her straight. "Miss Know It All," was going to have a new baby added to her family. She came running over to me with a braggish look on her face and said, "Laurel, I want you to know that we are having a new baby come to our house and you know what?"

She stopped talking for a moment, ripped open a pack of gum, and shoved six pieces into her big mouth.

"I know that you don't know that babies came out of a woman's private part." Then "Miss Know It All" blew a large bubble, just to agitate me further.

I could not believe what she just said! "Oh, no way," I defiantly spoke up, "You are wrong. Don't you know anything? Babies come out of a woman's betty button."

(I was also convinced at that time that boys had belly buttons and girls had Betty buttons.)

"No way! Are you that dumb?" my classmate said while laughing and taunting me. "Ask your mommy because she will tell you the babies come out of a woman's privates." At that moment my private started to hurt from the thought of a baby forcing its way out from down below.

All I could do was think, no way; she was somehow distorted in her thinking and I thought she could not be right on everything, could she? Well, "Miss Know It All," was finally wrong and I was convinced about that. I only lived a block away from my Tremont elementary school.

I wanted to prove her wrong right then and there but thought against running home to prove my point.

I decided that I would ask my mommy and she would know too that babies come out of a Betty button. I held out my hand and said, "I will bet you fifty-cents and have it ready on Monday." We shook hands and off she went giggling to herself. The need to know the answer to my dilemma was beginning to overwhelm me.

All weekend I had a hard time shaking it from my mind and when I would have to go pee, I would look down and say to myself, "There is no way that could possibly be true." I knew that with Mom, I was safe from ridicule and that she would not laugh when I asked. The only problem was when to ask Mom because I did not want to ask when someone may overhear me. I was on the alert waiting for a chance to ask and then all of a sudden my opportunity presented itself. Saturday afternoon had come and we were putting our dirty clothes into the two shopping carts for our weekend walk to the Laundromat.

I decided that that was the time because I really needed to know the truth and according to the old saying, "The truth that will set you free." And I hoped that I finally knew the truth about the "betty buttons." The sun had warmed the air, but it was not too hot or miserable for a walk. It was just right. Mom loved days like that because it was easy to walk and pull our shopping carts filled with laundry.

Mommy looked over at me and said, "Looks like you got something on your mind."

Mom knew me well; now was the time. I looked up at Mom and came up with the courage to ask. "Mommy how do women have babies? I bet a classmate of mine and she said babies come out of a woman's private part. Mommy can you believe that? I got fifty-cents on the line. Please, please tell me the truth."

Mom stopped pulling the shopping cart, looked at me, and paused for a moment, thinking over her words carefully and gathered her thoughts so she could respond in the right way. "Well, that is a lot of change to put on a bet."

"I know, Mom, but I got twenty cents at home in my pennies box," I said with confidence. I knew that I was right on this one and could not wait to go to school on Monday. And clear the air and set her straight.

"Well, Laurel, it is true babies do come out of a women's private part and the real name is called a vagina."

"Mom!" I cried out in disbelief and shock. "A vagina? What's a vagina?"

"Oh, Mom," I stopped. I was in a daze. I felt paralyzed as I held onto my vagina. "How can that be Mom? How does it happen?" I cried out begging to know more and trying to get a better understanding of all of this.

"Laurel, you are in second grade. We have time for that talk later," Mom said kindly and pulled her shopping cart straight ahead.

"Mom, wait! What talk?" I said, as my head started to spin with confusion.

Mom pulled her cart to a sudden stop and kneeled down on one knee so she could look me in the eyes and very patiently said, "You worry about being a little girl and in time we will have more talks on these types of issues."

Mommy assured me that I had a lot of time to worry about things of that nature. Mom very calmly reached into her purse and pulled out a fifty-cent piece and handed it to me. She never said a word of reproach as together we walked on to the laundry mat pulling our shopping carts behind us with Mom being fifty-cents less richer and I being a half a dollar wiser.

"Miss Know It All" was right again, but after Mom cleared it up for me, I knew the real name to the private part——vagina——and I bet she didn't. This simple learning lesson was only the first of many that I have learned over the years and I find that I am still learning. What a joy "life" can be at times with a mom who could help me through the most perplexing times! Not only in the debate as to the origin of babies, but also real-life traumas and bumps on the road that were to follow.

Chapter 2

New Arrival

The month of May was here at last and Mommy was in the hospital. She had our new baby sister, Veronica, and Mother's day was approaching. Back in the old days, women stayed in the hospital longer after having a baby than they do today. I was missing Mom so badly and agitated Daddy by asking him all the time, "Is Mommy coming home today?" Daddy looking tired reluctantly would say, "Soon they both will be back home. Laurel, we all miss them." I was not so sure that I missed the baby, but I missed my mommy and wanted her home desperately.

Taking over Mom's role around the house was not easy for Dad. My daddy looked a little out of place keeping the home together. Dad would say all the time, "Is this how Mommy does this?" I know that Dad tried hard to keep things up around the house and we all tried as well to help, but no matter how hard we worked, things were not the same, to the way Mommy ran the home. To me the days seemed long and lost without Mom around the house. Throughout the days that Mom was not home, I felt empty because I would have a question to ask Mom and it had to wait until we went to the hospital for our daily visit.

My father was a quiet man, tall and handsome, hard working, and very respectable toward others. Dad taught us to take nothing for granted and treat others the way you would like to be treated. Each one of his children loved and admired his strength to do a job right.

Not all Dads had a special name for their wives, but my father had a pet name for Mom. My dad called Mom, "Miss America." I know that many couples would call their partners "my old man," or "my old lady," or "my pain in the ass," but Mom and Dad never referred to each other in a disrespectful way. Every morning before walking out the door for work, Dad would say, "See you, Miss America," and give her a little peck on the cheek. I never saw my parents show a lot of affection in front of us, but we knew that they loved each other. The love was in their eyes when they looked at each other and when Dad would stop after work, at the corner store, just to bring Mom home her favorite chocolate bars.

It was time to go visit Mom again. Anxiously I ran ahead jumping into the back of the station wagon waiting for my twin brother Billy and Dad to get in, for our drive to the hospital to visit Mom. Once we got to the hospital and saw Mom in her room, I was so excited when I saw Mom that I would talk my head off and forget the questions that I wanted her to answer.

Mommy would smile and listen to me while I chatted on and on. Dad quietly held the new baby in his arms and Billy kept himself busy by playing with his army men that he had brought along in an old cigar box. I hated the hospital rules when it was announced over a loud speaker that visiting hours would be coming to an end.

We were the last to leave out of Mom's room because I held everyone back by not wanting to leave. I fought with endless determination, but I got nowhere. I thought it was not fair; I missed my mom and I wanted her back home now and I no longer wanted her cooped up in this hospital.

Our visit with Mom always went too fast, and in the end I would start pouting and crying, not wanting to leave Mommy. Mom looking sad would remind me, "I am coming home real soon and remember to be a good girl for your daddy." After every visit, Mom would stand by the window in her hospital gown holding Veronica and waving at us good-bye. I wanted to run up to her room and drag her home, but I was still not sure about the new baby or this *big-sister* business. With tears in my eyes and trying to catch my breath, I would keep waving back at Mom. My feet were like glue and I was too stubborn to move. I knew that I gave Dad a hard time, and he was at a loss not knowing what to do. Daddy was doing his best to calm me down holding my hand as we walked to the parking garage.

While I climbed into the back seat, still rubbing my red eyes, Dad stood near the back door looking at me and said, "Only one more day and Mom and our new baby will be back home." I loved it when Dad had a playful grin on his face, and knew that he was thinking over his next words. "How about we all put together a 'Welcome Home' party for Mom?" My eyes dried up fast and got real big and my mind started racing with ideas for the party.

"Daddy, that's a great idea," I said.

Daddy closed the back door and got in the front seat looking pleased that I would not be crying all the way back home. On the drive home, I continued to think of different ideas on how to make Mom's party special.

For as long as I can remember I enjoyed every holiday and knew I needed to get to work to make Mom's party a success. Once we were home I ran into my bedroom and pulled out my box of crayons and papers. I was busy making 'Welcome Home' signs and a Mother's day card with bright colored words on it saying, "I love you, miss you, and mommy you are the best mommy in the whole world." It had a heart on the front and flowers lined the border inside.

Daddy and Billy signed the card and I made my signature bigger than theirs to show Mommy that I missed her more.

After I had finished with the signs and the card, I realized that I needed a card that recognized Mom for having a new baby.

I was feeling guilty for not making a card for Mommy for having a baby; well I guess it was the honorable thing to do; so I went to work. I pulled out another sheet of paper and I worked on it a little, changing the words around until I was satisfied with the new card. It read, "mommy and baby we love you," and I drew a picture of Mom holding the baby with me right next to her, and put Daddy and Billy on the other side.

Dad, with our help, worked on getting the house in shape for Mom's 'Welcome Home' party.

The next day was Mom's big return home. Dad had ordered out for pizza and together we made a chocolate cake for Mom. Dad taped the 'Welcome Home' signs up and I put the cards I made on the table next to the balloons and flowers that Daddy had picked up at the drugstore. Daddy sized up the house looking happy with how it looked and said, "All we need is Miss America and our new baby girl." I felt like I was dying of anticipation of having Mommy back home. I just couldn't wait another minute. Daddy got us ready and together Billy and I raced to the station wagon being filled up with delight with finally having Mommy back home. I thought I was going to burst with excitement and joy.

Once we were in the car driving, Daddy said, "Mommy is going to love the 'Welcome Home' party, but do not tell her. Let it be a surprise."

"OK, Daddy," Billy and I said at the same time laughing. It was a pretty day in May and looking out the car window, the sky was clear blue with very little clouds. The weather seemed to fit the mood we all were in. I wanted to reach my hands up to the heavens and thank anyone that would listen, and say, "My mommy is coming home." Daddy looking back at me smiled and was relieved that I would not be fussy this time around.

I held it in not telling Mommy about the party. When Daddy opened up the front door Mommy walked in the front door looking around at the festive decorations, food, and cake. Mom's face was beaming with joy.

"Oh My! Thank you. Looks like everyone was busy planning a party for me?"

"Yes, Mom we all missed you and wanted to do something special for you," I said proudly.

"Well, thank you, I missed everyone too, and the place looks great, the food smells good. Let's eat." I followed Mom into the bedroom and watched Mom place Veronica down on the middle of the bed. I stopped dead in my tracks and starred at my new baby sister. Mom had the baby dressed in a pink sweater set. My baby sister looked to be the most beautiful, flawless, baby in the world. Veronica had a round small face, little nose, and big bright green eyes. Veronica was stretching her little fingers out to me saying, "Hi, big sister, here I am." I was afraid to touch her but could not move from her side because I was fascinated with this new life before me.

Mom put down the diaper bag and said, "You can touch her, but be careful for she is an infant." Reaching out I put my finger into my baby sister's hand. At that moment I fell in love right there and loved the idea of being a big sister. Billy ran over looking at us holding an army man in his hand. Billy placed it on the bed in a painstaking manner next to the baby. He kept looking at Veronica too with his mouth wide open in awe.

"Billy," Mom said, "It's OK, you can touch her." Billy being hesitant and not too sure said, "No way, she is too little."

We both stood next to the bed and watched and marveled at our new arrival to our family, frozen in place to the new wonder of new life before our eyes. Mommy standing near us the whole time looking pleased said, "I am going to need both of your help." Hearing Mom's words made my day happier than ever. I hugged Mommy. At last Mom was back home, and with my new baby sister.

Chapter 3

Unexpected Visitor

It was an uneventful Saturday until we heard Mom's startled voice, and Sheba ran to the back door growling and bearing her fangs. Until then it had been a typical Saturday. Dad had been sitting in his chair watching college football, and Billy, Veronica, and I had been outside playing in the backyard for most of the afternoon. Mom called us in, and together we all sat down and had eaten dinner. After we finished, Dad went into the front living room to take a nap. The three of us were sitting on the floor watching television when it happened.

Looking back now, Mom thinks it all happened to our home, for one reason. We had a rope tied around our gate because the fence latch was broken and Dad had not gotten around to replacing it. Or, when something happens there may not be any rhyme or reason behind the why. Mom always said, "It's how one handles a situation that comes your way that really counts," and Mom and Dad handled this stroke of bad luck really well. So, our Saturday evening turned into anything but typical.

Once we heard Mom's startled voice and hearing Sheba dash quickly to the back door growling, we knew where to find Mom since she liked to sit out back at the screened-in porch after dinner. Billy shot me a look and together the three of us almost ran each other over to get to the back door.

Sheba had her hair up on her back pawing frantically on the door to get out. Billy looked over at us, not sure what we would find once he opened the door. When Billy finally opened the door and Sheba darted out, I stopped frozen in fear. Right in front of us was a deranged woman with glaring eyes and wild, frizzy hair. She had a Vietnam army helmet on her head. She wore an army coat, and under the coat, a hospital gown. When I looked down, I saw that she had on old blue jeans and wore boots that looked a size too big. She looked hot in her heavy army coat and her arms were moving around in a nervous nature. This was the first time in my life where I actually felt a bone-chilling fear take hold of me.

Mom quickly grabbed Sheba's collar and pulled her back with all of her might to her side. Mom looking back at us calmly said, "All of you get back inside the house right now." Billy, Veronica, and I did move a half step back but by the doorway holding the door halfway open. Veronica was holding onto my hand so hard I thought she was going to break my hand. I could feel my little sister's hand tremble, or maybe it was my own hand that would not stop shaking. Mom then looked at the woman and said, "I am sorry, but your mom is not here. You have the wrong house."

The woman's eyes glared at Mom and she said loudly, "No, go get Mom. Tell her I am home. Go get Mom now."

That is when Sheba broke free from Mom's hold on her. Sheba jumped up on the intruder and knocked her down. Next, it looked like Sheba was going right for her throat. Mom moved quickly and took hold of Sheba's collar and pulled her off the woman while backing up to the door dragging Sheba in and locking the door behind her. Billy stood paralyzed in fear, looked out of the door window, and yelled, "She is still lying on the back porch floor." By now we were all crying and scared.

Mom spoke fast and said, "Go wake up Dad and tell him to call the police." Mom ran through the house and locked the front door while we ran over to Dad and shook him. I yelled, "Daddy, Daddy, get up! There is a crazy lady outside on the back porch and Sheba almost killed her. Mom needs you to call the police." Dad tossed and turned over looking at us like we were playing. While we were trying to get Dad up, Mom was busy closing windows and locking them. Mom scurried into the room looking over at Dad. Mom sounded worried and pointed to the window and said, "Look out the front window." Daddy jumped up almost falling over his two feet and went to the front window, looked out, and said, "Oh, my god!"

Then he grabbed the phone and called the police and told them that there was a deranged lady outside our home.

My father was telling them that she looked mentally ill, was wearing a hospital gown under an army coat, and she had an army helmet on her head.

"We need the police at our home now. We have children at home and we are worried for their safety," he explained.

I watched as Dad put the phone down, and that is when a rock came right through our front window. Glass shattered onto the floor and the woman starting yelling "Go, get my mom now!" Dad reached for the phone again, called the police a second time, and explained what had happened. Mom came over to us and said to us children, "Go upstairs and wait." Together the three of us all took off running up the stairs, two stairs at a time almost knocking each other over as we went. Once we were upstairs, we all looked worried and I felt sick. I hoped that the police would soon be at our home. Outside we could hear the woman's swearing and talking to herself. Dad and Mom came up and they both saw how frightened we were.

Dad picked up Veronica, holding her close, as she was sobbing so hard that she could not stop. Veronica said what we all were thinking, "Daddy is that crazy lady going to kill us?" All of us were looking nervous while we all sat on our parents' big bed trying to comfort each other. Downstairs, we could hear Sheba, pacing and growling following the woman's footsteps outside.

Dad said, "No, she is not going to hurt us. Sheba will stop her and the police are on their way to take her away and get her help."

Mom looked at each one of us and said, "We need to pray that God will protect us and our home and that the woman outside our home will calm down and do no more damage to our house." Together we all prayed hard, "Please God, protect us and our home."

Then Mom said, "We need to pray for her too that she has a mom and family out there somewhere and that she gets the help she needs to get well."

Daddy sat Veronica down onto the bed; she was calmer now and Dad got up and went to look out of the window, as we were all there right behind him looking out of the window. The woman had gone to our next door neighbor's house and pounded on Mr. Frank's door. Frank opened his door and stepped out, trying to calm her down. But it did not work. She yelled something at him that we could not make out and turned and walked down his steps rambling and mumbling incoherently to herself. Now she began pacing around and at times walking in circles in the street. The woman held up traffic and we could hear people yelling, "Get out of the way. Are you trying to get killed?" The sounds of car horns were going off as she looked up and down the street taking her time to move out of the traffic's way.

There were long periods of time when she got quiet and stood in front of our gate playing with the rope, putting it on and off our fence.

Dad said, "At least the rope is keeping her busy and calm." Dad looked down at his watch and said, "What is taking the police so long?" Dad called again and they said that being a Saturday evening, they were busy and running behind on calls. My father said in a firm voice, "I am with children at home. You need to come now. We have waited long enough. You must get here as soon as you can. You don't understand. We are in danger!" He placed the phone back down. Dad was doing his best to maintain his composure for us, but we could all tell he was near the end of his rope.

Together we sat back, praying on my parents' big bed that the police would come, and they finally showed up. We all jumped up in joy to see the police car. By now the woman had calmed down and was still playing with our rope on our front gate. The policeman had to pull her away from our gat, and then put handcuffs on her. She kept yelling when the police placed her into the back of the police car. "My mother is in the house. Go get her. I must see my mother! Please get my mother for me!" She kept on yelling to herself when the police slammed the door. She placed her face up against the back window and cried.

It was a very sad and scary time for us. I started to feel very sorry for her. I guess she really did need her mother now more than ever.

As a family we all walked down the stairs happy that she would soon get the help she needed and finally would be leaving our home and hoping that she would never return. The policeman told my dad that she had walked out of the hospital she was suffering from schizophrenia, and could be violent and aggressive at times.

"Well," Dad said, "We all saw that first hand." Dad pulled out his hand and thanked the policeman for finally getting to our home and resolving our problem.

The policeman apologized for taking so long and explained that after the last lay off patrolmen, they just could not respond to all the calls as fast as they needed to. Looking back on it now, it seems that once we started to pray, she calmed down a little and kept busy playing with our gate.

Dad was pleased that only one window had gotten broken. Dad got out a board and temporarily fixed the window to keep the cold out and told Mom that he would fix both the window and the gate first thing tomorrow morning. Mom and Dad could tell we were still worked up and nervous. Mom reassured us, "She is going to the hospital and will get the help she needs. And she will not be coming back to our home ever again." We listened as Mom said, "She was not herself and was very confused." We all needed to hear those comforting and reassuring words that we would now be safe. Veronica and I jumped up on our daddy's lap, feeling his safe strong arms around us. Billy sat next to Mom and said, "Look at Sheba still at the door protecting our house. She will not let anyone into our home."

We all started laughing and got up to let Sheba out to check the yard. Sheba had her nose down to the ground checking out everything, even the back porch. She sniffed and whined and growled at all the spots where this poor woman had been. Afterwards we all walked back in and Sheba lay down next to Dad's chair. Dad patted her, telling her, "Good Dog."

Together we all sat in the living room and watched a movie. Mom brought in popcorn saying, "This is one Saturday we will never forget." Looking around at my family it was nice to see us get back to a normal Saturday night.

It also really made me appreciate my mom even more after seeing this woman's need for her mother's love and comfort, but unfortunately, not being able to get it. That was not to say that we would all be crowded into Mom and Dad's big bed when it was time to go to sleep because our imaginations would be running wild that night.

Chapter 4

"The Miracle"

What Mom has not felt overwhelmed at times in her life? Raising children is a lifelong responsibility and is never an easy journey. The job of motherhood is now somewhat being recognized today for the difficult task that it has always been. I have never seen Mom get too worked up about things; and she was, for the most part, even-tempered in spite of the fact that life got awful complicated at times. She always had the belief in the Lord Jesus and prayed every night. I would watch Mom praying. Mom never knew that I would see her in her room holding the rosary beads in her hands moving her lips in whispers of reverence and quietly praying for all of us. Mom always kept her faith front and center, and she did her best in the most impossible situations. My mom not only did everything within her power, but she did it with a giving and loving heart and always put her personal needs secondary to her family.

Unfortunately, there were many times that Dad would get laid off from construction work; hard times would overshadow our family and the bills would come piling in. Dad would pick up side jobs because he was one that would never sit still. He was always on the go doing his best to provide for his family and our basic needs. Dad would put his ego aside and work at these small menial and humble jobs that would help us get by until Dad got called back to work.

Mom would often remind us and say, "Tell God our family needs and He will answer," and together as a family we hoped and prayed that the call would come in and that there was a job out there for Dad that would last for months that would keep our household going. Looking back, there were days when times got hard and the need to feed the family and having children to provide for made it next to impossible.

Fortunately, Mom seemed to know how to stretch a dollar. Mom would fix food in different ways that would fill the family up. I can remember we ate soup in every possible way one could think of. We even had, believe it or not, her famous "Hot Dog Soup." Somehow she even made that seem liked a fancy meal. Of course any meal from those loving and caring hands was always special. Mom may have burned a few meals and would never have a guest appearance on the cooking channel, but she did put her heart in every meal. However, there were times we would have to go to the free food line because the shelves at home were getting bare. After all, you do need hot dogs if you are going to make "Hot Dog Soup."

Together as a family we would go to the food distribution centers and get a box of food. There was this one item we received every time and we called it "Reagan Cheese." The eighties were a hard time for the working class in the United States. The fact that President Reagan was in office at the time, made our family give his name to the one food item that was always in the free food box.

This may offend some Republicans out there, but if a few Republicans actually lived in our neighborhood or waited with us in the food lines, instead of the lines at Heinen's, they may understand the struggle of the working man of that time. At first we loved the long hunk of yellow brick cheese. But after eating cheese and more cheese we could not even bear to look at "Reagan Cheese," no matter how hungry we were. As a family we ate cheese sandwiches, cheese and potatoes, cheese soup, and melted cheese on noodles. Often, when we were really hungry, we would cut off hunks of fattening yellow cheese and chase it down with Saltine Crackers.

Now, I like cheese but after eating cheese in every way one can possibly eat it, I started to hate "Regan Cheese" and the smell of the yellow brick cheese. However, in the free food box there were other food items to eat and one never knew what might be inside. It was like getting a surprise in each box—almost like when you open the cereal box and there is a toy inside. Mom would get us dressed and we would walk to the free food line that was four blocks from our home.

All of us took turns pulling the shopping cart. When I would look over at Mom, she looked so "out of sorts." The weather did not help out either. It seemed like every time we would have to walk to the food distribution center the weather would be awful.

It had rained hard most of the morning that we headed out, and there were puddles of water near the curbs. The sun tried to peek through the storm clouds but was not successful. All of Cleveland looked gloomy and the two men that passed us on the street dropped their head as they passed. Everyone seemed to be in a bad predicament with no work and low on food for their families. I felt that the dreary wet day and the sad men we saw were getting to Mom.

Billy, Veronica, and I loved getting all wet and splashing around in the water near the curb. The three of us were getting loud, wet, having a grand time, and getting on Mom's nerves. Mom yelled out, "Stop it right now! All I need now is for one of you to get sick." Mom had enough and was afraid that we would get sick if we got all wet. The three of us knew we upset Mom and felt bad; so we stopped and marched on in silence, like three little soldiers, and I kept looking over at Mom's sad face and feeling bad for her. As we continued to walk on, I took a turn pulling the shopping cart down the wet sidewalk and did not utter a sound. All of a sudden Mom stopped and looked down. Lying near a puddle was a little worn, black pocket Bible.

It was not soaking wet through to the pages and only the cover was wet, like someone had just dropped it a minute ago. Mom looked around to ask if anyone had lost their Bible, but no one was around. She then took a double take up and down the block.

Mom then picked it up, wiped the moisture off the small black, holy book on her coat. She then smiled to herself and her whole mood changed. Looking up toward the sky, Mom softly murmured to herself, "Thank you." Then Mom said to us in a calmer more relaxed tone, "If we get cake mix in our food box, we will go home and make a cake and if here is no cake mix, I have something at home that I can make up. How about chocolate chip cookies? I think I have enough flour and chocolate chips to make up a batch." Together we all started jumping up and down hoping there would be cake mix and other goodies in the box. Mom and Dad didn't know where the next house payment was going to come from, if they could keep the lights on, or if the heat would stay on till Dad got back to work.

But all of us kids had joy in our hearts because of the promise of chocolate cake or chocolate chip cookies.

As an adult I now am ever so grateful to Mom and Dad for making sure that we kids did not have to carry the burden of their trials. They both made sure that somehow or someway things would get better for us all.

Mom always had, throughout our childhood, a strength and firm faith that helped pull us through another miserable day. Together as a family we walked back home pulling our shopping cart with our old faithful food item, "Regan Cheese," and a mom's love that always seemed to shine when we needed it the most.

Chapter 5

Our Home

There is one house on every street in America where all the kids on the block come over and play, and that was my home on Starkweather in Cleveland. There was always a knock on our front door, with young, eager faces asking Mom if Billy, Veronica, or I could go out and play. Mom was a firm believer in the idea that children needed to get out and play, get dirty, and use their imaginations. Mom was always approachable and friendly, making children feel comfortable around her, and she made us kids feel like what we had to say mattered; so her natural, loving way with children made for a busy house with lots of kids in and out of our yard.

Mom let us all play in the backyard, and for a city lot we had a long, big yard with a large oak tree that provided us with a shady play area. Mom allowed not only her children, but others to dig a huge hole in the backyard next to the oak tree. Laughter would fill the air while we all got filthy from head to toe relishing our carefree childhood youth. Together we all worked hard maneuvering the shovels into the ground moving dirt from one place to the next. All of the kids would end up with large piles of dirt, and our family dog, Sheba, would jump right in alongside of us pawing up the dirt. Sheba was a tough German shepherd, who was always on the look out to protect our home and family, but she was good with all of the kids that played in the yard and she just kind of palled along with us. The best part was dragging out the hose and Sheba would run for cover not wanting to get wet. Of course, as little kids we all loved to get wet and dirty. Getting muddy and dirty was a childhood dream and the messier the better. We all played endless hours in the backyard. It was our wonderland because Mom left us alone and we were able to make up games and create our own little world out back in the yard.

One day Billy and Jose started a new game. My twin brother, Billy, was "all boy" and at an age where some kids feel invincible.

He had brown hair and soft, hazel eyes that lit up wide when he had a new idea. Because he was my brother, I felt he was great in everything that he did, and in all honesty he still to this day has great athletic ability and excellent coordination. We took out a long, wooden board and placed it over the hole we had dug. We then rode our bikes over it, all taking turns going in a circle. And we all tried to "Pop—A—Wheelie," riding on the back wheels of our bikes and popping our front wheels as high in the air as we could go without falling off. Billy and Jose had it "down pat." They could "pop up" and ride on the back wheel, and then would see who would last the longest up in the air. We all would get loud with excitement each time we "popped" the front wheel of the bikes in the air. I tried but never seemed to get my front wheel in the air for very long.

So, I would sit next to Veronica on one of the dirt piles we had formed that day, wide eyed in astonishment and awe, and watched the two of them go up and ride and make the bikes reach for the sky. One time Mom came out of the back door, looking confused as she looked around the front and backyard. She looked puzzled and a little disoriented and looked like she wanted to ask us a question.

I stood up and I said, "Mom, what are you looking for?"

"Well, you guys keep yelling 'Poppa Willy, Poppa Willy' and I don't see Dad anywhere." We all started giggling out loud. Mom, good natured as she was, didn't get mad at us for laughing at her.

Mom looked at us very confused and said, "What are all of you up to and what's so funny?"

"No, Mom," I explained. "We are saying 'Poppin a wheelie' and not Papa Willy." Billy was right on cue and gave Mom a demonstration on what poppin a wheelie really was.

"Well, I see now. I thought Dad was home and off work.

And please kids be careful. I know you are all having fun, but it does look dangerous and we do not want to take anyone to the emergency room."

In unison we all chanted back, "Don't worry, we'll be careful." Then she turned around, offered us a gentle smile, and went back into the house.

Every day at around six I would go to the front yard and stand anxiously by the gate waiting for my father to come home.

When I saw him at the corner, I announced loudly, "Daddy's home! Daddy's home!" and take off running full speed after him. My father was a good-looking man, with a quiet nature. Dad was a tall man with a muscular, thin build and carried his Slovenian heritage proudly. He wore his hair in a crew cut, which was fashionable for the times, and had broad shoulders. Dad would look worn out after using his physical strength on his construction job all day. But every day, Dad, strictly for my amusement, would turn around in his work boots and run playfully away from me to tease me. I would yell out to him, "Wait Daddy, stop, stop."

Then he would yell back, "Who are you?"

I would then say, "Daddy don't you know me? I'm your little girl."

And he would say, "Oh, I guess you are." That is when I picked up my pace and ran faster until I caught up to him and grabbed him happily. The best day of the week was Friday and Dad would feed all the kids in the neighborhood. Dad was an orphan at a young age; so he spent a lot of time in orphanages and foster care. Needless to say, there were not many special treats in either of those places. So because of Dad's generosity and his love for children, and payday, the best day in a working man's week, we ate pizza and glazed doughnuts every Friday. This meal, of course, was a nutritionist's nightmare, but was our favorite.

Every one of us kids would always look forward all week to our Friday evening smorgasbord feast. There were a lot of hungry kids, who had fathers that had left most of their paycheck at the corner bar. They had their best meal of the week on Fridays at our house.

Every Friday at around 4:30 p.m. is when Jose from across the street would start asking, "Is Papa Willy home yet?" I heard this dreaded question every week and I always wished he would get away from us and leave us alone for our special time with our Dad.

Jose was a little on the chubby side, with big brown eyes, and it seemed to me that he was always hungry and ready to eat. Like so many of the neighborhood boys and girls, he came from a troubled household and found the love and attention all kids need at our house. It seemed that on Fridays there were more and more kids over. So, every Friday I had company at the gate waiting for Dad to come around the corner. I would push Jose away, feeling that he invaded my space and my special time with Dad. But Jose being larger than me pushed me back. We moved around awkwardly and I shot him dirty looks, but he never moved. Once I saw Dad, Jose would start yelling, "Pappa Willy is home! Pappa Willy is home!" That is when I hit the ground running after my father. Daddy would have candy bars in his pockets and he would pass them out to all the kids that surrounded him, and he always had a box of glazed doughnuts in his hand.

Once he walked into the house, he would say, "Hi, Miss America. Order the pizza." Dad would then hand over his weekly pay to Mom. Once the pizza arrived, Mom lined up the boxes on the ironing board because Mom had a non-stop, always-open kitchen for anyone who was hungry. That meant there were always dishes in the sink and on the table. Fortunately, there was no fanaticism for a spotless house.

We lived in a well-lived-in and comfortable home that always seemed to need a little more cleaning because of all of the traffic in and out at all times. The ironing board became our smorgasbord. All the kids lined up, some pushing to get to the pizza, while others grabbed the doughnuts.

Mom would say, "No pushing. There is enough for everyone. My mom was an ordinary woman on an ordinary city street like so many moms out there that seemed to be overlooked for all of their selfless and gentle giving hearts. However, she was a mom to many young lives that came and played at our house. She touched the lives of the young on our Starkweather Avenue home with a meal, a loving heart, and Friday pizza parties that were always the best of times.

Chapter 6

Snakes

To feel fear of something is a common thing to most of us. If we are being honest, we would all say, "Yes, I am afraid of something." Even though Mom is a brave woman who endured many hardships, my mom was no exception. Mom too had her fears.

We had a small five-and-dime store on Professor Avenue. Many times while on a stroll through the neighborhood, we would stop and Mom would allow us to pick out a small inexpensive toy. The store had rows of wooden bins filled with affordable items from kitchen wear to tools to toys for kids. Naturally, all of us kids would run straight to the two bins filled with toys. Billy found some army men and I found a jump rope with red plastic handles.

"Hey, Mom. How about this jump rope? Can I get it?" Veronica's tiny hands were outstretched trying to grab a baton made of glittery, shinny aluminum.

"Oh, I guess it will be OK," she said. I then went to the next bin and held up a large plastic rubbery snake that had bright glossy realistic colors that made it look, at first glance, pretty real. I held it up in the air and said, "Hey, Mom. How about this toy?" Mom's eyes dilated to double their natural size and began to back up and stutter and mumble, "Snakes, snakes, no snakes!" The three of us had to stop her from bolting out of the five and dime.

I can remember if she even saw a snake on the television, Mom would start to tremble as she closed her eyes wishing the picture out of her mind. She would then plead for whoever was in the living room to change the channel. She would then take deep breaths to try and calm down and talked herself into a calmer state.

I remember it being a hot summer day in our Tremont neighborhood. A neighbor boy came over to show my brother Billy his collection of snakes that he had caught and put into a glass aquarium. Mom was always working in the kitchen, either preparing a full meal or working on making snacks for us and the kids in the neighborhood. With the hot summer weather in full force, Mom had chopped up fresh fruit for a fruit salad for all of us to munch on. Mom called out to us as she walked out on the front porch walking to the front yard to tell us the fruit salad was done.

Billy and I were on our knees surrounding the aquarium and admiring the snake collection. Mom tapped me on the shoulder and I turned to see what she wanted. Mom got a good look at the snakes. Mom stopped and let loose a scream of terror like I had never heard before in my life. My usually well-composed mother took off running up the street, with a large-bladed butcher knife, stained with the juices from ripe fruit, screaming and yelling like a wild banshee, frantically waving the large knife over her head. Since it was the hottest days of summer, a bunch of boys had just left the swimming pool at Lincoln Park.

These punks thought they were tough guys and often had started trouble around the neighborhood. I saw that the boys were walking down the middle of the street with their usual swagger and cockiness. As soon as they saw Mom yelling and screaming with a butcher knife in her hands they dropped their towels that they had over their shoulders, and all of the boys, took off running in several different directions screaming for help. I was running after Mom, yelling at Mom to please stop running. She ran through the neighborhood all the way to the freeway ramp on West Fourteenth Street. Thank God, she ran out of breath from all of the screaming and running. She stood at the ramp with her hands on her knees panting and mumbling incoherently, "Snakes, snakes! Get away! Snakes, snakes!" It took both Billy and I to coax Mom back down the street and try to get her into our house without drawing any more attention to us. Billy took his shirt off and then gently eased the knife out of Mom's panicked grip and rolled it up in his shirt. She kept mumbling to herself all the way home, "snakes, snakes, make them go away." We both keep reassuring her that the snakes were gone. Mom started to calm down once we got her home and put a cold wet towel on her neck.

We gave her some ice water, and finally relief sat in, until she let out a nervous laugh asking, "I had a knife in my hand running down the street yelling and howling the whole time. I must have looked *nuts!*"

Billy and I started laughing too, "Yes, Mom. You looked nuts!" Funny thing is that every time we saw those trouble-making boys, they put their heads down, ran to the other side of the street, and went the other way.

Later in the week, I was helping Mom put away the groceries. She had bought fresh strawberries, blueberries, and watermelon. This was the same recipe that produced the bloody knife that she ran down the street with terrorizing the neighborhood. I looked over at Mom and we both started laughing.

"I guess I made a spectacle of myself the other day," Mom said as she blushed. "Ya know Laurel, we all have something we are afraid of and sometimes you just have to pick up your feet and run." Together we both were laughing again and I felt the warm trusting spirit of my mother while we both put away the groceries.

It was truly a lesson in bravery for me to see a grown woman laugh at her deepest fears. Mom always told us that throughout our lives we are going to have a lot of laughter and a lot of tears. But life can go a lot easier when you can laugh at yourself.

Chapter 7

Last Minute Gifts

I was ten years old when mom and I took the Christmas Eve bus trip. I will start by saying that Cleveland sure can have some brutal winters and when you have to use public transportation, it could be a downright nightmare with lake effect snow and wind showing no mercy. We did not have a family car from the time I was six years old until I went to work and bought my own. After the station wagon got stolen in front of our home and was later found stripped and burned to the frame, Dad said, out of frustration, "No more cars!" And from that day forward, we traveled around Cleveland on the bus. Dad went to and from work each day, on the bus, near and far, and never missed a day or was late.

Mom was from the generation where many women did not learn to drive. She was also from a small country town where most people walked to where they needed to be. Consequently, Mom never learned to drive, and if she did, well, I would simply worry for the other drivers. She would follow every rule to the max, read every sign, and in the end would only hold up traffic.

So on to our trip to the K-Mart, in the need of last-minute gifts for Christmas, oh man did we have a lot of snow, cold, and blustery wind, the kind that goes right to the marrow of your bones and you remain cold for several hours after you get out of the cold.

We were out in the open, exposed to the elements, waiting for the bus and we were moving our feet back and forth to try to keep warm. Snow covered up the roads and we were truly in a winter wonderland. There were not too many people out in this weather; the only person I saw was the mailman. He was strolling by and his mustache and beard were frozen to his face. His nose reminded me of Rudolph's because it was a bright cherry red. He gave us a nod and said, "What beautiful weather we are having and have a Merry Christmas." I looked over at Mom and we thought we were dressed warm enough, but the love to make Christmas special in our home kept us warmer. I watched as Mom pulled the bus schedule out of her coat pocket, looked it over, and said, "If the bus is on schedule, it should be coming soon." In a hesitant voice she said, "Boy, I don't know Laurel, maybe we have no business being out in this weather."

I replied in a cheerful voice, "Look Mom, the bus is coming," and we both let out a sigh of relief. When we got on the bus and there was only one person on the bus.

He was not dressed too well and had a large brown shopping bag. He was continuously babbling to himself and occasionally singing out loud to an audience that nobody could see but him. The troubled man was looking over from time to time saying something that I could not make out, and he had a mean look on his face that showed the years of problems and heartaches he had in his life.

All of a sudden he jumped up and said in a loud gruff voice, "Dam it driver! Stop this bus right now! This is my stop." So the bus driver stopped and he got off and we were all pleased to see him go. It was typical of the Public Transportation scenario. We always seemed to get one disagreeable lout when we rode the busses like so many other big cities across the nation. Because it was Christmas, deep down, I did wish that this mean man did have a Merry Christmas or find a little peace of mind somewhere. We had our usual seats up close to the bus driver because we never knew what we could expect to see on a city bus line. Our stop was approaching and we stood up to leave. Then, the bus driver turned to us, smiled, and said, "You are very brave to be out in this storm," and wished us both a Merry Christmas. Mom turned to him and replied, "Merry Christmas to you and yours."

Once we got into K-mart, there were a few last-minute shoppers on this cold and bitter Christmas Eve, but not many. Most people had enough sense to stay out of the Christmas Eve blizzard. I noticed that the area off to the side that was Santa's seat was empty and there was not an elf to be found. It was so terribly cold that the manager of K-mart had to put space heaters by the front windows to keep the windows from freezing over with ice. Mom and I once again held onto the shopping cart filling it up with goodies and gifts for our Christmas holiday.

Part of our shopping tradition was to stop in the K-mart cafeteria to get a warm cup of soup and our usual two pieces of chicken that we shared. We looked out the window only to see that the winter storm had gotten worse and the snow kept piling up. Mom said wearily, "Maybe we should have stayed home."

"No, Mommy I had fun. It looks like this Christmas was made for me and you." Mom smiled and said she was happy too. My mother had the true Christmas spirit—she shopped for gifts for everyone all year long. Together we pushed our shopping cart filled with love and the gifts we found to make our Christmas a blessed, festive, holiday. Mom pulled the shopping cart to the front cashier line and I helped put each item up on the checkout counter. Mom always brought three strong plastic shopping bags. She made sure that I always got the lightest of the three bags. Mom always carried the two heaviest ones.

Once we got out to the front of the K-Mart, a man was ringing the Salvation Army bell, and wishing everyone a Merry Christmas on this bitter, cold winter night. His face was half covered with a bright red Christmas scarf and the below-zero weather did not affect his friendly Christmas spirit.

Mom looked over to me and said, "Laurel drop this change in the kettle." No matter how tight money was or how low our food money was when Dad got laid off, Mom always found a way to open her generous heart and meager pocketbook to anyone in need.

We then headed out to the bus stop making fresh tracks in the newly fallen snow. Our near Westside neighborhood had a sense of beauty and stillness with this fresh blanket of snow. And to this day, that Christmas Eve will always be special to me even though I thought I was going to freeze to death.

Chapter 8

The Accidental Fans

During the end of summer, which was not my favorite time of the year, we were getting ready to go back to school. Mom would take us shopping for all the school supplies and clothes that we would need. This time of the year would set off different emotions. The leaves were changing and brightly colored carpets of fallen leaves stretched out over the landscape. Here in Northeastern Ohio and neighboring Pennsylvania, it was one of the most special times of the year—football season. Grade school, junior high school, high school, and college teams became real special at this time of year because Americans could follow their beloved sport of football. And on every Sunday afternoon in almost every household, three important things happened—people went to church, had a great Sunday meal together, and huddled around the TV to cheer for their favorite NFL team.

Everybody at this age wants to fit into their peer group. Consequently, not only was I anxious about going back to school, but getting the right clothes to wear made my head spin to think about it. Just like the kids of today, back in the seventies, kids were very aware of what they wanted to wear to school. I never made shopping trips easy for Mom because I was particular about what I would wear and sometimes very stubborn. I have a twin brother Billy that I looked up to and at times idolized.

Together we played army men and got all dirty in the backyard. My brother's world seemed better to me then playing with dolls and being a "girly girl." And with me being a tom boy, I just hated clothes shopping.

Mom would start with Billy in the boys' section, and then next, the girls' department where I gave Mom a hard time because I was not sure what I wanted. To me, the boys' department seemed like it was more streamlined and not as much lace and color going on like the girls' overstated clothing. With me standing right next to my brother, I watched Billy pull out a football jersey with the number "12" on it, with strong colors of black and gold. Billy eyed up the jersey and said, "Mom, can I get this football shirt to wear to school?"

Mom walked over to Billy and held up the shirt, "Sure you can and you will look nice in those colors."

I spoke up, "Mom, I want one too with the number "12" on it too." Billy looking annoyed with what I had said and replied, "No way! You can't copy me. You can't get the same football jersey like me. You can't have two of the same numbers on the same team. Get this one," and Billy pulled out a jersey with number "88" on it. I felt that if these clothes were good enough for my brother, then they were good enough for me. Both of us were feeling pleased with our football jerseys. We both asked excitedly, "Mom, can we wear them on the first day of school?" I know Mom would have loved to see me in a dress and in a more lady-like outfit.

However, she replied, "Sure you can," with a little hesitation. Together we walked over to the girls' clothes department in the hopes that I would change my mind and find something more suitable for a girl. I impatiently went through the aisles, and I picked out blue jeans, while Mom picked out a light, sky, blue blouse with flowers running down around the sleeves and collar. I could tell Mom was happy that I was being somewhat agreeable on my second outfit.

On the morning of the first day of school we were getting ready and Mom had brought both outfits out. In a pleading tone Mom said, "Laurel, you would look so nice in this outfit. Look at the pretty flowers around the sleeves and collar."

"No, Mommy," I cried out. "I want to wear my football jersey like Billy on the first day of school. I will wear that outfit tomorrow." Mom gave in to me on my choice of outfit for the day and was keeping a close eye on the clock.

She finally said, "Fine, Laurel. Get dressed fast or we will be late." Going to school that first day I felt proud and I was holding on to my brother Billy's hand knowing that we both had on the same football jerseys even if the numbers were different. It was a warm and sunny September day, and the gold numbers on the jerseys glistened in the sunlight and were brought out even more by the rich, black, background. The first day was uneventful and the class lined up to go home. And I will never forget what happened once we were on our walk back home.

There was a big, husky, bearded man, who was the father of a boy who was a couple of years older than us in school. This man and his older son started calling us names for no reason that we could figure out. The duo became louder, and I think the father said, "That team sucks!" followed by his son repeating every word that his dad had said. Billy turned to me and said, "Laurel, are they talking about us?" I never got a chance to answer Billy and was still not sure if they were talking about us, but it became evident when the older boy ran up behind me and spit on the back of my football shirt.

Then he turned back and ran back to his father who celebrated his bad behavior. "Way to go, Son, right in the middle of the number." Billy grabbed my hand and we both took off running for our dear lives. What a way to start the first day of school, to be scared and breathless on day one!

I heard both Father and Son laughing and yelling at us as we ran to the safety of our home. Billy made it to the house first, and I ran in after him crying and it was hard for me to talk. Mom looked worried and got down on her knees to hold onto me. I could feel Mom's shoulders droop as she held onto me. Then she asked frighteningly, "Laurel, what happened?" I was still out of breath and could not talk. Billy was scared too and blurted out, "Mommy, a crazy man with his son was calling us really bad names and the son ran up to Laurel and spit on her football jersey."

"Mommy!" I cried out. "Why would they do that to us and why would someone spit on my shirt?" At that time, my mom did not know anything about the NFL.

She said, "I have no idea. I will call the school and report what has happened. Don't worry, everything will be fine. Tomorrow I will walk you both to school and after school I will walk you both home." Even though we lived a short half of a block from the school, this was comforting to hear.

Later we all learned from Dad that this is Cleveland, and it is "Brown's Town," and that we had inadvertently picked the arch rivals of the Browns, the Pittsburgh Steelers Jerseys, to wear to school that day. Mom was still trying to get a hold of the idea that a grown man would encourage his son to behave so badly over the colors of a jersey. Mom said with her feisty Irish spirit, "This is America, and the two of you can wear whatever colors that you both like." Dad was not sure what to say. "Well, maybe only wear it around the house and not to school." Then Dad said, "As a matter of fact, the Brown's and Steelers are playing on TV this Sunday." That Sunday was the day Dad explained the game of football to us.

We all listened while Dad talked about the offense and defensive lines and what each player's responsibility was on the field. Dad talked about the number "12" who was Terry Bradshaw, the quarterback at that time and the number "88" who was Lynn Swan, the wide receiver that Bradshaw would throw passes to.

Together as a family, we sat back and watched Terry Bradshaw and Lynn Swan playing the game, and we were having a ball cheering for our teams. Both Billy and I jumped off the couch and I yelled out, "Way to go," when Lynn Swan caught the football and each time a little revenge set in thinking to myself, "Back at you, Spit Boy."

Dad sitting in his chair said, "Well, I guess I will have company each week watching football." I smiled big at Daddy and said, "Is it OK, if I liked the Steelers over the Browns?"

"Sure," Dad said. "It looks like I will be the only one for the Browns in our house."

Mom, looking a little worried, said, "How was I to know about this football stuff? Look what I did to our children."

"Aw, Doris, don't worry about it. They are OK now." So all because of our Mommy and back to school shopping, we became Steelers fans.

Later on in the week in the laundry mat, I was on the lookout for the man and his son. Mom, feeling that I was uneasy said, "Laurel, I will never let anyone hurt you." I relaxed a little feeling safe next to Mom. Together Mom and I were folding our clothes and I tried to hide the football shirts so no one could see them. Mom stopped folding clothes and looked me in the eye and said, "Laurel if you like that team, wear that shirt with pride, but never put down any other team or anyone who roots for another team because a true fan never hurts another fan. And remember, just because someone acts or looks a little different, that doesn't mean they are a bad person." Packing up our shopping cart to head back home, I felt taller somehow and to this day still love the Steelers, but I only wear my Steelers jersey around the house, not like my brave twin brother Billy who wears a different Steelers shirt all through the whole football season.

Billy along with his whole family truly live and breathe Steelers football to this day. It's always a special event over at Billy's house when the Browns and Steelers play. It's good to be a part of something larger than yourself and lose the "me-ness" for a sense of team and group affiliation.

Our family and friends all gather around the big screen TV in Billy's front room and cheer for our teams. It's a great time with good food, good people, and sometimes a great football game, depending on who you are rooting for. Sometimes the back and forth banter gets a little out of hand, but it is always in good fun and not taken too seriously. And after all, even though it has become a huge rivalry, in the final analysis, it's still just a game.

Chapter 9

The West Side Market

It has always amazed me how we all traveled around Cleveland on the bus with our bulky shopping cart. Mom and we kids had it down to a science when it came to traveling on the city busses. There was a certain way of pulling the grocery cart on and off the bus. Mom would pull up the steps and Billy, Veronica, or I would hold onto the bottom and walk up the two steps, one at a time, to get onto the bus. Mom, with the three of us, most of the time used the bus to get to where we needed to shop. But there were times when we had more kids if one of us wanted to bring along a friend, which was usually the case. We always got noticed by someone, but then again there was a line of us following Mom with the shopping cart. We looked more like a marching band without their instruments than a mom out shopping with her kids.

We always got the annoyed and critical looks from the grouchy folks who just didn't like kids, but Mom always was indifferent to them. She had a shopping task to be done and was not going to let their fuddy-duddy criticism, ruin her day with her children. We all enjoyed going shopping with Mom and she had a way with us that kept us busy and in line. She had made up games for us to play to keep us occupied. And Mom was always prepared with the bus schedule on her at all times, so we never waited too long. While waiting, Mom creatively made up fun games for us to play while waiting for the bus to arrive.

One of Mom's games was to pick a number from one to ten, and then we would count the cars passing by until your number landed on a car. We could keep or trade in the car that passed us and landed on our number. We all took our turns counting and laughing out loud. Sometimes we were happy if our number got us a cool-looking sports car like a Vet or Thunderbird. But if our number that we picked landed on a garbage truck or hearse, we would all start giggling and yell out "Keep or trade!" Then Mom would jump into the game and say, "Keep or trade?" Then we would all shout out in unison, "Trade, Trade!" We were having a great time, so time went by fast and before we knew it, the bus was coming.

Once we got onto the bus, we tried to sit close to each other because there was always someone on the bus that was loud, rude, and out in their own little world. Mom would tell us, "Try not to stare at them." Then she would give us a special look that said, "Remember we are all God's children." When we got restless, Mom would always pull out a large traveling bag with books and toys in it to keep us busy and quiet. If we could, Billy would sit next to me, and Veronica next to Mom, and our friends sat together. One of our favorite shopping places is a landmark of Cleveland. It is the West Side Market on West Twenty-Fifth Street.

The market is a fresh open market with endless fruits and vegetable stands with all of the different veggies and plants one could ever think of.

What also made it fun was that each one of us was allowed to pick out one item we would like to eat and Mom would get it for us. The market was always bustling with people walking swiftly by going to their favorite stand to buy their produce. There were people from all over the world, it seemed, talking in different languages all under one roof. Without failure we always stopped in the meat market next to the open produce stands. And there was every type of meat one could ever desire from veal, beef, and pig to fresh fish stands. It was not unusual to see someone carrying out a whole pig for a pig roast, which always tended to gross me out. We would always turn to each other and say, "Ewww, that is just too gross."

In the summer heat, the aroma from all of the butchered meats and fresh fish would at times overwhelm me. Sometimes, I just had to stop and breathe slowly to keep from getting sensory overload. My quick gag reflex would force me to slow down or the worst would happen and I would lose breakfast and lunch. One of our favorite stops was the smoked meats stand. Everyone looked forward to this stand because Mom would always buy us a dozen smokies to share and munch on. This was our last stop. Mom said, "Looks like we bought out the whole market. What do ya say kids? I guess it is time to head home."

The West Side Market was close enough to home, so we would walk back home and pass on taking the bus to get a little exercise and not have to deal with a crowded bus that would usually have only standing room at that time of the day. We walked on a long bridge called Abby Bridge. On one side you can see the skyline of Downtown Cleveland, and looking down, you could see the famous Cuyahoga River that actually caught on fire. Everyone took turns pulling the grocery cart as we laughed and talked and gobbled down our smokies on our walk back home. All of a sudden a dark blue four door, late model station wagon rumbled by us. The windows were down and loud music and voices blared out at us.

The back seat was filled with kids our age bouncing around in the back. One of the wise-ass kids rudely yelled out of the car, "Hey, what's wrong? Too bummy to own a car?" They all laughed at us, which made it worse. I got angry and flipped them a bird. Mom said, "Now Laurel, don't do that. Don't stoop to their level."

"But, Mom, that wasn't right, of that man to yell that mean stuff at us. Anyway, who are they? Are they rich because they own a car? And does that mean that we are poor because we don't have a car?"

Mom stopped pulling the grocery cart and turned to me and said, "No, Laurel, you can own three cars and still be poor in your heart. The fullness and fulfillment of the heart is the true richness of the earth."

"I guess so Mom, but I think life would be a lot easier for us if we even had an old car that ran good."

"But, Laurel, stop for a minute. What do you see around you?"

I did what she asked and took a closer look at what was actually going on around me. Billy and Veronica, along with our friends were getting more out of hand by the minute, laughing and teasing each other and having a grand time. I looked over the bridge and saw the crew teams rowing down the river, gliding gracefully by.

Mom caught me noticing all of this and said, "Look at all of the seagulls circling on the wind currents trying to catch a fish for supper, and look how pretty those clouds are just above one of our most famous land marks the Terminal Tower. See, Laurel, those people who flew by us in their fancy car were not able to see any of that."

"Oh, Mom, I guess you are right."

Billy tapped me on the shoulder and said, "Aw! Come on, Laurel, those jerks were nobodies. You can't pay attention to chumps like them." I realized Mom and Billy were both right and I was so grateful to have a brother and a mom like them who managed somehow to look at the world around us in a different light.

Once we got over the bridge we were back in our Tremont neighborhood and very close to home. Mom would stop at the corner store and buy us soft drinks to wash down our spicy smokies and before we knew it, we were back home, putting in the fridge all the bright-colored fresh vegetables that we had gotten and looking forward to eating more good food from the West Side Market.

And once again, both Mom and my brother Billy had given me a healthy perspective on who we were and why we belonged where we were at, and how important it was to enjoy that time and place in our lives, on that particular day when we took our trip to the West Side Market. I learned that one of the true riches in life was to remain comfortable in your own world and whatever place and time you were in at that moment.

Chapter 10

Out of Sight

Going shopping with three children was never easy for Mom. Getting us on and off the city bus until we reached the store was always a challenge, and on this particular day, it was extremely muggy and hot out. While waiting at the bus stop, a neighbor friend pulled over and gave us a much needed ride. Because of Mom's independent spirit, she never asked for rides and never took a ride from strangers. She accepted rides only from people that she knew and only if they offered. Mom believed it was her responsibility to get around to the stores on her own. However, if someone offered, she would be happy to take the ride, but never for free. She always gave money toward gas, and each one of us was truly grateful for the ride in a car because we would be able to be close together and not be around strangers on a public bus.

On this day we were going to Sears and Roebucks. Mom liked the clothes better at Sears than some other department stores. Mom felt that the clothes held up better and were more durable and each one of us always seemed to find outfits that we liked because each department was neat and orderly and it was easy to find our different sizes. Also, Sears had a lay-a-way plan at that time that made it easy for working-class families to purchase clothes. The lay-a-way plan was ideal for working-class families because you could lay an item away and pay on it with no interest and pick up the item when you paid it off in reasonable installments. Today we have credit cards, which in reality are, loan sharks. Once we were dropped off in front of the store, we walked back to the lay-a-way department. Mom kept us close and kept a watchful eye on us at all times.

There was usually a line because this was a popular way to buy clothes. Finally it was our turn to pay.

My little sister, Veronica, was around three years old at the time. She moved around fast, and always had a big mischievous smile on her face and seemed to be always looking for trouble. She would always get silly in line and entertain herself by bending over and looking at the world from an upside down view. I could tell that the lady waiting on Mom was annoyed because she gave us all a look like, "Look at that child misbehaving. She needs to get under control." The sales lady wore a shimmering black blazer with a bright red-colored blouse, and off-white dress slacks. The sales lady had her hair piled up high on her head and it did not move because of all the hair spray that froze it in place. She also was overloaded with overlapping bracelets and necklaces. We could hear her bracelets making noise as she took Mom's money and put it into the cash drawer.

She handed our lay-a-way number to a younger sales clerk with her hair pulled back in a pony tail that looked to be fresh out of high school. She walked in the back to retrieve our lay-a-way bag. Mom moved us to the side of the counter, and the three of us tried to wait patiently until the young lady came out from the back and smiled at Mom, handed over our shopping bag, and said to us, "Have a nice day." Mom smiled pleasantly and thanked her.

All the while the other women looked harshly and glared at us because Veronica was impatiently tapping and moving around the counter getting into whatever she could get her hands on. Mom kept taking the bell, lay-a-way slips, and moving them away from Veronica's reach. The big-haired lady was quite relieved to watch us as we walked out the door of the lay-a-way department. Another part of the shopping ritual was watching Mom's wishful eyes scan through the marked down bargain racks and to look at the different dresses that she knew she could not afford, and hold up the lovely dresses close to her and admired each dress as it reflected back to her in the mirror. Mom never spent too much money on herself. Only if there was a special occasion like a wedding, or Easter Sunday, would she ever consider getting anything for herself. The needs of her family always came first. And if Mom did buy a dress it was from a bargain basement room and on sale.

Veronica was moving around a little but staying close by. Occasionally, I would grab her hand if she drifted too far away from us. Mom looked around a little and said, "Time to get going." Looking around, she said, "Where is Veronica?"

I frighteningly said to Mom, "I just had her right by my side. She was just here." We all started looking around the aisles at the dresses but no little sister could be found.

Mom was staying calm, but looking worried she said, "We will find a sales clerk and report her missing." Even though I was very young, I knew the danger my little sister could be in. I tried to calm the knot that was churning in my stomach and hoped and prayed nothing had happened to my little sister.

To my relief, the loud speaker came on to say that they have a little girl lost, and she has long dark hair and her name is Veronica. "Would the parent of Veronica report to the office next to lay-a-way in the back of the store please?"

Mom let out a sigh of relief and grabbed both Billy and I by the hand and then we walked back to the office to pick up Veronica, and once we walked into the office, there was my little sister sitting up on an office chair, grinning to herself, swerving around in the office chair while eating a lollypop that she must have gotten from the store manager. Veronica looked like she loved sitting up on this big chair and acted like she was the "Queen Bee" looking around at the people as they walked in and out.

She sat there like royalty ready to be crowned the royal head of her kingdom. Her big, bright, green eyes and charming smile were saying, "Gee, look how much fun I had getting away with this." And right next to the manager's office, was the lay-a-way department. The lady with her perfect hair was staring over at us with a nasty scowl of disapproval on her face. The store manager, who was a gentle, grandfatherly type of guy, gave Veronica a little push, so she could twirl around in a circle in her chair. Veronica giggled and was having the time of her life and loved all of the attention she was getting. Mom walked over to the store manger to tell him that Veronica was her little girl. Then the phone rang and the manger excused himself, picked up the phone, and said, "Please hold." He told Miss Perfect that she had a call.

The big hair lady scurried over and picked up the phone that was on the desk where Veronica was sitting. Veronica jumped down and inadvertently grabbed a hold of her white dress slacks pulling herself down and leaving a sticky, gooey mess of little girl slobber and icky green lollypop smear on her leg. The woman started mumbling obscenities under her breath about a bratty, out-of-control, little kid who ruined her expensive slacks. She looked appalled beyond words and ran off to the wash room to try and wash of the stain and get her image back to Miss Perfect. Mom picked up Veronica and held her close to her.

Veronica said, "What's wrong Mommy? You look sad."

Mom held Veronica at arm's length looked her in the eye and sternly said, "Please do not ever go away from us like that ever again."

"Why Mommy? I just was having fun."

"Please don't because there are bad people out here that do bad things to little girls when they catch them alone."

"Oh! I didn't know Mommy. Please don't be sad. I promise I will never do it again. I don't like to make you sad, Mommy."

The big-haired lady came back and looked disappointed that we were still in the store. She stood there mumbling to herself and shaking her head as Veronica sweetly smiled at her and waved good-bye. The young coworker in the pony tail was thoroughly entertained by to the whole incident, and had a good laugh while waving good-bye to my little sister.

Most parents would have given their child a beating or a severe tongue lashing. Mom remained cool and spoke to Veronica in a controlled, stern, no-nonsense voice that let us know that she cared deeply for us and did not want to see any harm come to us. None of us kids ever wandered off again. We always kept a safe visual distance so that we would not upset our Mom.

Chapter 11

Dreadful Words

School—some kids get it and others like me tried, but didn't get it. You know the ones in class that get straight A's on every spelling test. They seemed like they have it together all the time! Well, I was not one of them although I tried hard to be one. I had my spelling words on hand all the time. I wrote them out on paper over and over again. I felt prepared and ready for my test on every Friday morning. I would study hard and work all week on the words, take my test, hand it in, and get it back with most of the answers wrong, and sometimes all of them were marked wrong. It was hard to imagine, but it was true. I thought, "Boy, I must be dumb." After all the endless work and sweating over these words, and I still didn't pass. I was feeling tired and beaten down that all my hard work over my spelling words ended up with red ink on them each week. When I got home, I decided that I needed a nap because I was feeling overwhelmed, frustrated, and a little sorry for myself.

I fell asleep and heard my mom's soft, soothing voice. I thought maybe I was having a dream about my sweet, gentle Mom who came to me in a dream to share some important fact of life with me or maybe even give me the mysterious secret that was behind the art of spelling words correctly. Then I thought, I really am dreaming. I am dreaming and I am just going to turn over and go back to sleep.

Then all of a sudden I felt Mom get close to my side near my ear saying words ever so softly and very clearly and carefully to me. "Broken, B-R-O-K-E-N," she said softly. Well, reality hit me when I sat up in bed and there was Mom, on a chair right next to my pillow, leaning over me and whispering spelling words and their correct spellings over and over again into my ear while I was sleeping. I rubbed my eyes to make sure they were clear and looked at Mom strangely and said, "What are you doing?"

"Well, I heard a doctor talking on TV and he said if you have children with a learning disability, try reading and spelling words to them when they are sleeping while their minds are at rest. So, I wanted to give it a try to see what would happen."

"Gee Mom, I never heard of that before, but who knows it might work." With all the extra help this past week, and with Mom trying this new experiment, I felt more ready than ever before when Friday's spelling test came around. Knowing that I worked extremely hard, my confidence level was at a new high. Sometimes, you just know when it is your week, and I felt that this was my week. After all, I had advice from a leading psychologist that came straight from a morning show on TV.

When Friday came I took out my #2 pencil and was feeling properly prepared. The teacher said to the class, "Take out a sheet and write the numbers one though twenty on your paper."

I did what I was told and waited for the teacher to mix the twenty spelling words up and began calling them out to us. She would pronounce the word very slowly and then use the word in a sentence. After I took one last glance over my spelling words, I brought my sheet up front to the teacher's desk and stood by her side while she graded my paper. I stood a little taller this week and kept a slight smile on my face until the teacher pulled out her red pen and went to work scribbling those dreadful red marks again.

All I can say is that this experiment and all of Mom's hard work did not work. Well, when I got my spelling sheet back it had those familiar red ink marks all over it like a painful toothache that won't go away. I always tried to hide my red-inked paper from the other students in line waiting their turn. I was feeling ashamed and discouraged for not passing another test. This one really hurt because I thought Mom and I had really solved the mystery behind the myth of spelling that constantly eluded me.

Once I got home, Mom was eager to find out my spelling grade for this week. I was feeling a little out of sorts and started to wonder deep down if there was any hope for a spelling-challenged person like me.

Mom walked over to me and asked, "How did your test go today?" I pulled out my test from my jeans pocket. I hoped that if I shoved it hard enough and deep enough into my pocket that the wrinkles would make the red marks and bad grade a little blurred and less overwhelming. I took out my spelling test with all of the red marks and couldn't say a word. Mom took it from me and looked it over and said, "Well, I can see that just maybe that doctor didn't really know what he was talking about. But look on the bright side. You did get a D instead of an F."

"I guess so, Mom, but we both worked so hard. I was sure it would be better than this."

"I know, Laurel, but you'll get it next week I am sure."

"But Mom what if I don't get it next week or ever get it for that matter?"

"No, Laurel, you'll do better next week. I know you will."

Another week passed and I worked even harder than before. Unfortunately, the results were the same. I did poorly again. My heart was heavy with disappointment and I was so frustrated that I was going to make Mom sad and upset that my spelling was still terrible. I pulled out my sheet filled with red ink and handed it to Mom. Mom looked at me in her loving understanding way and said, "Well, Laurel, I guess this didn't go the way we thought it would. We will try again this week to study the words and maybe do better on the next test. The funny thing about disappointment is that we always get another chance to try again. There is always a next time if we are willing to go after it." At the end of the week it was time to go shopping again. When we got to the Stop-N-Shop Mom said smiling, "Pick out something you like to eat because you worked so hard on those words and you deserve a good meal for your hard work." That was easy, I immediately said, "*Oh* Boy! I want cabbage rolls!" The disappointment seemed a little lighter with the thought of fresh bread, cabbage rolls, and blueberry pie for desert. While heading home from the Stop-N-Shop, pulling the shopping cart with food for the week, I looked over at Mom and said, "Mom do you spell cabbage like this? G-A-R-B-A-G-E."

"No, Laurel I think that is what the men from the city pick up every Friday in those big cans we put out in the front yard."

"*Oh* darn it," I said. "I thought I knew that one."

"But you were close. Both words have the same ending," she said.

"Do you think I will be able to spell some day?"

Mom said, "Of course, Laurel. You already knew how to spell. You just sometimes put the letters in the wrong place. Just keep working at it and you will improve. You are a bright young lady. Besides, you are a gentle person with and old soul and have a grown-up-ness about you that most kids and some adults never get.

As you get older you will come to understand that spelling tests are only a small part of your life and later on you will face the real tests in life that I am certain you will pass because of your strong spirit and good heart."

"Really, Mom," I said in astonishment.

"Oh, yeah," she said reassuringly. As we pulled into our front yard Mom stopped dead in her tracks. I was a little scared cause she had a troubled look on her face for the first time in our whole trip to the store.

"But what I am really worried about now is I can't remember where I put that big roaster pan we need to make the cabbage rolls."

I really liked the healthy way Mom put her list together of important items on that list in her head. In her mind, spelling, we would get that later but right then cooking a good meal for my sad and disappointed daughter was much more important than any spelling test. As usual, Mom was right.

Chapter 12

Dandelions

I was in the sixth grade and by now in special education classes. I did not resist being placed in these smaller classes. I found that I started to like my pint-sized class and I became curious about the different topics that came up. Looking back, I know that I was smart and intelligent and was able to do anything I put my mind to in spite of my disability. We were having a classroom election for class president and vice president. I placed my name in for class president, and why did I run? Well, I thought just maybe I could win. Besides, even at that early age, I started to develop an interest in our political system that lasted clear into my adult years. It may have something to do with my Irish heritage and the fact that we endured six-hundred years of oppression at the hands of the English.

Now that I was in the running, I had prepared all week to give my speech in front of my class. I knew I was ready. I wrote my speech over and over again until I was satisfied and knew each word of my speech by heart.

It was Friday and the big day was there at last. I had my sheet in my hands and glanced over it nervously. The teacher was telling the class to pay close attention to both speeches because every vote was important and counted. I heard my name called. At first I felt sick and my body sat still not able to move from my desk.

"Laurel, please come to the front of the class and present your speech," my teacher said.

I pulled myself up, and in what seemed like a hundred steps, I reached the front of my class; I could feel each classmate looking at me. When I reached the front of my class, I began my speech, but only nervous quivers started coming out of my voice, which was an incoherent mumbling that I never had heard before. I stopped myself, let out a breath, and with my tongue, I wet my lips and said, "This is why I want to be your class president." After I said all that I liked to do as class president, I felt relaxed and confident with how my speech turned out.

I smiled wide at my classmates, thanked them for listening, and walked in a normal pace back to my desk and sat down and was relieved that it was over. Now it was time to hear from my opponent. He walked up looking as nervous as I did and stood in front of the class moving his feet from side to side. I could tell his nerves were getting the best of him; he looked like he might throw up or run out of the class room. No such luck, he pulled himself together and began his speech. We both had similar ideas for our class, and to be honest, he did a better job. The teacher smiled and told us how pleased she was with both of our speeches.

She told the class to make a conscious effort to vote for the best candidate because by the end of the day we will have our class president and vice president. The teacher gave us both a round of applause that was followed by the whole class applauding us.

I could feel my face warm up as I shifted my head looking down at my shoes and was very thankful that it was over.

Since we only lived a block away from our Tremont school, every day my brother Billy, Veronica, and I went home for lunch. We all enjoyed being able to break up the day by having lunch at our home. Once we were home, Mom had made egg salad sandwiches, opened fruit cocktail, and put it in three small bowls. With the nervousness of giving my speech, I was feeling a little tired and ill at ease and passed on the egg salad. I told Mom I needed to lie down and took a short nap. Mom came into my room to wake me up and insisted that I ate something before we all walked back to school. I ate a little fruit cocktail and drank a large glass of apple juice. Feeling a little better, I could feel Mom looking me over and said, "How did your speech go today?"

I sat my glass down on the table and said, "It went really well and I was happy with how it turned out."

Mom reached over and touched my head and said, "I hope you are not getting the flu bug."

"No, Mom, I am fine, I'm only a little tired."

"We need to head back," Mom said to us. Together as we were headed back to school, I turned to Mom and said, "I feel uneasy voting for myself. Mom I am not sure if I would be a good class president; maybe I would be a better vice president because either way I was in."

I told Mom how we both believed in the same things and we were on the same level on class issues like no homework on Fridays. Mom patted me on my back and said, "Laurel, you would be a great class president or vice president and you should vote from your heart to whom you believe was right for the job."

Once I was back in my classroom, the day went fast. First, we had math followed by social studies. Finally, it was time for our class election. I watched as each classmate walked up to the front of the class and put in their vote and dropped it into the box. Finally, it was my turn. I walked up and saw my name and my classmate's name. I felt unsettled and the room started to spin. I felt like I was going to lose my balance and fall face down on the floor. I took in a deep breath and grabbed hold of the table, almost knocking over the class election box. Looking back down again at the sheet, I checked my opponent's name and placed it in the box. After a few more students went up to the front, the teacher took the box and pulled out each vote onto the table; she then put our names on the blackboard and took one vote at a time reading aloud the name and making a check mark by their names on the board. Right there on the blackboard I saw the results and I lost by one vote. I was really fine and almost happy to be vice-president and taking on a new role.

The teacher called us back to the front of the class. Together we both congratulated each other and shook hands in front of our class.

The teacher handed out cookies and milk, and before I knew it, the school day was coming to an end.

Everyone lined up by the door waiting for the school bell to ring to end the school day. I looked up at the clock feeling sick again and before I knew it, I collapsed and was falling backward onto a classmate. I woke up to see the vice-principal holding a cold cloth on my forehead. I wanted to tell him that I was a vice-president. He said, "Hold on, the ambulance is on its way." I passed out again. I woke up feeling exhausted and weak. Looking down at me were two firemen pulling me up and putting me on a stretcher. I could hear my teacher saying with a concerned voice, "Where is the ambulance?" No one answered her and the fireman said, "Take in slow breaths." I could feel my body being lifted up in the air as the firemen walked me down the halls followed by the stairs. I kept my eyes closed feeling a wave of sickness and nausea take hold of me again. I could hear the ambulance sirens blaring in the distance and pulled to a stop in front of my school.

Before I knew it, the paramedics ran over and took over, putting me on another stretcher. I was feeling nauseous and turned my head and vomited all over myself and the stretcher. "Oh, dear," the paramedic said and cleaned me up and put the oxygen mask on my face.

I closed my eyes as I was once again lifted up in the air and walked outside. There were people standing around and I heard someone yell out, "That's Billy's twin sister. Is she dead?" Some kid replied with the certainty of a medical professional, "Yeah, she looks dead to me." Then I felt someone reach for my hand. Mom was looking over me and right by my side telling the paramedics that she was my mother. Once I was in the ambulance, I was being examined and Mom was holding on to my hand. I heard Mom tell Billy, "Sorry you cannot come. Go home and watch Veronica." Billy just stood there defiantly and I could tell he really wanted to be with me. The bonds that bind twins together are strong. The paramedic said, "Sorry, Son, you need to go." Billy reluctantly went home.

The doors were closed and we took off toward the hospital. Mom was right by my side and I felt better by Mom being near me. She pulled back some hair that had fallen on my face and told me, "You are going to be fine."

Finally, we were in the emergency room and the tests began. I had a dry mouth and kept falling off to sleep. I wanted to tell Mom about the class election. There were doctors in and out examining me. I had one test after another. I fell asleep for a little while, only to wake up and see another doctor. Mom patiently sat by my side the whole time. I was hungry and exhausted.

I looked over at Mom and she looked worried and tired too, but she held my hand keeping my spirits up, by just knowing that she was there close to me and that made the ordeal bearable.

A nurse walked into the room and said, "There is a young man outside the door very worried about his twin sister and he has something he would like to give to you."

Billy walked in looking bashful and worried. He walked over to my hospital bed; he had pulled some yellow dandelions and placed them into my hand. "I thought you were dead!" Billy let out a tearful laugh. We all started laughing in relief that I wasn't dead like Billy had thought. The doctor walked in telling Mom that I was going to be staying in the hospital for a few days. He informed Mom that I had a convulsion and I needed to rest. Looking over at Mom and my brother, I knew that I was going to be all right. After the doctor walked out of the room, I said, "Billy how did you know what hospital they took me to and how did you get here so fast?" Billy looking around my emergency room in wonder said, "I ran home and grabbed my bike and followed the sounds of the ambulance to the closest hospital to find you. Oh, I picked you some of the flowers on the side of the hospital. Do you like them?"

"Yeah, I like them. They're great." I closed my eyes feeling the love and concern coming from my brother and having Mom there, I knew I was going to be all right.

"Guess what?" I said. "I am the vice-president of my class."

"That's great, Laurel, but you need your rest," Mom said worriedly.

Billy spoke up, "Hey, Laurel, that meant you came in second out of the whole class?"

"I sure did." So as it turned out I survived the rigors of a presidential campaign and a life-threatening medical trauma all in the same day. And of course, I came through it all because of my loving and caring Mom and my special twin brother.

Chapter 13

Mishap

I wonder if most Mothers realize that when their children are growing into their preteen years and the development of a whole new personality emerges, do they hold their breath and hope it's a steady and a pain-free experience? I was no exception to this situation. In my early teen years, I had given my mom many headaches and heartaches.

I remember how Mom and I were always a good cleaning team around the house. However, I was one who liked to be left alone when I cleaned. "Stay out of my way," was the message from me because I moved fast when I worked and it did show in my cleaning. I'm sure it did because I was the one that surfaced cleaned hastily. Of course, with age and maturity, I have improved in this area and I am a much more serious cleaner in my own home. In one minute, I would be wiping down the stove and taking it apart and scrubbing all the parts in the sink and the next minute, I would be swinging the mop across the kitchen floor. My goal was to get it clean and get it done because I knew there were better things to do than clean.

Mom and I worked well together even though Mom was more patient and methodical when she cleaned. Many times Mom would just leave me alone by going into another room, and leave me to my hasty cleaning, and then she would go over and do it again in a manner that never showed disapproval.

On this typical cleaning day, Mom was working in the kitchen washing dishes while I was running the vacuum in the living room. When I walked into the kitchen, I saw that Mom had finished the dishes and took out the garbage to the backyard. She had stopped to say a few words to our next door neighbor. So I started sweeping the floor and then filled up the bucket with pine cleaner.

I used to use too much soap when I cleaned and it was never the required capful for me. It was always the too much capful. I would bustle around the kitchen mopping up the floor because I wanted to get to the TV, to see the show "Facts of Life" that was coming on; it was one of my "must see" shows. But in reality, what I learned at that young age was the true meaning of facts about budgeting and running a household. After I finished, I left the dirty bucket of water in the doorway between the dining room and kitchen. I turned the TV show on much too loudly and was munching on some cookies. That's when I heard Mom yell out and I knew right away what had happened. We had a household safety rule to inform the whole house that the kitchen floor was wet.

It was an old, black-and-white, worn-out tile surface that was dangerously slippery when it was wet, and with my excessive use of soap, it made the floor much more slippery than usual. I got up and ran to the kitchen to see Mom lying down on the wet floor. Mom's arm looked twisted and out of place, "Oh, Mom," I said, "I'm sorry. Let me help you up."

I tried to help Mom up off the floor but with no success. Mom looking up at me in pain said, "I will be all right. Just give me a minute." I felt awful seeing my mother on the floor and seriously hurt.

Billy and Veronica came running down the stairs, and both gave me an accusing kind of look that said, "What did you do?" The three of us tried again to pick Mom up. But every time we tried, we were unsuccessful and we were only making her injury worse and hurting Mom more. Mom said in a cringing painful voice, "Billy, pull a chair next to me." Billy grabbed a kitchen chair and placed it next to her. Mom took her good arm, pulled herself up, and crawled up onto the chair, holding in her breath as she moved further up and finally sat down on the chair. I watched my mom moving in pain and felt her pain.

Billy had a worried look on his face while Veronica gave me an angry sneer and I could almost read her mind on what she was thinking. It was a look that said, "It's your fault. You broke Mom's arm."

I said sadly and shamefully, "Mom, what can I do to help you?"

"Bring me a glass of water," Mom said with a wince.

"Veronica," Mom said, "can you get an ice bag?" The three of us were working and doing our best to help and ease Mom's pain. Mom sat and rested and I was feeling so bad about what had happened to Mom. I started to cry saying, "I am so sorry. It's all my fault that you got hurt."

Mom said, "No, Laurel, you were helping me and it was an accident."

We were not sure what to do next. Then the door opened and Dad had just walked in from a hard day's work and saw Mom sitting on the kitchen chair holding her arm in pain; he reached for the phone and called his brother for a ride up to the hospital. In that moment, I felt so awful. I went upstairs and let my tears fall onto my pillow. The person I had cared the most for was hurt because of me. I hoped that Mom would be all right and that it was not too bad. In my head I kept on saying, "I'm sorry" over and over again.

Later at the hospital, Mom had an X-ray that showed her collarbone broken on her right side. The only treatment was a sling and the doctor wrote out a prescription for the pain. The doctor could not put a cast on the area where the bone was broken. When Mom walked in, she looked tried. I said, "Mom, I am so sorry again that it happened."

Mom said, "Laurel, this was an accident, but I will be needing more help around the house."

"Yes, Mom," I said. "I will help you with anything that you need done around the house." I wanted to do all that I could to make up for what had happened.

My mother was a determined woman. She still got a lot done around the house in spite of the broken bone in her shoulder. My mom would keep on working with her good arm, trying to keep up our home.

I watched her move around, cooking, and cleaning and she would often wince in pain. I offered to help with the cleaning and cooking. When I tried to jump in to help and tell Mom to relax, she would tell me that she was fine and could finish it herself. I would kind of ignore her and would pitch in more than I ever did before. I guess that is what guilt does to a person. I felt the strong need to help to ease my guilty conscience. All three of us kept asking Mom what we could do to help and Mom would always answer, "I'll be fine," or "Don't worry, I got it."

Mom's right arm was in a sling and it was hard for her to write; at times, she had uncontrollable muscle spasms in her shoulder. I was frightened when I would see that happen to Mom. The sight of Mom suffering so badly was terrible to see. I felt so sad and so helpless. This is when I felt the worst about her accident. Mom never complained about the injury or never blamed me for it happening. This, like so many other wonderful things about her, is what made her such a special Mom.

Well, it was that time of the month when all of the bills were due. I watched my mother with a concerned eye when Mom pulled her chair up close to the dining room table and pulled out all the bills. I could see her wince in pain when she tried to write out the checks for the companies that we owed money to. This was the first time Mom ever asked for help.

In spite of her poor uneducated background, she was such an independent woman and at times very stubborn in a sweet kind of way. She was not able to write clearly with the broken collarbone and her handwriting was like a bunch of scribbles that we could not make sense of.

Mom finally asked me for help and said, "Laurel, I need your help with writing out the bills. I just can't do it." I could not believe my ears. I was so proud that Mom asked me to help her. I jumped up so fast I almost knocked the table over. It was a real milestone in my life because I was asked to partake in one of the most serious adult activities concerning the management and well-being of our household. That is when Mom taught me how to write out bills and balance a checkbook. As I sat next to my mother, she patiently explained in great detail how to balance a checkbook. She was such a good teacher that to this day, I have never bounced a check in my entire financial life. Mom had a spiral notebook and I had to write out each bill and the amount to be paid.

I had to add up all the utility bills and other bills that were due, and then put money away for food.

If we were lucky enough to have anything left, we would put it aside for any other unexpected expenses that might come up with having a family. If the budget would allow, a little was put aside for savings, which was not much at all considering we had to raise a large family, and it seemed like we were growing out of our shoes and clothes all the time. All this information was placed in an updated financial journal that Mom kept; entries were added to this journal every payday that Dad had. Mom knew where every nickel and every dime went that Dad brought home every payday. Mom explained to me in a caring way, how to write out checks and balance our budget. She showed me how to record account numbers and where each amount of money was going in the financial journal that she kept.

Having my mom involve me in important family business was when I really felt like an adult. Mom had a simple one, two, three, method of budgeting. First, pay all the bills, then put aside food money, and if any was left we would put it in the family savings account. Now that I am older and have a household of my own, I am doing the same thing that my mother lovingly taught me years ago while she was in a tremendous amount of pain. Mom taught me how to balance a check book and budget, save for a rainy day, and most of all, to live within one's means.

The most remarkable thing about this whole incident was that Mom never got cantankerous or mean and nasty because of the pain in her shoulder. And the most impressive thing about the situation was that she never once blamed me for the accident even though it was clearly my fault. I really appreciated her not making me feel worse than I already did about the incident. She was truly a grand and gracious lady, no matter what the situation was.

Chapter 14

Temptation

When it came to moral lessons, Mom laid down the law and taught us right from wrong by her guidance and her good, religious example. Mom's moral compass always seemed to be pointing north. Mom had a caring way that never showed judgment. Mom would say, "We really shouldn't judge anyone cause that job is already been taken. God is the only judge. Besides, people know in their hearts if they have done right or wrong." And how true; I guess we all live and learn from our mistakes.

We were at the mall shopping for shoes for my little sister Veronica because she had outgrown hers. I was fifteen years old at that time and saw a cute shirt that I wanted. I was at that awkward age where I was preoccupied with my appearance. Every clothing item I saw that I thought may look good on me, I wished that I could buy it and have it in my closet. "Mom, I like that shirt. Can I get it? Can you buy it for me?"

Mom let out a weary sigh and said, "Next time, or you could save your weekly allowance and come back at a later time and buy it yourself. We are on a tight budget. I wish I could buy it for you, but I just don't have enough to get it right now." I had a side job dog walking and doing odd jobs for a neighbor lady. Mom was right. I could save up and get the shirt later when I had the money from my earnings. I worked for an older lady named "Miss Kitty."

That is what she went by. She took a liking to me and the feeling was mutual. I liked working for Miss Kitty, but she was very particular and wanted things done right. I always took my time when cutting her grass and made sure I trimmed the edge nicely and neatly and would always sweep up all of the grass shavings from the driveway and the sidewalk. I would do other jobs as well, like washing her car and going to the store for her. Miss Kitty would always check my work before she paid me, making sure it came out right. And if she was not pleased with something, I would have to do it over again. At times, I thought she was being too fussy, but I did what she said so I could earn the extra money.

I received a weekly three-dollar allowance and Mom always took care of my personal expenses so that whatever I earned, I could spend on whatever I wanted to. Mom was right. I could save and wait, but being young and not thinking, I wanted that shirt that I saw in the mall. To me it seemed like my friends always had new clothes all the time. So why couldn't I? I knew I would look good in it with my slim, teen figure. Plus, this weekend I could wear it with my girlfriends to the movies. My teenage hormones were raging and it was a hot day in the middle of August, and I kept thinking about that shirt. So I went into my mom's pocketbook and took out sixteen dollars.

I wrote a note saying, "Mom, I am taking sixteen dollars out of your wallet and I am going to the mall. See you in a few hours, and I am going to pay you back." I signed the note, "Love, Laurel." I took the bus to Parmatown Mall. It was about forty-five minutes to get to the mall from my home. Once I got to the mall, I went and bought the shirt. After I tried it on and looked into the mirror, I was very pleased with how good I looked in the new shirt. I wandered in and out of a few stores looking and wishing I had more money to buy more clothes that I, in reality, didn't really need.

By now I was getting hungry, so I stopped at the food court. I ordered three soft tacos and a large glass of lemonade. I paid for my food, but I realized I had only fifty-nine cents to my name. At that time, the bus fare was eighty-five cents to get back home, and it took forty minutes to get home on the bus. Looking back down at the tacos, I no longer felt like eating and my stomach felt sick. I thought that maybe I could ask someone for twenty-six cents, but I felt too shy and funny about asking a total stranger for money. I threw out the tacos and grabbed my lemonade and bag and headed out of the mall entrance.

Once I was outside, the sun was blazing down and I started to cry knowing that going into my mom's wallet was wrong and that I was going to be in trouble when I got home. I was dressed in a T-shirt, jeans shorts, and sandals that were not good for walking. This was going to be a very long walk back home. I figured it was going to take two hours before I reached home.

I was about an hour into my walk and the heat was getting to me. My feet hurt and the lemonade I had was long gone. I was sunburned and tired. I took off my sandals and walked in my bare feet; the cement burned my feet as I walked. I was sweating and looking down at the bag in my hand. I no longer thought this shirt looked cute. By now I hated it and myself for what I had done.

Guilt and grief engulfed my mind for what I had done to my sweet Mom. "What was I thinking?" kept rolling around in my head. I was also upset knowing Mom was worrying about me. I needed a drink and my month was dry. So I decided to stop at a corner deli. Before I reached the store, I heard a voice yell out, "Hey, sweetheart you need a ride?" I looked over to see a shirtless man with his windows down with a perverted look on his face. He pulled over to the curb and said, "Come on, Honey, I don't bite. I am as safe as Santa Claus, so come on in here and sit on my lap." I hollered back at him, "No, thank you," and took off running into the corner store. Once I was inside I felt safe and I realized I had fifty-nine cents on me and I could buy a soft drink. I killed a little extra time in the store to make sure Mr. Santa would be long gone before I began the last hour of my long walk home.

The little store was air-conditioned, so I hung around a bit to try and cool off before I hit the oppressing heat. Once I was back on the sidewalk, I saw a car pull over and honk at me. I got scared and picked up my pace and walked faster, thinking it was another "weirdoe" wanting to give me a ride. I also knew that there was no way I was getting into a stranger's car no matter how overheated and miserable I was from the August heat and humidity. The driver honked again and I heard my name being called. "Laurel, Laurel, what are you doing walking alone in this heat way over here?" It was Miss Kitty; I was relieved to be able to get in and sit in an air-conditioned car. Miss Kitty looked at me and said, "It's a hot day to be all the way out here walking. Are you OK?"

I was in no mood to talk; I only wanted to close my eyes and relax my muscles after walking for so long in the heat. I started to cry again and I began telling her the whole story of what I had done and how wrong I was. She listened to me and finally said, "Well, looks to me that you learned a valuable lesson and you got a lot of explaining and apologizing to do when you get home." We drove the rest of the way in silence and I had a feeling of an overwhelming sense of guilt. Miss Kitty dropped me off in front of my home and I thanked her for the ride. She said, "Go and tell your mom the same thing you told me because your mom is a good woman and things will work out."

I got out and walked up my steps and walked into the house. My leg muscles ached and my skin was burning from the long walk in the heat. Without saying a word, my mom looked at me and went directly into the bathroom and got some lotion and came over and put it onto my burning arms and face. After I felt a little relieved, she told me how wrong I was and my punishment.

First of all, I was going to pay her back and secondly no phone and no going out for a week. Finally, I had to return the shirt that I really could not afford and I could not stand looking at it anymore. I gave Mom the money. No friends were allowed to come over and no going to the movies.

This I felt was fair. I said to Mom, "I swear, Mom. I will never go into your purse again." I wanted to say more, but Mom stopped me and in her own selfless practical way and said, "Laurel, did you eat?"

"No, Mom, I felt too bad to eat." Right at that moment in my young adult life I knew my mom was not only Mom, but my best friend and I felt worse knowing what I put her through. She went into the kitchen and I followed her in.

Mom said, "Get busy and help with the dishes. You got a lot of money to pay back and I will fix you something to eat. You need to put back the fluids you burned up in that long walk in the heat. I'll make you some cold ice tea." I felt like the "Prodigal Daughter," returning home and given a feast in my honor. In a lighthearted and teasing manner she said, "Do I have to put a padlock on my purse?"

"No, Mom," I replied. "I'll never do that again." And that was the end of it. Mom graciously never brought it up again. I felt so bad for what I had done and I think I punished myself with guilt more harshly than Mom punished me. Incidents like this and so many other times when Mom had every right to be harsh and cruel but was very sensitive and caring, is what made her the special lady that she was.

Chapter 15

Girl's Weekend

There are people out there who love to get around and see new places and Mom was one of them. She craved a new road to travel on and I know she deeply wanted to someday travel out of the country to see new lands if she ever could afford it. Mom loved to collect old *National Geographic* magazines and she was an avid map collector. Mom would find an old map of a state or country and she would, with a gleam in her eye, try to locate the capitals and the main sightseeing towns and places on the map. When she was involved in this activity, she would be lost in the actual town or city she was studying. As for me, I enjoyed travel as well, but only if it was short lived and I could be back in the comfort of my own bed that evening. Consequently, watching the travel specials on Public Television satisfied my curiosity about distant lands. Mom, however, would have jumped on a plane and would have gone to the far ends of the earth if she had the money. This could never come to be a reality, but it never stopped her from dreaming.

I was around fifteen years old at the time and I said to Mom as she was engrossed in one of her maps, "Let's take a little trip and maybe we can take a greyhound bus into Pittsburgh, PA." Mom gave me a playful look of approval and smiled saying, "Yes, Laurel, that sounds like fun!" Without hesitation, Mom immediately reached for the phone and called the greyhound bus station and inquired about the price from Cleveland to Pittsburgh, PA.

Mom said, after hanging up the phone, "Laurel, it is in our price range. Maybe we will go this weekend. What do you think?"

"Mom," I answered, "It will be fun." I immediately ran to my room looking for outfits to pack. Mom asked Billy if he wanted to go and he said, "No thanks, Mom I'll stay home with Dad." However, Veronica was jumping up and down all excited about a bus trip and was wondering what she would take with her.

Our get-away-weekend was here at last. The three of us were getting onto the bus and Mom said cautiously, "We will all sit up close to the driver." Mom was always concerned about safety but she was never too far into her own shell to open up and talk to someone whom she did not know. I sat next to Veronica and we both were so happy to have Mom all to ourselves for a few days. I remember the bus was half filled and Mom was sitting next to a young woman, who had visited her family for a week in Cleveland and was going back to Pittsburgh because she was a student at the Pittsburgh University. Mom asked her if she felt safe traveling by herself. And she said confidently, "I only take the greyhound in the daytime and sit close to the driver." Mom had a way of making even total strangers feel at ease. I could see that she liked Mom. The young woman talked a lot about what she was taking at college and how she missed being home, but liked being on her own and stepping into her own dreams as a young woman.

As we passed Lake Erie on a warm June day, people were fishing outside on the docks and we could see the sailboats out on the lake. The water looked light blue and the waves were moving steadily up and down the shoreline. Veronica and I kept our eyes glued on the scenery that was out of the window. I then glanced over at Mom. I could see that she was soaking everything up as we passed by. Seeing Mom's light green eyes light up made our first bus trip special.

To Mom there were no ordinary sights; they were all special and unique to her. I could tell we were going to have a great time together this weekend. Once we were in Pittsburgh, PA, we got off the bus and took a taxi to the hotel. Mom said to the taxi driver, "Take us to a nice hotel in a safe area of town" and he did. He dropped us off at the Hotel Hilton by the Three Rivers Stadium, which is now Heinz Field. We all got out looking around as the people passed by in a midday rush. Mom walked in confidently and we followed her up to the front desk to check in. Mom never had a credit card and paid with check or cash for everything we brought. Mom had her ID card with her as well. The middle-aged man, who had on a pressed, tightly fitting blue uniform, behind the counter said smiling, "How can I help you? Do you have a reservation?"

"No," Mom said, "we do not."

He smiled and said, "Do you have a major credit card?"

Mom stood up closer to the counter and politely said, "I would like to pay for our room with a check or cash and we will need only two nights" and thanked him. He was looking on the computer and asked Mom where she was from. Mom said, "I am from Cleveland and I am visiting Pittsburgh PA, with my daughters and we are Steelers fans as well as my son."

That is when Veronica excitedly said, "It's a girls' weekend. My brother stayed home with my dad." He smiled at us as his manager overheard what Mom and Veronica had said. The man at the desk then replied, "I'm sorry, Miss, we only accept major credit cards." The manager heard this and he tapped his employee on the shoulder and took over on the computer. He then told us, "Welcome to Pittsburg PA." Then he said, "We have a room on one of the top floors that has an excellent view." Mom handed the manager the money and he called for someone to get our bags. As the manager took us up to our room, he was telling Mom a few things that we could do while in PA. Mom smiled at him and thanked him for his help.

Looking back now I think we got the room for a good price. It may have been something to do with being a Steelers' fan and the manager being impressed with Mom's tall stature and good looks. Or, it may have been that he noticed Mom was a special woman eager to spend quality time with her daughters. Whatever the reason, he was much more hospitable than the first clerk.

The manager opened the door and we walked into the room. It had two beds and a nice big fancy desk in the corner. Looking out the window we could see houses that were up on the hills, the three rivers, and there were a lot of crosses poking out into the sky from the top of the church steeples. We all sat on the bed feeling like high-class people and we thought we were something because whatever we wanted, all we had to do was call for room service and it was there.

Of course, we never used room service because it was too expensive and we had no credit card. Once we were settled, Mom, Veronica, and I ventured out of our room and walked down by the river and around downtown, loving every minute of our walk in a strange, new, and exciting city. By now we were getting hungry. Close to the hotel was a little chicken wings place with a small eating area. There was a line to get the wings and Mom said, "It must be good, if people are waiting in line." Not to mention that we all loved chicken wings.

After we ate our early dinner, we took a short walk around looking in a drugstore to buy postcards. Walking back to our room, it was early, around six o'clock. I said to Mom, "Can I go next door to get more wings?" as a growing teen with a ferocious appetite, I needed more food. Mom said, "OK, Laurel, but get only wings, a large salad, and soft drinks." Mom handed me the money and told me to come right back. I felt like I was a grown up walking out the hotel door to go and order food in a strange city all by myself. Walking out the door, I noticed that it had cooled off a little from being outside walking around earlier in the day.

With the money in my pocket, I walked into the little Mom and Pop's eatery and put our order in and stepped aside picking up a magazine and tried to look interested in what I was reading. For a teenager, it's all about appearances. When my order was ready, I paid and walked out feeling important, walked out into a new city that I was never in before, and walked slowly heading back to our room. I went directly to the fancier elevators in the front of the lobby to see if they would bring me to the same place. Curiosity had gotten the best of me and I punched in our floor, but when the door opened I was somewhere different and it was not looking familiar. I turned around to go back down to the lobby when the door closed on me. I could see that in the ballroom there was a dinner party that looked to be an art auction going on with a lot of formally dressed people.

As I was waiting by the elevator door two young girls around my age came out of the bathroom. Looking over to me they started laughing and one of the girls said,

"Did you order takeout from the restaurant in the lobby?"

"No, I didn't," her friend said giggling, "but I bet it is better than what we had to eat," she put her fingers by her mouth and made a gagging noise to show her disapproval of their expensive supper. I was very self-conscious because they had on expensive evening gowns and I had a t-shirt and jeans with an order of take-out chicken wings to go. I nervously kept hitting the elevator button like it would open up faster for me. Finally, to my relief, the door of the elevator opened and I started to walk toward the other end of the lobby that would take me to the elevators that would lead to the section of the hotel where our room was. All of a sudden, a well-dressed couple in fancy evening apparel approached me and the woman said, "Please hold the door." Looking over at me she said, "Are you going up?"

"No, I am going to the lobby," and I tightened my grip on to the take-out bag. They both were dressed up; he had a black suit on and his shoes were shining. She had a long black dress that came over her shoulder. It had some shimmer to it. Looking over at me she said, "Dear, what is in your take-out bag? It smells wonderful." I held on even tighter to the bag and said, "Chicken wings from the small restaurant a few doors down from the hotel."

I always felt the rich had an unfair advantage over the working class because they had the power of negotiation from all of the so-called "disposable income;" whereas, working people needed every nickel they had to make it from paycheck to paycheck. I was waiting for her to say, "I'll give you fifty bucks for that bag of wings" and I was scared that I would give in because to a broke teen fifty bucks is an awful lot of money.

She said looking over at her husband, "Honey, can you go get some wings from next door? I am still hungry and the auction dinner never gives you a proper portion."

"Yes, Dear," he said annoyingly as they walked out of the elevator door. I was glad to be alone with my wings knowing they were safe from hungry, greedy, rich folks. Once I was off the elevator and on the right floor I felt relieved.

I tapped on the door and Mom opened looking worried. As we sat by the table near the window I told Mom what had happened and we all had a good laugh. Looking out the big picture window the sun was setting and glistening on the three rivers. The sounds of laughter continued as we ate our greasy chicken wings. Mom had all of the brochures out on the bed of interesting places to see in Pittsburgh. I could see that Mom was thinking of what we could do tomorrow, but being by her side was enough for me and my little sister too. Even though we were on a small tight budget with not many frills, it was one of the best vacations of my life. We had Mom all to ourselves and we girls had a chance to be just girls all weekend long.

Chapter 16

Used Car

I was turning the magical age of sixteen and had my driver's license in my hands, but no car to drive. I felt that it was my right to have and drive my own car and I would be happy with an old used car that ran well. Who cares what it looked like? I just wanted a car to get me from point A to point B. I had my share of public transportation headaches, and I had enough "weirdo" passengers to last two lifetimes. As I saw it, my girlfriend had a used car that her father had bought for her. So why not me? Maybe I was a little self-centered and selfish with my typical teen attitude and behavior.

Somehow I got up the courage and walked right up to my dad while he was reading the newspaper. Without thinking, I spoke too fast and said, "Dad, I want you to buy me a used car because Diane's father bought her a used car." I waited for his answer, but Dad just ignored my foolish statement and kept looking at the paper. "Dad," I said again, waiting for his answer that I thought would never come. Dad folded the newspaper and put it onto the floor. I could see the answer in his eyes without a word being said. "But, Dad, I am sixteen years old and I got my driver's license," I pleaded with my father. I watched as Dad picked up his coffee, took a sip, and placed it back down onto the coffee table. He started shaking his head.

"No!" my father said, "I will not buy you or your brother or sister a car."

Then he picked up his paper to find the article he was reading. "But, Dad, please, I really want a car," I cried out. Being an overly dramatic teenager, I felt an overwhelming pain on the inside of the pit of my stomach. I could tell that I was getting nowhere with my father. "Well," Dad said in a firm manner,

"I said no. And if you really want a car, they are hiring at the corner Deli. You can earn your own money, save up, and buy your own car."

I felt an attitude coming over me and a childish temper tantrum overwhelming me. I turned and marched into my room, closing the door behind me and feeling sorry for myself. I stewed and wallowed in my own self-pity and self-righteous anger toward my dad. I was wishing that my friend's Dad was my dad, and he had bought me a car. I felt that life was not fair and wondered why other parents could buy cars for their kids, but not mine? I kept on pouting throughout the day in my room, complaining to myself that life is just not being fair to me.

I eventually came to my senses and took my father's advice and that is just what I did. I went to work and I saved my money for a used car. I did everything I could in the Deli to keep my hours up and the tips coming in. I prepped meals, bussed tables, and ran the cash register. The really tough part was not wasting the money I earned on things I did not need. Life may not be fair at times, but now that I am older, I can and do appreciate the value of a dollar.

My father had really helped me by teaching me to be responsible and to think before I buy and to wait and ask myself whether or not I really needed something. In actuality, I really needed a car to get around because public transportation was a real risky venture in those days. As I was growing into womanhood there was always some pervert on the bus or in a car cruising the bus stops trying to pick me up and other young girls. I don't think Dad understood this.

When my Deli job ended, it took some time and effort and I worked and saved. I then found a job at a donut shop. I still worked for Miss Kitty walking her dog and other odd errands. I loved every minute of taking care of Miss Kitty's dog. It was fun being outside with my big, black, fuzzy-faced K-9 friend. Mom helped out and took over walking the dog when I got too busy with my work schedule.

Back in the eighties, poor and working-class people could buy an old car at a reasonable price and at that time there were no E——checks or inspections. I finally had saved up five hundred dollars and brought an old brown Cutlass Oldsmobile. It ran most of the time but it was old and loud, and it needed some work. I had a religious experience every time I tried to start it up. I would look to the heavens and say, "Please God, let my beater start." But for city driving it was reliable. So, even though my first car was old and ugly, it got me around Cleveland.

Image is everything to a teenager, but I could not have cared less because I had a car and I was fed up with riding the busses.

Dad saw that I had worked hard and saved up and got a car; he gave in and helped me by putting on a new exhaust system and muffler. This was great because before that you could hear me coming two city blocks away. Yes, there was a great feeling to going out the front door, and parked there on the street is an old, ugly car that is all yours and will start up and get you to where you needed to go. For me it felt like Independence Day each time my car started up and to be able to pull into a parking lot and walk a few steps into a store instead of jumping in and out of busses and facing all the freaks and weirdoes that came with the territory of Public Transportation.

Mom and I loved to head out in my car and drive to the grocery store. But what we loved to do most was to shop at second-hand-shops and pull over if we saw garage sale signs. As a new teenage driver, Mom kept a close eye on the road, telling me to slow down or watch out for a car pulling out. Mom was co-pilot, even if she never drove herself. She had a watchful eye and saved me from a number of accidents and close calls. In my young woman stage of my life, my mother and I grew into becoming best friends as well as Mom and daughter.

At the end of my teen years we were just two close "Gal Pals." We loved to talk, laugh, and sometimes cry together over every topic we could think of.

She was that one person who I knew that no matter what happened or what mistake I made, would love and listen to me and not judge, preach, or criticize me. And in those early driving days, the two of us would get lost in the moment just shopping and talking together.

"Mom," I would tell her as we drove through different neighborhoods, "Keep an eye out for garage sales signs."

"Oh, not to worry, Laurel, I got it covered."

"I know you do," I said smiling to myself and the day would go on with us pulling over and looking at all this stuff and a lot of plain old junk too. We never knew what we might find.

With a little money and patience, we would bring back home something we could use and that was the fun part. Mom had a keen eye for things, while I would only see junk for sale. Mom would pull something out like a new pair of slippers that were never worn and still in the box they came in. There was something special about our time together buying for the whole family with a few dollars in our pockets. The hours would pass by and before we knew it, the day turned into evening.

After a whole day of "junking," as Dad would call it, we could not wait to get home and show off all of our bargains that we had found.

When we finally came home, Dad would say, "Six hours! Where have you two been? Did you forget your address?" We had a trunk full of bags of finds from our garage sales and second-hand shops. Dad helped to bring in the bags and laughed to himself. In a teasing manner he would say, "All this junk." But he kept that grin on his serious face.

"Look what I have found," Mom would reply. Mom would pull out something for Dad like a tool box that was still in great shape. Dad looking it over would say, "Well, Miss America, what did you pay for that tool box?" Even though Dad would tease us, he always put to good use all of the things we found.

"Two dollars," Mom would answer in a, "I-told—you—so" tone.

Mom was the best shopping partner I ever had. She would go her way and I would go my way, and we would meet in the middle. Then we would look over at what we had found, and then we would talk it over with each other if we should buy it or not. Mom was much more patient than I was on these shopping trips. I would tire out much sooner than she would. No shopping excursion was complete without stopping into a family Mom and Pop's restaurant to eat. We avoided the franchise restaurants because they just did not have the same atmosphere as the little out-of-the-way places we found. Together we would build up an appetite and enjoyed a meal there.

It was special for Mom not to be laboring in a hot kitchen preparing meals for our big, hungry family but just sit and relax. That first old car of mine got us around our city and the memories of the trips with Mom are dear to my heart. Mom also loved looking at every house as we passed by. She always loved to drive down a new street, shopping in new stores, and eating in small cozy different restaurants. We each became our own restaurant critics and rated the price, the food, the menu, and the service, and then decided if we would come back and eat again. If the food or the order was not right, Mom would not complain. She would just smile and say, "Well, she got the order wrong, but I know firsthand how tough it is waiting for tables."

What I remember most about driving in my old "beater" with Mom was Mom would often say a little prayer for total strangers we passed on the street especially someone pulling a shopping cart. Both of us could easily remember those days out walking and pulling a shopping cart ourselves. Not too long after I got my car, Mom said, looking over at me, "Laurel, it's nice to go shopping in a car and a lot easier."

"Yes, Mom it is," I answered. "But back when we were out pulling our cart, I had fun. To me, in a way, it was a shopping cart filled with love and we always had the best of times."

Mom looked over with tears filling up in her eyes and said, "Yes, we did." In every city across America, that was how many people got around to feed their families by pulling shopping carts filled with groceries up and down city streets. With both of our hearts being opened to what we had shared, and on a day out driving and shopping at garage sales, the rain clouds were coming across the sky to spoil our fun day. The sky had dropped the soft blue color it had held for the day and was turning dark and lightning had lit up the sky around us as we drove. Now the rain started to come down hard.

We felt a sense of relief, knowing we would be home safe in a few minutes. Then we both saw an older lady pulling her shopping cart filled up with brown paper bags with groceries. Since we were living in the city, Mom would always tell me be careful and not to give a ride to strangers. Mom said, "Laurel, it's raining hard and that little old lady is pulling a cart and she is getting all wet. We should offer her a ride home. I remember how hard it was for us when the weather would get bad on the way home from shopping."

"OK, Mom," I said as I pulled my car over to a stop. I got out and spoke to her and tried not to alarm her, "Excuse me Miss, I would like to give you a ride home." She had on an old dark green sweater, had a round Slavic face, and on her head was a babushka. The lady was soaking wet, and with a heavy Eastern European accent her answer was, *"Yes I ride."* I opened my trunk and put in her wet brown paper bags carefully, folded up her shopping cart, and closed the trunk.

Mom got out and said, "Please sit in the front." Mom sat at the back. The older lady slowly got in the front and sat down while I ran around and jumped in the driver's seat. By now the rain had picked up and started coming down with a harsh force again. I put the key into the ignition and as always said a silent prayer. "Please, let it start."

Looking up to the heavens when it started, I would say, "Thank You, Lord Jesus." I turned to the older women and asked, "Were do you live?"

She answered, "I liveth on West Twenty-Fifth Street of Clark." I pulled over toward Clark Ave, and Twenty-Fifth-Street. Mom tried to make small talk but the lady looked over at me and very rudely said, "You needed new car. This car no good, too old."

I was a little taken back by her rudeness. After all, we were giving her a ride.

"Well, yes, in time," I politely said holding back my anger. "I am happy to have this old car. It gets me around." With a sour look on her face she obnoxiously repeated, "No this car is no good, too old. You needed to go get new car." Looking back in the mirror I gave Mom a look that said, "Can you believe this rude ungrateful woman?" Mom gave me a little bewildered shrug with her shoulders and moved her lips saying, "She'll be out of the car in a few minutes."

I was getting angry, and truly wanted to yell at this woman but held it in. I said in a calm voice to the old lady, as I reached Twenty-Fifth Street, "Where do I turn?"

"Turn, Turn, my side now, the white house, three from corner." I pulled over to the older lady's home, which was so run down. It looked like it needed everything. It needed new paint and her porch had rotting boards that caved in on the one side. Her windows had plastic garbage bags and duct tape to keep out the cold. I so much wanted to say to her, "You need a new house, go buy new house." Mom tapped me on my shoulder, "Laurel, go and help with her bags." I got out, opened my trunk, and opened up the shopping cart placing her wet brown bags back in it. Then I walked up her stairs with her cart. I was afraid that her rotted out porch would cave in as the boards creaked and sagged when I walked across them. At any minute I thought the boards would collapse and I would be trapped in this witch's dungeon forever.

Once I got to her front door, I quickly turned around and ran to my car. The old crabby lady could not open the rusty door to my car so I pulled open the door and helped her get out. I told her to have a good day and I wanted to get away as fast as I could. She stood there and arrogantly gave me that sour look again. She pointed her finger at me and said while the rain let loose and poured down on us, "Car no good, too old, no good, you go get a new car."

I ran fast to get away from her pointed finger and I so wanted to give her a finger of my own. I got back into my car and watched her slowly walk up her steps to her porch. Mom got back in the front seat and we both let out a crazy laugh.

"Mom, can you believe it? We tried to help and be nice and help out someone and all she kept saying, *'Your car no good, too old, go get a new car.'* I wanted to dump her off in the middle of the street in the pouring rain—run out and open my trunk and throw out her shopping cart and bags right out in the middle of the street. And look at her house! Like that old hag got no room to talk. She lives in a dump," I said as I was ranting and raving about our obnoxious passenger.

"Now, Laurel, remember that our intentions were good and she is the one with the problems not us."

"OK, Mom," I said laughing out loud, "Old witch need new home, home too old, no good." We enjoyed one more laugh at the expense of our guest passenger.

I started up my old car and was relieved that it started. We then headed home. We vowed that if we ever saw the nasty old lady again, we would say a prayer for her and keep on driving. Once again, my mom was nothing but manners and class.

As obnoxious as that lady was, Mom by her good example kept me calm and kept me from being as ignorant and rude as our passenger.

Chapter 17

Determined

There are days, weeks, and months when things turn out wrong and just don't seem to go your way. I think we all have been in, from time to time, what is called a rut. I was in one and I found it to be a comfort and that scared me. I had dropped out of school, not because it was the right thing to do. I was getting nowhere by going to Cleveland public schools. Many of my friends' parents were putting their kids into private schools or moving out of the city to get away from the rapidly, rising crime scene. For us, moving to the suburbs or Catholic school tuition were options that were not in our family budget.

Sadly to say, racism and uncalled for hatred toward people of any color was out there and to this day I believe it was truly wrong on any side of town. Where I was raised in Tremont, we were already a mixed area with different ethnic groups and races of people—living, playing, and going to school together and somehow just getting along and getting by, most of the time. But around my junior high school years, Cleveland city schools started moving kids around into different neighborhoods and putting children onto buses and taking us across town to attend different schools in neighborhoods that we were not familiar with.

Many parents and school kids were experiencing a great deal of anxiety by being forced out of their own neighborhood schools and were bused to schools and learning environments, out of their neighborhoods where they were not always welcome. Later on it was admitted that this blunder was a huge, costly mistake. Busing is now voluntary.

The adolescent years are hard on everyone. Teens face peer pressure, an identity crisis, and the need to fit in somewhere. I was tall for my age, had big, green eyes, was extremely shy, and a late bloomer with the boys. I was really not interested in the "girlfriend boyfriend" craze that my friends were all wrapped up in. I was always on my best behavior and listened to all of my teachers, to the point of being a stickler for the rules. I felt sorry for most of my teachers who were constantly trying to control noisy, and at times, violent students. The teachers at the junior high that I was bused to were in a losing battle trying to maintain a sense of order, only to get cussed out and assaulted for their efforts. Their full-time job was not teaching; it was trying to stop the class from getting out of control. Time passed and little to no work was getting done at school. I can remember days where the class would open a book to the day's chapter of work and the teacher would spend the whole period being a cop or a baby sitter.

Days like these were very common and I was truly frustrated and was a little bewildered as to how this could really be a school. On those days we never had the opportunity to learn anything.

I also had to try to block out the hurtful names, nasty sexual and vulgar comments, and the deliberate bumping into my shoulders while trying to get into my next class. All of this mistreatment was because of who I was, not because I had done anything to anyone. Every day that I walked into school, a fear for my safety came over me because of all the fights and the violent outbreaks around me. I became anxious and scared to go to school. I gave Mom a hard time every morning before going to school. I started crying and got panicky, and did not want to go knowing what I had to face every day. It simply left me overwhelmed.

I had reached the age of sixteen; I quit school and was working part time at a donut shop. It was a mutual and difficult decision made by my parents and me. I felt work and working on getting my GED in my own time was better for me than having to face chaos and danger every day. Mom felt my pain and knew what was going on with school, and she knew that I would work hard to get my GED. So, as usual, she supported me totally. Her constant reinforcement and support was always there no matter what I got myself into.

"Laurel, I know you will work hard and get your GED."

I jumped into action and went to a place called Project Learn for years. Yes years; I had low reading skills and a learning disability.

I was way behind in my learning, but I never let it stop me from soaking up everything that the program had to offer. It was truly a life saver for me to have a safe place to learn and be supported by kind people. In a way, Project Learn was my new high school experience. It was very comforting to go to school and actually learn rather than constantly fear for my safety. A lot of helpful volunteers made up the teaching staff. They were dedicated and committed to learning. Most of us students were not what you might call, "the top of the charts" type learners. We were mostly strugglers who wanted a fair chance to learn and succeed. This created a relaxed learning atmosphere that suited all of us. As for me, I achieved a great deal from this program, and to this day I will remain most grateful for my opportunities to learn at Project Learn.

I was still working and going to Project Learn, and it helped save me in many ways. My confidence level was rising each day that I went there to learn. I began reading and writing much better. Every spare minute I could find I had a book in my hand going through the pages with ease. To this day I still love to read and enjoy the wonders of good stories on a written page.

An overwhelming sense of pride would set in knowing that I was "getting it," and I felt ready to take the next step and get through my GED test. After years of study and catching up on subjects I missed or did not learn in school, I felt confident enough to try and take the test.

I saved up the money and took the test. I hoped and prayed that I would pass. I went in and took the test, feeling confident the whole time.

Next came the anxious waiting game to see if I had passed. Every day when I got home from work, I would check the mailbox. In our home, there was a window that faced the street and was next to our mailbox that was mounted on the wall by our front porch. I would daily watch anxiously for the mailman to come. He was never on a regular schedule. I became accustomed to listening to the sound of his footsteps onto the porch. I would listen for the mail carrier to open and close our mailbox, and then run out to see if my GED test results had come that day. Mom reached the door first that day and I walked up to her; Mom handed me the envelope with the GED test results. We went and sat on the living room couch. It was a surreal moment for me.

Finally, I had the results in my hands. I sat motionless unable to move, holding the envelope in my hands for a minute. Not wanting to rush or tear it open too quickly, I took in a long breath and opened it up. Mom once again reassured me and said, "Laurel, I believe you made it and I am here for you no matter what the results are." Once I opened it up, I got the news I was waiting for every day—I did not pass the test and missed it by a few points. I sat there on the couch not wanting to believe what I had read and dropped my head on the pillow in my lap and cried. I was devastated. How could all that hard work not pay off? Was all that work for nothing? I thought I gave it my best.

What do I do now, knowing that my best was not good enough? I felt Mom move closer to my side; she held onto me and steadied me with a warm embrace. Mom picked up the results of the test and read it. Then Mom said in a reassuring way, "Laurel, you will get it next time. Look here, you only missed it by two points. Keep up your studies and you will get it. Look how close you are."

"Mom," I said crying, "I don't feel like talking and I got to go. Look at the clock. I will be late for work. Besides, I really don't know what else I can do. I gave it my best. I don't know what else I could have done differently." I was giving into a negative, defeated attitude, and self-pity.

Mom said, "OK, Laurel, I understand how disappointed you are and I know you worked as hard as you could, but remember good things come to people that keep trying, and I know you will make it next time. You must never give up." I really was not listening to what Mom was telling me because I was too busy feeling sorry for myself. I got up and went in my room, put on my uniform, and went out the front door without saying good-bye to Mom as I left.

Outside there was a light dusting of snow on the ground and the sky was a typical gloomy, gray Cleveland winter day. I got in my old car and thanked God when it started up and pulled off. I always took my time with my old car and drove slower in the snow.

I turned the corner and out of nowhere a cat ran out in front of my car. I tried to stop but felt my back wheel hit the cat. I heard the hit, felt awful, and pulled over and got out. I called for the kitty and looked down on the street covered with snow only to see no blood. I checked the tracks in the snow and saw that there were three paws moving normally while one looked like the cat was limping and not walking right. I walked around and up and down the street, looking in the front and back yards calling for the cat. Then a man, walking past me started laughing,

"That cat took off running like a bat out of hell."

"I hope that his back leg his not broken. I was not driving fast," I said to him with a pleading and apologetic voice and still searched the grounds for the cat. The man had a tooth missing, a scraggly looking beard, and looked like he had slept in his clothes for the last month.

He let out a sadistic laugh and said, "So what if you did? One less stray cat running around is fine by me." He turned around and mumbled something to himself, let out another cynical laugh, and went down the street. He did not say a word to help the sad mood I was in.

I walked up and down the street looking and calling for the cat. With no luck and shivering from the cold, I got back into my car and burst into tears. For over a half hour, I was desperately searching for a cat that never came back. My eyes were swelling up and red and my head hurt from a pounding headache.

I sat in my old car trying to calm down and knew that I was late for work; I had to somehow pull myself together and get to work.

I walked into the donut shop and saw that I was written up for being late and was told that next time I would lose my job. I signed my name on the warning slip and went and got my cash drawer and went to work. No matter how hard I worked or how much of a responsible worker I was, I always understood that there were ten people waiting to take my job in a minute. The only good thing that happened that day was that it was payday.

It was always great to get that envelope and rip it open and see that check with my name on it. But I always thought, like every underpaid and overworked working stiff in America, "I wish I was earning a little more." Mom's words of comfort kept replaying in my head and this motivated me to keep on trying, and I knew that someday I would get it. No matter how discouraged I got, deep down in my heart, I knew that I could never give up. I also knew that my mother would never let me call it quits because she was also driven to see me succeed and support me in the earning of my GED and to me that made all the difference in the world.

Chapter 18

Comfort Food

Getting back to my studies was not easy for me. I had a day off at work and told myself I need to open up my GED book and get to work, but opening the book seemed more of a challenge on this particular day. I kept attending Project Learn, and that kept my educational drive going, and I was hoping that things would turn around for me. But my enthusiasm had taken a nose dive when the reality that life never goes as you planned smacked me right in the head when I did not get the passing grade on my GED test. I needed a break from my studies if only for a day to rejuvenate my energy and kick back and be a little lazy.

Being a practicing and fervent Catholic, we were in the Lenten season and it was a Friday, which meant a no-meat day. This was my favorite time of the week because we could eat fish, fries, and pierogies. These are my favorite foods that I love to indulge in. I would feel a little guilty by "pigging out" every Friday, but I did it anyway because the food tasted so good, especially the cheesy mashed potatoes' center with a thin layer of dough, smothered in butter and onions. I could easily destroy a dozen of these tasty delights in one sitting. These two dishes are truly my "comfort foods."

I did follow the Lenten rules as best as I could and as my religious duty I gave up chocolates and my favorite candy of all time—peanut buttercups.

Mom would often remind me not only to give up food but to work on something to improve my life or someone else's. I thought about what she had said and for this Lenten season, chocolates and peanut buttercups were the best I could come up with and to me it was hard enough. Not only was I not in the mood to study, I was "PMSing" so badly and in the desperate need of the comfort of peanut buttercups. They seemed to relieve my monthly woman's pains and agony that visited me every month. But I held back my urge and took two Midol to help my menstrual cramps and moodiness. I lay back on my bed still wishing I had peanut buttercups to eat. I thought to myself as the guilt snuck in, "God must think I am weak," when Mom opened up my door and gave me a worried look, "Are you feeling well?"

With a sigh I answered, "No, Mom, I'm not, but I'm OK. I'm just PMSing. I kept thinking about food."

There is this little place down on Professor Avenue in our old neighborhood where you can buy the best pierogies in town, where a little old lady worked diligently all week to fill the stomach of many happy customers.

"Hey, Mom," I said, "do you feel like some pierogies?"

"You know, Laurel, that sounds like a great idea and everyone loves Jefferson Inn pierogies. But I need to stop at the bank first to get some money and that will be fine because that is only a block away from the little corner bar and restaurant."

We got into the car together, and Mom could see that I was having a bad day and still feeling down about not passing my GED test. Mom in her loving way said, "Well, Laurel, I can tell the way you are acting that things aren't going too well. Try to understand that there will be days like this to come and learn to be thankful for what we have and not be sad about what we don't have." I would sit and listen to Mom and see all of her goodness and kindness pour out in each word that she would say to me. She also told me, "Don't worry about this problem you have now about passing your GED. It won't stick around too long and tomorrow you will have something else to worry about and something new to feel good about." "Mom," I said, "Life is never what we think it is going to be."

"No, Laurel, it's not what we might think it will be but only what we make it to be. And in life, there are stepping stones that we must cross to get to the better side of life, especially the side of the street that has pierogies."

I laughed and appreciated Mom dragging me out of my bad mood. I just felt better somehow listening to Mom's soothing words. I looked and there were no parking spots near the bank. So I dropped Mom off in front of the bank and then I drove around the block looking for a parking spot to open up. Mom had her bankbook with her to take care of her banking business. I drove around again and finally a place opened up in front of the bank.

It was a Friday and a lot of people were coming in and out of the bank cashing their weekly paychecks. Next to the bank was a corner store.

One thing that was nice about our neighborhood was that, even though we were in a big city, it felt more like a little village. Everybody in our little corner of the world knew everybody; so Mom always liked to stop and take a few minutes to visit with the tellers.

It was early evening by now and the February snow was coming down. It looked beautiful and I opened my window to get fresh cool air and watched for Mom to come out of the bank. I was feeling better now about not passing the GED test and planned to look over the areas where I needed to study more for my test next time around. But I was very tempted to satisfy my immediate chocolate fix that was nagging me all day, but the Midol was kicking in and my cramps had eased up. Thank God! I was about to get out of my car to buy a candy bar when a young man came out of the store; he had a little bag of chips. For some reason, unknown to me, I turned back and went into my car, closed the door, and locked it. I kept a keen eye on him because something seemed a little off about this guy. He opened his mouth and poured the remaining chips into his mouth while a few dropped onto the snowy ground. Next, he opened the can of Coke and drank it down in a few gulps and then tossed the Coke can to the ground.

I took another long, close look at this guy and I kept my eyes on him the whole time because I noticed he had a kind of wild, crazed look about him. The next thing that he did was to take off his coat and hat. He then folded them nicely and neatly and put them on the wet, snowy bench that sat in front of the bank. He seemed, in a way, harmless to me, but one can never tell and he did have that bizarre look about him.

I was hoping Mom would come out so we could get out of there because I started to sense trouble. All of a sudden he started moving fast. Next his shoes came off, followed by his blue jeans and his sweatshirt. All that was remaining were his boxer shorts and his sweat socks. He then raised his hands in the air and twirled around in a circle humming something to himself. I thought to myself, *"Oh hell! A 'nutzo' is on the loose and Mom may be coming out of the bank at any minute now."* A middle-aged black man turned the corner and his eyes got as big as saucers; he said, "Hey, man, are you crazy? It's freezin out here!" Our exhibitionist paid him no mind and the older fella crossed the city street, shaking his head in disbelief. He stopped twirling around in a circle and removed his socks.

Then he dropped down his boxer shorts, put them on the bench with the rest of his clothes, and walked down the street. Mom, unfortunately, came out exactly at that time and came face-to-face with this poor, troubled lad.

The two of them met on the sidewalk in front of the bank, and Mom stepped aside and said calmly, "Oh please, after you, young man," and I could tell that Mom was totally embarrassed and was trying to not look down at this man with no clothes.

Mom then hurried to my car, jumped in, and said, "That poor young man in going to catch a terrible cold with no clothes on!"

"Boy! That guy needs help!" I said. I then saw her stop and say a little prayer that she often did when she saw someone in trouble or in need.

I could not help myself as silly laughter got hold of me. People were out on the street watching him parade down the street with no clothes on in the middle of a Cleveland Winter. I then heard the store owner say he called the police. "Mom, that man is going to freeze that little pecker right off."

"Now, Laurel, try to be nice. That poor man is troubled."

"Mom, what do we do if he comes into the Jefferson Inn?"

"Drive slow so we can give him time to walk farther down the street or maybe the cops will catch up to him and give him a blanket."

I said kiddingly, "I don't think he will need too big of a blanket to cover up what he's got!"

"Now now," Mom said smiling over at me, "let's just go get a delicious pierogies dinner and pray for this young man and his misfortunes."

With this good hearty laugh and a dinner with Mom my mood immediately changed to a better one, and for a little while, I got a break from the GED blues. And of course, the pierogies were delicious as usual, and as usual I overate. I guess I felt kind of sad for the man who felt like he had a need to parade down a city street in his birthday suit. Sometimes, the senseless acts of other people can somehow make your own life more sensible by comparison. Then again it's probably not good to compare or judge anyone because I guess we are all on the brink every day from doing something we will regret later on. All in all, I felt really lucky to have a mom that was not judgmental and also had a warm and caring sense of humor.

Chapter 19

Relationship

My teen years went by like a blur at a speed that I hoped would slow down and become a little more manageable. I had grown into a young woman in my early twenties and was still living at home, working, and I kept putting off taking my GED test. I kept up my studies with the hopes of some day earning my GED, then moving on to the next step, which would be college. I stopped myself and realized there was a time and a place for each goal in my life. I realized that life was not that easy, right? Or are we the ones that made a mess of it all by ourselves? These types of questions haunted my mind at this time in my life.

My relationship with Mom was at its best because I was able to talk over each dream and fear that would pop up in my head. I must have driven Mom nuts with, "What do you think, Mom?" type of questions. Mom would offer up advice such as, "Well, Laurel, you know each person holds that answer in their heart and when you're at peace with something, well then there will be something else for you to work out and solve."

"Mom, why can't life be a little more easy? You know, you work hard and see good things happen."

"Life, is not easy, Laurel. You know the saying, 'When life hands you a lemon, make lemonade.'"

"I know, Mom, but wouldn't it be nice to be handed the lemonade once in a awhile?" I said pleadingly.

Mom always provided me loving support but kept that delicate balance between demanding to run my life and letting me work out my own personal dilemmas. She left some problems up to me so that I could learn to make my own decisions. But I always knew I had Mom to count on when I got myself into a jam.

The big number twenty came along for me and I was no longer a teenager. I was an adult woman now and in a disappointing relationship that was not healthy for me. Most women know the ones, the relationships that you think you can fix, and turn it into something better for the both of you. Everyone, but you, can look at that person and say "Run like hell!" But you look at the person and say, "Maybe I could fix this."

He was really sweet, funny, and so nice. At first, there seemed to be more good in him than bad. Then again who of us is perfect? So, I kept putting a lot of effort into this relationship and the times that I did, I became overwhelmed and disappointed. Mom was open and honest enough to tell me what she thought of my situation. I knew by what she had told me a number of times that I was in trouble, "Laurel, I am worried. Remember you can never really change a person. The only way a person can change is if they can fix what's wrong themselves." I was young and always gave people a chance, but I tried to keep my eyes open to what was really going on.

I knew I had it in me to turn away from a relationship if it was going nowhere or not good for me, but I often worried if I was too late and stayed too long before I walked away and had a lot of heartache, which seemed to be a likely scenario if I kept this relationship going. I always had faith and prayed that God would guide me to the right person someday. I truly offered up that prayer daily. I guess we mess up the free will part, and God is waiting for us to see the mess we put ourselves into and then gives us the strength that we never knew that we had inside our souls, to get free of the trouble we stumbled into.

I met a young man at this time who was only two years older than I from my neighborhood. He was tall, bright, and a hard-working construction worker. On the other hand, he also loved his drinks and had a temper when things did not turn out his way. I could tell both Mom and Dad were not pleased with me dating him because his father had a history of drinking and domestic violence, and history has a way of repeating itself. Maybe the old saying, "The apple really doesn't fall too far from the tree," has some truth to it. Mom looked more and more concerned as we keep on dating. As they say, we live and learn, and I learned in my relationship with this young man, the hard way. The months went by, and we were together for over a year. There were signs, but I put them aside and tried to hold onto the good and stick it out.

One day I started feeling tired and sick and I wanted to sleep more and more. When I missed my period, I thought *"Oh, God! I could be pregnant. Wait a minute*" I thought. I am only late and told myself not to jump to conclusions. I picked up a pregnancy test at the local drugstore and followed the directions. The news was not good—I was pregnant; I was not sure what to feel, so I went right to Mom. You would think that bringing a new life into the world would be a joyous occasion. However, after I told Mom the news, we both sat and cried. I waited for Mom to say something, "Laurel, you are going to be a Mother and you need to think hard about what is best for the two of you. Remember you have two lives to think of and don't rush into anything. I'll be here to help you the best that I can."

There were feelings that were situated deep in my soul and that was motherhood, what is best for me, but most importantly what was best for my baby that sat inside of me. The summer was moving along and July 4 was here. Time has a way of moving fast when you are under a lot of stress and confusion. Summer was almost half over and I was nauseated most of the time, drinking a lot of water, and running to the bathroom all the time in my early months of pregnancy. I lay in my boyfriend's bed and just listened to the sounds of the world outside the bedroom window. The smells of barbeque grills and the sounds of loud music, as the cars drove past West Fourteenth Street, filled the hot humid July air.

I turned over and listened to hear the voices getting louder on the front porch at my boyfriend's house. There were a lot of people that I did not really know drinking and setting off fireworks, and I heard my boyfriend getting louder and more vulgar with each beer that he poured into his body. I thought I should be outside on the porch with my boyfriend but I was not up to it or in the mood for a group of people that I did not know getting smashed.

I laid my head back down onto the pillow and touched my stomach, holding back the tiredness in my heavy eyes and just thought of my baby, "God, help me do the right thing for my baby and be a good Mother." I turned over feeling the warm, stagnant, summer humid air, making me feel like I was going to vomit. I took in deep, long breaths, letting them out slowly until the sick feeling passed over me. I got up and turned on the fan on high letting a cool breeze comfort me while trying to block out the noise outside on the front porch. Do drunken people know how stupid they sound, I wondered while I climbed back into bed? I heard, *"Fuck You"* followed by laughter. Next I heard a woman's voice crying out in pain yelling, "What the hell is wrong with you? Why did you hit me in the head?" Great, I thought, what is going on outside on the porch? I feared that something terrible was happening.

The mixture of heat, alcohol, and hot tempers made a toxic mixture that only ended up in an explosion.

And sure enough, it exploded. I got up feeling queasy again and went to the front door and walked out onto the porch. What I saw was my boyfriend with a beer bottle in his hand, and he had a wild, out-of-control look about him that scared me. It was a look I had never seen before. One of his brothers held the woman's head that was cut and bleeding. I turned looking frightened and said, "What did you do?" I had only gotten out the words, when my boyfriend grabbed me, not saying a word pulling me near him, and my bare feet were off the porch floor, and the next thing I felt was pain in my side and lower back; then I vomited all over myself. He threw me off the porch and I landed on my back on the sidewalk. I only looked up to see him turn running into his house slamming the door, while I lay in pain on the sidewalk.

That was all that I needed to happen. I knew at that moment that I never wanted to see him again.

"*Remember, what's best for you and the baby,*" came back to my mind. "*I am having his baby and look at me lying on the sidewalk!*" I thought to myself, "What the hell? This is not right! No one deserves this!" People were looking down on me lying there and then tried to help me up. I looked up at all those people and said while in pain, "No, please leave me alone. I can get up by myself." I got up and said, "Look. I am fine," holding in the pain and walked away from him and the drunks and headed back to the safety of my home.

With each step that I took away from him, I knew that I would never turn around and walk back into his life again, a life I did not want any longer. I had a new strength that washed over me and as I touched my stomach I told the baby, "I am sorry. Mommy is not going to let anyone hurt you or me like that again." My bare feet walked over some leftover fireworks on the street that burned the bottom of my feet and I jumped up only to feel the bad pain in my ribs. "Oh, god! Please help me." I let out a breath and was pleased to see I only had one more block to walk.

I reached the corner of the street, of my home, and there were people out setting off fireworks. I wanted the loud noise to stop; I wanted the people to go back into their homes. I just wanted to be alone at that terrible moment and collect my scattered thoughts. I wanted to run from the pain. I wanted a place where I could just sit in silence and think. I needed my mother, and I did not want anyone to see me like this. Once I walked into my house, Dad immediately realized something was wrong, jumped up, walked me to my car, and took me to the hospital to get checked out. Mom was sitting next to me telling me, "You are going to be all right." I then watched her pull out her rosary and she started praying. Dad pulled the car to the front of the emergency room and Mom got out and helped me into the hospital. A nurse took me right to the back and a doctor came in and examined me. He then gave me a shot in the attempt to stop early labor.

He was a young medical doctor and touched me softy and kept telling me, "Try to relax. You have two bruised ribs." I held in my breath while he put the medical tape around my ribs. The pain was excruciating and all I wanted to do was hurt someone to relieve the anger and pain I was feeling. He looked over and said sadly, "Sorry there is not much we can do for bruised ribs—only rest and you will heal in time." Before he stepped out of the room, I asked him, "Can my mom come back?"

"Sure," the doctor said, "what's her name? I'll go get her."

I told him her name and he came over and touched my hand in a sympathetic way, "I see women going back to men like yours every day. Please be one of the smart ones and don't go back." I cried as I nodded my head in agreement. I already knew down to my very soul that I would never be with him again. Even though I knew we were wrong for each other, I was still sad with the fact that it was truly over for us. I was going to be a Mother, and a Mother wants the best for her baby. I promised my baby that what had happened to us will not ever happen again.

Mom walked in and came over looking exhausted and grabbed my hand and said, "Laurel, I will help you get through this."

"I know you will, Mom," I said. I closed my eyes and fell off to sleep. Once I was released from the hospital, I was told I needed to get a police report and was given a card with several listings of different women's groups that I could talk to for help. I took the information and had a sense of hope that there was help for me and my baby out there.

When we finally got back home, I was so tired and in need of sleep. We were only in the house a few minutes when we heard glass shattering outside. I went to look out and there was the father of my baby, jumping up and down like a crazy man breaking out my car windows with a baseball bat and screaming obscenities! There was a car waiting, idling, for him. And typically, like most cowards, he struck while no one was around. He jumped in and the car sped down the one-way street. Dad called the police and they said they would be there right away. Dad went to the door, saw the damage, and said, "I better clean that mess up. I don't want anyone getting cut." With a broom and a trash bag he swept up the glass around the sidewalk and street. My father walked back into the house looking frustrated, angry, and exhausted and said, "I will clean the inside of the car in the morning."

"Thanks, Dad," I said.

I was so ashamed. I was ashamed of what had happened because I had all the red flags right on my face but I didn't do anything about it. I never should have let this happen. I should have never let it get this far. I then remembered all the temper tantrums he had in the past. What was I thinking?

I knew better; Mom raised a bright woman. The words "I messed up, I messed up" kept filling up my head. Dad walked upstairs to go to bed. Mom stayed by my side and waited for the police.

I told the police what had happened earlier in the evening and about my car. They wrote out everything and told me that I needed to get a restraining order and gave me the same cards I received from the hospital for women's groups.

The man that I thought was going to help me raise my child was now not legally allowed to be near me, for my own sake and my baby's. "What a night!" Mom said sleepily. "We both need some sleep."

I tried to rest, but I was unsuccessful. I was turning over in pain throughout the whole night. When you bruise a rib, every breath you take is painful.

I got up quietly and put on my shoes while still in my PJs, and went to get the broom and trash bags to clean the inside of my car filled with glass. I kept working early into the morning and cleaned out my car in silence. When I looked up, there was Mom with another, smaller broom and bags helping me clean up the mess that was all over the inside of my car and helping me cope with the mess I had gotten myself into as well. I got a cut on my hand and Mom said, "We got a lot done. Dad will get the rest." I did not want to stop cleaning, so Mom pulled the broom and bag out of my hand.

"Laurel, please, you need some rest." Mom put her arm around my shoulders and walked me back into the house, washed my cut on my hand, and put a band-aid on it. I felt her love not only then, but in the days that have passed and will keep feeling it in the days to come.

A mother's love for her child is a bond that is hard to break. I needed my mother now more than ever and she was right there to see me through this passing tragedy. I nervously talked to my mom all night to try and make sense out of the mess I put myself into. Of course, there is no logic or reason as to why we do the crazy things we do, and I guess all we can do is learn from them and try to move on. However, I was so glad to have my mom sit with me and comfort me all through the troubled night.

Chapter 20

Expanding

W as I day dreaming or in a dream? I was roller skating holding onto my baby in my arms and a feeling filled me with love and overwhelming tenderness. These days it seemed I was dreaming all the time and that one dream played in my head many nights as I slept. It seemed that all through my pregnancy I was exhausted and I wore my emotions on my sleeve. There were days I would cry and I could not stop while other days I felt strong and more energetic and ready to face the world. Mom, as always, was there for me, and on one of the days that I was very emotional, Mom said, "Laurel, you are having a baby and your body is changing. Why don't you get a book at the library about having babies and I will also help you answer any questions that may come up." I took Mom up on her advice and went to work reading anything I could find on the topic of having a baby.

I had all this new information in my head and I felt overwhelmed. There is so much going on in nine months until it is time to give birth to a baby. Every time I looked into the mirror and watched my stomach expanding to a new size, the fact that I was experiencing motherhood would set in. I knew that I needed to protect the life growing inside my womb and the first priority in my life became my baby.

I knew that together we could make it. The responsibility and expenses of having a baby was something I also needed to take care of. It was not easy for me at first to go on welfare, but it needed to be done.

For me going to the government office for help was embarrassing. To a working-class person, it feels like you have given up and are somehow inadequate. I know that there are people who try to take advantage of the system, but the reality of it is that most people do this because of a desperate need or a situation that is short term. I had always worked and paid for what I received. I did not want to become a government number. I wanted to be free of that if I could. However, life was not easy and my job at the deli at that time had no benefits at all. I had to stop working in the middle of my pregnancy and make sure I could be covered with health insurance. I had wanted to get back on my feet as soon as possible, but knew that I needed time and help because I was about to be a new mother with an infant. This is a common dilemma that many single Moms have to face in our modern times. Things are not like they used to be with two-parent households.

When everything piled up in my head with having a new baby, I stopped and just thought of a new beginning that would be hard at first, but a new beginning with a new life growing inside of me, and with my mom I knew my newborn and I were somehow going to be fine.

I was very concerned and worried of what I took into my body and I made sure that I ate healthy foods. I never smoked or was a drinker, so I checked this off my list of things that a Mother should not do. I was doing all the right things and relaxed until my baby would be born.

There was this one thing that I was extremely funny about; I would not let anyone touch my stomach or feel my baby moving inside of me. Not even my mother was allowed to touch me; I was selfish and only wanted those special moments like that for only myself. The feeling of life and the life in me were too hard for me to put into words and somehow explain the bond my child and I had together to other people. It was like, "It's you and me kid, and no one is going to impose on our special time together." I really felt this when my son would start to move and flutter inside of my stomach, which let me know he was full of energy and life. This also included doctor's appointments. I felt uneasy having a doctor close to my stomach, but I knew it was all part of what needed to be done when having a baby.

The day had come to have an ultrasound. I had to drink cup after cup filled with water. I needed to pee; I was holding my legs as tightly as I could together while a cold gel was put onto my stomach. To me it was astonishing how so many people get to touch and see life right within you; people you don't know, but I wanted to reach out to this stranger and tell her to be careful when looking for my baby. The woman giving the ultrasound finally spoke, "Do you want to know what you are having?"

"Yes," I said, with a smile so big it filled the room.

"You are having a boy."

I kept smiling to myself and I said, "I thought I was having a boy, but now I know for sure."

Lying there I knew the name I was going to give my son—it was Nicholas. I chose this name because of Santa and Saint Nicholas and the spirit of giving that goes along with the name that my mother, over the years, nurtured within me. Then a doctor walked in and said, "Everything looks good and the baby's heart is strong." Then the doctor said, "Would you like to hear the baby's heart beat?"

I immediately said," Yes! Yes! I'd love too!"

He put on a special handle device onto my stomach and the room filled up with a strong-sounding, beating heart. It was the sound of my baby's life; the life inside of me. I started to fill up with emotions when the doctor said, "You can get dressed now."

Before he walked out of the room, I said, "Where is the bathroom?" He answered, "Two doors on the right." I got up and dressed fast, walking swiftly out of the room and into the bathroom. Before I got my pants down all the way, I tried to reach the toilet, but I started to pee on myself. Well, I was pleased that I had a long coat on to cover up the wet spot. I was sure I smelled of pee.

I walked over to the front counter with my folder in my hand. There were brochures on the table. With my need to know everything I could about having my baby, I picked one up and saw that the hospital offered Lamaze classes. Looking the brochures over before checking out, I asked the receptionist, "I'd like to sign up for the next Lamaze class." The lady behind the counter said, "Let me check the list. It might be filled up." She pulled out a book and opened it. I saw that there were two more spots open before it was filled. I was relieved and I wanted to do all the right things, and the class sounded helpful. She said, "I need your name please." Then she said, "You need to bring a partner. It will be this Thursday evening at 7:00 p.m., and the class is an hour and a half long." I knew I was going to ask Mom to be my partner because at that point I knew I could count on her. I walked into the house and Mom was busy in the kitchen like she always was.

"Mom," I said, "will you be my partner for Lamaze class?"

"Sure, sounds like fun, you know I never had it offered to me when I was having babies. It will be helpful to know."

"Mom, I need all the help I can get," I said as I picked up a bowl and ate some chicken soup Mom had made. I sat down looking over the brochure again. It said to wear comfortable clothes and to bring two pillows.

Thursday evening was here and I had only a few clothes that fit me by now since I was getting larger by the day. I put on a big blue sweat shirt and black jogging pants. My feet were swollen, so I wore tennis shoes, but tucked in the shoe strings. I had my two pillows ready and I went into Mom's room. She was taking out the last bobby pins out of her hair. I sat down and watched Mom comb out her hair. "Well, I guess that is as pretty as I'll get. Let's go," Mom said in a light-hearted manner. We were on time and about fifteen minutes early. Some of the women were already there on the floor on their pillows next to their husbands. Mom and I took a spot on the floor together on our pillows. In came more couples, and the room filled up.

Right on time the instructor walked into the room and introduced herself. Then she wanted each one of us to say our names and introduce our partners. She started on the right side and we were sitting closer to the middle of the floor. I sat and listened to all of the people call out their names and introduce their husbands. My turn had come and I said, "I am Laurel. My partner is my mom and her name is Doris." I was the only pregnant woman without a husband there. A few people gave us weary looks of disapproval and then looked away. The class began with a natural birth video. I sat watching it wide eyed. I was scared and a little overwhelmed seeing it for the first time, watching how a baby is actually born into the world seemed almost surreal to me at times.

I felt a little scared but told myself that women have been doing this throughout the ages of time. It amazed me how women could hold life so long inside of their wombs and then release this life when the time was right. Next, the instructor talked a little about what to pack for the hospital stay. Then we all got to work on how to breathe and relax while our partners were there to help us to stay calm by holding our hands and touching our stomachs in relaxing ways.

Mom knew how funny I was about the whole thing about touching my stomach. I gave Mom a look that said, "If this is going to help then touch all you want." Mom touched me hesitantly at first because she knew how uneasy I was about touching. Mom listened to every word that the instructor was saying, like there was going to be a test at the end of the class. She handed us handouts and went over each one. The class was moving close to an end when the teacher said, "Our class has come to an end. Do you have any questions?" By now I was getting hungry and wanted ice cream badly. I hoped that not too many questions were going to be asked. There were a few questions asked, like when to get pain medicines if needed in labor. With a long, drawn-out answer, the teacher finally said, "Thank you for coming out tonight and there are cookies and juice in the next room. Feel free to stop in and visit." I looked over at Mom, "What do you think? Do you want to stop in for a few minutes?"

"Sure," Mom said. Some people took their pillows and left while others went next door and left their pillows on the floor. There was a long table with cookies and juice. A few women started talking right way.

I overheard them asking each other when they were due and some were giving out phone numbers. Mom and I went over to the table and I smiled at the lady and her husband; she smiled back only to pull her husband away and started talking to some other couple. It was clear to me that I was an outcast.

I was a woman having a baby out of wedlock. Mom said something to another woman, that she liked her blouse. She smiled back at Mom and said, "Thank you," and that she had gotten a lot out of the class.

Mom said something like she did too and in her days they did not have classes like this. I looked around the room and I tried to make eye contact, but no one was looking back at me because I was a young unwed mother. Mom walked back over to me by the cookie table and I was now on my fourth jumbo cookie. "Mom, I feel like ice cream. How about we stop at the store? Are you ready to go? And ya know, I am not really comfortable here and no one has bothered to make me feel welcome."

"Ice cream sounds good and I need to pick up some other items while we are there," Mom said.

We pulled up to the grocery store and as we walked in Mom pulled the shopping cart while I went right to the frozen food section to pick out ice cream when unexpectedly, two buttons popped open on my coat. It was the strongest leg kick I had ever felt. Next to me was an older woman with some gray hair pulled up on her head in a bun. She had a nice, round, brown warm face. She saw what had happened and said, "You got one strong baby in there and I can tell you both like ice cream." Holding onto my stomach, I smiled back at her proudly and said, "I guess we do."

She wanted to know more about me and my baby. She said looking me in the eye, "Honey, what are you having?"

"A boy," I said.

"When are you due?"

"Less than a month."

"Do you have a name picked out?"

"Yes, 'Nicholas.'"

"May God bless you and your Nicholas."

"Thank you." I watched her smile at me then pull her shopping cart away when she turned back and she said again with a warm and friendly smile on her face, "May God bless Nicholas."

I desperately needed some conversation and concern that I did not get with the other pregnant ladies like I should have. Here I was receiving love, support, and concern from a complete compassionate stranger, in the frozen foods section of a super market!

It warmed my heart for my baby and my situation to be acknowledged even though I did not have a husband to share my life's work of raising this child. This was a random act of kindness that I'll never forget.

Chapter 21

What's This?

Time was drawing near to when I would have my baby boy in my arms and I would look at him for the first time. Anticipation had its grip on me in these last few weeks. My stomach was so huge that I felt like I was going to pop. I was at that very uncomfortable stage where I hurt all the time. I tried to keep my swollen ankles propped up most of the time. My lower back ached all of the time too, but even though I was hurting, I was getting a little nervous and excited all at the same time as motherhood was soon to be upon me. Nicholas was on the move wrestling inside of me. This feeling brought me peace and wonder. I spoke to my unborn child and said, "Well, Nicholas, maybe today will be the day you come into the world and we will look at each other for the first time." It seemed that when I touched and talked to my baby boy in the womb, Nicholas went into overtime moving around in response of those words and that always brought joy to my heart. I checked the calendar every day and if Nicholas was not born, I wound X-out the date on the calendar. I held my stomach saying to my baby boy, "When you are ready, I will be too!"

If there was a word I would chose for those days in waiting for my baby, it would be eagerness; the eagerness to have and want my baby now, but I understood that the first born always takes a little more time and I knew that somehow I had to find the patience to wait a little longer.

I loved to fold and refold all his baby clothes over and over again. I would pick up his bottles and baby toys, look at them fondly, and put them back again into their proper place. But what kept my heart smiling was the baby's crib. The crib, when we first got it, was old and in need of work. My brother, Billy, sanded down and varnished the old wood. The oak crib looked beautiful, waiting in the corner of my room for the new baby boy. I was overjoyed thinking of the day my Nicholas would soon be the new member of our household. The thought was so charming that I smiled to myself and tried to relax my anticipation. Even though I was hurting pretty bad, I had vigor in my step. I could spend the whole day looking over all the baby items. I walked from one corner of my room to the next, thinking to myself, "What is he going to look like? Will he be into sports? Will I be a good Mother?" These thoughts would fill my mind and Mom would reassure me, "You will not only be a good Mother but a great one." I thought to myself, "*I hope so. There is so much to learn and do. What if I mess the whole thing up?*"

I had to stop my routine of spending my day lost in baby sleepers, blankets, and bibs. I had a doctor's appointment and I needed to get moving if I was going to make it on time. I put all the baby clothes back into his dresser and then I went into the bathroom to get washed up. We had an old-time cast-iron bath tub, the kind you need to climb into and soak with big crow's feet on it.

I loved to go into the bath tub at night and soak for over an hour and relax. I was in the mood for a soak with bubbles falling over the side of the tub. But not today; I needed to get going. I filled the tub half way and climbed in. I washed in a hurry to make my appointment on time. I stopped myself from washing when I reached down below. I felt something that seemed different. "What's this?" I said to myself. I was in no pain and feeling fine, but my lower back did hurt a little. I thought it was from my weight gain. I never felt anything like this before on my body. It was small and round. Then I thought, "Can it be the baby's toe? No, that can't be it, but what then, and why was it sticking out down there?" I was young and yes, at times, a little naive and did not understand all the complicated parts of a pregnancy. After getting out of the tub and getting dressed, I knew I wanted to ask Mom what I felt down below. Walking out of the bathroom, I said, "Mom, I have a question for you. It's about being pregnant and the baby." Mom was busy in the kitchen breading chicken. She looked up at me, walked over to the sink to wash her hands, and said, "What's on your mind?"

"Mom," I said, "I feel something." Then the phone rang, and interrupted me. Mom reached for the phone and said, "Hello," breaking off what I wanted to ask Mom. I looked up at the clock and I needed to leave if I wanted to be on time; being on time is important when going to the doctor's, even if they keep you waiting.

Mom smiled at me, holding her hand over the receiver, and said, "We will talk after you get back."

"OK Mom," I said, as I rushed out of the door.

While I was waiting in the room for the doctor to come into the examination room, I would look at the posters on the wall showing a picture of babies inside the womb. And if I was left in the waiting room a long time, I passed the time looking inside the cabinets to see what was inside of them. It was always the same old stuff: paper gowns, gloves, and long swab Q-tips. Well, don't ask me why, but I felt better knowing it was the same items each time I looked inside the cabinets. Maybe the feeling that the hospital was prepared helped me to relax. I got back to the examining table and heard the doctor tapping on the door and then he walked in.

He smiled and asked, "How are you feeling today?"

I told him that, "I was feeling fine, and I had more energy, however, my lower back is hurting me from time to time, and my ankles are swollen."

"The lower back pain is to be expected. It's all part of being pregnant and carrying the extra weight," he said. He opened my folder and wrote out what I had said.

Before he left, he told me to put the paper gown on, and he would be back in a few minutes for my examination along with a nurse. I stopped him and said, "Doctor, I have one more question."

He pulled up his glasses, "Well, what is your question?"

"Well, maybe it's not important, but while taking a bath I felt something different down below, something I've never felt before."

"Oh, well what did you feel? Can you explain?" he asked.

"It was small and round," I replied. "Doctor, do you think the baby's toe may be sticking out?" I was very serious, but his face turned a little red in embarrassment, and he went for the door, chuckled a little, and told me he would take a look. I undressed and put the gown on, feeling nervous because I had to wait for an answer. *"Is the gown getting smaller?"* I thought. I felt more naked than ever with my stomach taking up more space than I wanted it to and I was feeling cold; the paper gown and cover were not keeping me warm.

The door opened up again after a tap, with a nurse and the doctor coming in and closing the door behind them. The doctor told me to lie back and put my feet into the stirrups. With all of the advances in medicine, I still wonder why they can't find a better way to do this. I hated doing this. It felt awkward and embarrassed to have a strange man so close to me down there with my legs spread apart and flung up in the air. But he never seemed to mind or make a big deal out of it. It seemed so routine to him. I guess he saw many women from down below every day. Women of all shapes and sizes in rooms with feet up in stirrups and all that they owned exposed to him.

I wanted to say, "Hey, after me how many more vaginas do you have to look at before lunch?" But of course I didn't.

I don't have that kind of nerve. The doctor was putting on plastic gloves and put gel on the tips of his fingers. I felt his fingers moving around inside of me and he told me that I had not dilated and that he was hoping to loosen me up, in the hope of getting me going. He then told me he was going to schedule an appointment to have my labor induced since I was only seven days from my due date. However, if I went into labor, I was told to come in before the scheduled date.

The doctor also told me to try walking a little more to get my body ready for the delivery. He then let out a hysterical laugh telling me he was sorry, but as for the baby toe I asked about, "Well, it's no baby's toe, but you do have a hemorrhoid down there."

"I never had a hemorrhoid! I don't understand. What are they?" I immediately felt sorry right after I had said it, but it came out and now I really felt foolish. I had heard about people getting them, but I never had one. So how was I to know? I thought only old people got hemorrhoids. I needed to learn to think before I talked. Now, both the doctor and nurse where holding back their laughter and I was feeling more embarrassed by the minute. The doctor turned toward the sink, washed his hands, and said, "You can get the cream over the counter at any drug store to help you with your hemorrhoid. It is a very common ailment for pregnant women. You have been fortunate to have such good health this whole time." He smiled and started to walk out and then turned and said, "Even though it can get really uncomfortable it is not a serious health concern for you right now. Do you have any more questions that I can help you with?" In response, I shook my head no. I was too embarrassed to ask him anything else.

I got dressed and took my folder up to the front desk. I heard a group of nurses giggling in the corner of the hall. I tuned so red; I knew they were laughing at me. "That's OK," I thought, "we all need a good laugh from time to time." I scheduled the appointment to have my labor induced and then I walked out of the doctor's office and thought to myself, "I do remember reading about pregnant women getting hemorrhoids throughout their pregnancy." I told myself to stop and think before I speak. I guess we all have lessons to learn about life and its complications.

When I walked into the house, Mom asked, "How did your doctor's appointment go?" I turned red and giggled out loud. Mom said, "What's so funny?"

"Well, Mom, you know the question I wanted to ask you? Well, I thought the baby's toe was sticking out below. I learned I have a hemorrhoid and boy I do feel so dumb and silly."

Mom, looked at me, and let out a laugh and said, "You know, Laurel, it's OK to laugh at yourself. We all make mistakes of some kind every day. We live and learn."

"I guess so, Mom, but I just feel so dumb and wish that I had never asked."

"Now, Laurel, you should not feel dumb. Yes, I agree even though you were a little embarrassed, I bet you helped lighten up their serious workload with a little laughter."

I pulled out the cream that I had purchased at the drugstore to help with my hemorrhoid problem and said, "Excuse me, Mom, I got to go take care of a personal problem."

"Make sure you put enough cream around the swollen area," Mom said with loving care.

I rolled my eyes toward the ceiling and said, "I know, Mom. I think I can handle it."

"I'm only trying to help," Mom said in her motherly way.

"I know, Mom."

I then closed the bathroom door, wishing more than anything that I could somehow change the events of the day, so that I wouldn't feel so embarrassed. Fortunately, Mom took the sting out of my embarrassment and once again made a difficult situation bearable.

Chapter 22

Time

Is it here at last? There is a funny feeling like menstrual pain in the front side of my stomach. Can this be the beginning of labor? I lay back in my bed a few minutes until it happened again. I wanted to make sure before I went into the hospital that I was in real labor, not just a passing funny feeling in my stomach. It was a cold January early morning and I lay under the layers of blankets feeling warm and cozy. I looked over at the alarm clock and it read 3:10 a.m. when my eye caught sight of the baby's crib. Well, this may be the real thing; time to give birth. The feeling put me in a state of well-being, knowing that it soon would be coming to an end and my baby would soon be here at last. I lay back very still in bed. I wanted to see how close the contractions were coming. The contractions were far apart and not too hard or painful. I knew I had time.

Hoping that I could get my contractions going, I got up out of my warm bed, thinking, "What can I do and not wake up the family?" I had a few days to go until my scheduled appointment to have my labor induced. I started marching quietly in place over and over again until I reached one hundred. "What next?" I thought. Then I started walking up and down our stairs several times while swinging my arms. Mom called out in a groggy voice, "Laurel, are you OK? What time is it?"

"Mom, I'm fine. Go back to sleep."

"OK, Laurel, but wake me if it's time."

"I will, Mom." I thought there was a little more discomfort, but there was not a lot of pain and my contractions were not coming too hard. Well, by now I had warmed up and worked myself into wanting a night snack. I still did not want to disturb my family until I knew I was ready to go and I felt bad already that I had woken Mom up, but still there was not a sound in the old house and all seemed quiet at this early morning hour. I hoped that Mom would go back to sleep. I walked into the kitchen and poured a glass of tap water and drank it down. Walking over to the refrigerator door, I opened it, and before I knew it, our family dog was by my side begging for some of the food I was about to eat. She was a mixed breed named Star. Good old Star, she was a sweet girl with some German Shepherd in her and was always ready to eat. And she knew what was going on because she had some puppies last year and wanted to comfort me.

I looked over at all of the leftovers in containers to see what I could pull out to eat. There was leftover cold chicken in a dish. I pulled out the dish and put it onto the table. I sat down and next to me sat Star. She put her paw onto my leg giving me that look like, "I hope you are going to share."

"OK, hold on, Star." I took a bite and shared some with her.

After we both had two pieces of chicken legs between us, I said, "Well, Star, I haven't felt any more contractions. I guess I'll go back to bed. What do you think?"

Star followed me back up the stairs even though Star usually slept downstairs. She was looking out for me and I loved the feeling of having her near me. I got back into bed and patted the bed so that Star could jump up onto the bed with me. She leaped up and bunched the covers around and moved in circles a few times before she finally plopped down to go to sleep. I curled up next to her to keep me warm. I tried to sleep, but I could not get comfortable on my side. My mind was spinning around in circles in my head. This might be the time. Star, feeling my restlessness, moved down around my feet.

I turned over to my other side and closed my eyes to try and relax. "Relax, Laurel," I was telling myself and thinking of what is called "positive thoughts." Boy, I had a beauty! I was walking on a long beach holding Nicholas in my arms and the waves were rhythmically easing into shore, making that relaxing swoosh in and out of the shoreline. Then the pain hit me again. This time I knew it was time to go to the hospital.

I got up fast and Star jumped down looking to go back down and eat some more. Star turned back looking me over, then sat down on the floor, watching me rest my hand on my belly. "Sorry, Star, no more food. It's time." I then put on my roomy pants and sweat shirt and shoes.

I tiptoed into my parents' room to wake up my dad and Mom. Mom immediately heard me walk in.

She was already awake and sitting up in bed. In a sleepy voice she said, "Laurel, is it time?"

I nodded at her and said, "Yes it is."

"Dad" I said, "I think it might be time for me to go to the hospital." Dad got up swiftly with his pajamas on. He spoke fast and said, "I will get the car warmed up." I watched Dad put on his boots with no socks on, followed by his coat and hat. Looking back at me he said, "Laurel, go sit down and where are your bags?"

"Dad, it's OK. Mom and I already put the overnight bag in the trunk days ago."

Dad said in a hurried voice, "Good, but go and sit down." He was looking worried and concerned for me.

"I'm fine, but I'll go sit down if that makes you feel better," I said, while smiling at him watching him moving quickly down the stairs. I was following Dad down the stairs, when Mom called out from the bathroom, "I will be a minute." She already had her clothes out and ready to change into and go when the time came. We were prepared; I simply was happy that this would be the day for me to finally meet my baby boy. I sat down on the chair, looking outside as Dad swept and scraped the ice and snow off the car windows, and Star sat next to me putting her head onto my knee in a caring sympathetic way, as though she understood what was going on.

"Good Girl," I said and I patted her a few times on the head.

There was a light dusting of snow, but it was bitter cold out. Mom dressed fast, walked down the stairs, and looked a little breathless as she walked over to me.

"How do you feel?"

"Fine, Mom."

Mom looked out the window then said, "Looks icy outside." Dad walked back in and said to us, "Be careful there is ice out on the ground." I thought two minds think alike sometimes. Here I am, a grown woman, and my two parents are fussing over me like I was fine china. In reality, I think I am more like a cast-iron skillet. Dad walked over and helped get me up, while Mom held my other arm and the three of us walked outside together.

"Oh, it's cold out here," Mom said,

"Oh boy, you're not kidding," Dad said.

January in Cleveland was always bitter cold, but this year we were blessed with not too much snow. Both of my parents were holding onto me, like I could not walk myself or I might break. This protected feeling shielded me with love and overwhelming support. Once we got into the car, Mom sat in the back with me, and Dad got in and pulled out fast, heading toward Metro hospital, which was one mile from our home. Together we drove and I looked out at Lincoln Park; everything looked frozen in time. Old Man Winter had a good grip over Cleveland and the frosting of ice left stillness over the park.

There was no one out, and driving on the early morning roads it almost made one feel isolated. Then I finally saw two cars passing by on West Fourteenth Street as we drove to the hospital. The deep freeze outside did not affect the warm joy I felt inside of me, knowing that soon I would see my baby. Mom touched my hand and broke my train of thought. Then out of nowhere, a sharp pain came over me.

"Oh dear, are you all right?" Mom said. "How are you feeling?" I could tell she was overly concerned for me.

"Not too bad," I said. "Only some pain a few minutes apart." Dad pulled up and jumped out and walked very fast into the emergency room and returned with a nurse pulling a wheelchair. Dad opened the trunk and handed over the overnight bag to Mom. He helped me get out of the car and into the wheelchair. Dad, looking down at me, stopped and kissed my forehead, telling me he would see us soon. Dad told Mom, "Call us as soon as the little fella is born."

Mom reassured him and said, "Will do."

Dad nor my mom were not the kissing type of parents, but that kiss from my father put me a little more at ease. I know he wanted the best for his daughter. I smiled back at my father and he gave me a grin followed by a wink. Mom kept up the pace with the nurse, walking beside me in the wheelchair. After we were placed into the birthing room, Mom set down my bag and came over to my side. A doctor came in to examine me.

I was in early labor and had dilated to about a three. I had a different doctor than the one who had been seeing me over my pregnancy.

"Well," the doctor said, "Do you feel up to walking the halls?"

"Sure." I said. "Mom, if you are tired, you can wait in my room."

Mom stood up, "No, Laurel, remember I am your Lamas partner."

"OK, Mom."

Together we paced up and down the halls for over an hour. With all the weight gain around my belly and my tired legs, I was ready to go back into the room when Mom said, "Let's take a little rest and go back to the room."

"Mom," I said, "that's what I was thinking—time for a little rest." We were in the birthing room only a few minutes when the doctor walked back in to see how I was doing. I hoped that he did not want me back to walking again. He checked me and I still had not moved. I was still only dilated at a three.

I smiled up at him, saying, "Can I take a little rest? I will get back up to walk, I promise."

"Take rest and when you're ready, walk again, and the more walking the better to get things going." Then he walked out of the door.

"Mom," I said, "I like the doctor."

Mom agreeing with me said,

"He seemed very conscientious"

"Mom," I said, "I guess babies take time when it is the first one."

"Yes, babies come when they are good and ready."

When we got back up to walk I asked Mom, "What about taking the stairs?" I asked.

"OK, we will walk the stairs a little, but we can't get too carried away. We need to stay close to the room." I could see that Mom worried that I might overdo it. I was eager, and hand-in-hand, Mom and I walked up and down the stairs and through the halls. I watched as the nurses walked in and out of the birthing rooms. One of the nurses smiled over at us and said, "Keep walking! You are doing great!" I felt comforted and safe as Mom held onto me and stayed close to me. It made me feel special and protected like things would just turn out just fine.

"Thank you, Mom, for being my partner, and being here with me."

"You do not have to thank me. I wanted to be here with you, but you sure are wearing me out," Mom said. We walked this time for over an hour and a half and by now, I had a backache as the pain was getting sharp and my legs hurt.

"Mom, let's go back to the room."

"Sounds good to me," Mom said a little out of breath. Together we walked back into the birthing room and in walked the doctor asking me how I was feeling.

I told him that the pain was a little sharper and closer than it was before.

He said, "I will take a look." I had a nurse on one side and Mom on the other.

"Well, you are moving along now. You dilated to a seven." The doctor, I could tell, was pleased with how my baby and my body were moving along. He had a nurse put a monitor on me to check on my contractions, and the nurse put another sheet over me and said in a caring tone, "How about ice chips?"

"Great! I'd like some. Thank you." And I made a face to hold back the pain that came over my body.

"If you need anything for pain, push the button, and I will have a doctor order up something to help you with the pain," the nurse said.

"No, thank you. I am fine for now." I was hoping to do the all natural birth. Mom sat down on the recliner chair next to me and turned on the T V. Either one of us were able to watch the TV. We both stared up at the tube changing the channels around and turned it off when we heard a baby cry out in the next room. A new baby had just been born, as I closed my eyes, telling myself maybe my Nicholas would be next. Mom looked over at me and could tell that the pain was becoming unbearable.

"Mom," I said, "You know me well. I would keep going with the pain if I could, but I think it is wearing me down." Mom then handed me ice chips to suck on.

"Laurel, if you need to push the button, it's fine. It may be a long night." The early morning had passed and already it was the end of the afternoon. I then realized that going all natural may not work for me; I hit the button and the nurse walked in. I told her holding back wanting to yell, "I need something for the pain."

"I'll go get the doctor and he will order something."

"Thanks," I said trying to hold back the pain that had a solid grip on me.

The doctor walked back in and checked me again. I was still at a seven.

"Well," he said, "I am ordering an epidural and it will go into your back. It will be here soon." Then he explained to me not to be scared that I would feel numb from the waist down and my legs may feel heavy.

By now I was hurting real bad and in pain. I was only allowed ice chips, but I tried keeping my mind off the pain the best that I could and Mom was doing her part to help me out. Mom kept helping me work on my breathing exercises and together we did it over and over, passing the time together, waiting on my new arrival. I stopped and thought that Mom had not eaten anything all day. "Mom, go to the vending machine and get something to eat," I said pleadingly.

It made me feel much safer to know that Mom would be by my side throughout the whole labor process.

"Don't you worry about me," Mom said patiently. "Let's get back to the breathing again."

Then we both went back to working on the breathing techniques that we had learned in Lamas class. I then turned over to my side and Mom rubbed my stomach.

I looked over at Mom taking in breaths and letting them out, I starting laughing out loud. "Mom," I said, "you look so funny." Then a sharp pain went right through me.

"Dear God, help me." I let out a breath, when finally a middle aged man walked in and put the epidural into my back. I wanted to rejoice when I saw him and yell at him, "What took you so long?" Once I had the epidural in my back, I started to relax, and I did feel heavy and numb from the waist down.

I fell off in a deep sleep, only to wake up at 1:30 a.m. the next day. I was sleeping for over six and a half hours. "Oh, baby boy you sure are taking your time." Just then I heard another baby cry out from somewhere down the hall. I turned over and looked over at Mom, and I could tell that she was not sleeping. "Mom, I think another baby has been born. Do you think it will be me next?"

Mom got up and stretched, and said, "I hope so Laurel." Mom went into the bathroom, while I lay back in bed hoping that I would be next and able to hold my baby. By early morning a doctor woke me up.

He was a different one from the other day he was moving very fast and seemed like he was in an awful hurry. This doctor was in and out of my room in a matter of a few minutes. He seemed preoccupied with something else.

I wanted to ask him how things were going, but he impatiently left my room. I thought I should maybe press the nurse's button and get the doctor back into my room, but choose to let it be. I was still at a seven and had not dilated at all over the last fifteen hours. No one seemed worried or concerned because it was my first baby and these things can take some time. However, by late afternoon the doctor came in to check on me again.

He said, "There seems to be some stress on your baby but not to worry." I was then hooked to another monitor and was told to lie on my left side and then lie on the right side.

I moved from side to side several times and Mom stayed right by my side looking worn out, but doing her best to help me. I know that we both were feeling the same thing, hoping that I would be the next Mom to deliver a baby boy. It was just taking such a long time.

The anticipation was getting to me by now and I was so hungry. I wished I had eaten the whole dish of chicken and packed food into overnight bag. I was not allowed to eat, so I bit on more ice chips wishing it was food of any kind. By now we both were getting tired of being in the birthing room.

Mom kept up my spirits by passing the time talking, telling me stories about when I was a baby. Time was moving slowly and I was getting a little anxious, keeping my eyes on the wall clock; my epidural started to wear off.

It was early morning when the doctor decided to break my water and he loosened me up hoping to get things moving along. I dilated to an eight and my epidural had worn off completely. By now, I was fully aware of each pain that came over my body. Mom got up and put a cold cloth on my forehead. I tried to focus the pain out of me by closing my eyes and praying to God with all the fervor I could muster up. I must be dilated close to a ten by now, I hoped. I was letting out long deep breaths and Mom was doing her duties as my Lamas partner. "Please, God, let this come to and end," I thought.

Finally, the hours seemed to trudge on and I had reached the magic number of ten—time to push. I pushed and pushed for over an hour, giving it all I had each time I would bear down. Then I cried out telling the doctor, "I don't think I can push anymore. I am exhausted."

He replied in a cold manner, "No, we make our girls work in here. Keep pushing."

"What did he just say?" I wanted to slap him in the face, but had no energy in me. His words hurt me because I was working and gave all that I had.

I had been in the birthing room for over two days by now, and he should have known more than anything I would do my part as a mother. I could tell he had an attitude like, "You got yourself into this, you single Mom, on Welfare, now get yourself out of it." What a jerk! I tried hard to change my thoughts to having my baby and not this cynical doctor.

Mom spoke up and said in a stern annoyed voice, "My daughter has been doing her apart over the last two days. Maybe she needs more help."

He did not answer Mom. He looked at me with a disrespectful glare and said, "Push again" and I pushed down as hard as I could when I tore my flesh open from my vagina all the way to my rectum. I was quivering and shaking in excruciating pain. I thought I was dying right there in the birthing room.

I closed my eyes and held in my breath. I let out a little air and yelled out, "Someone please, please, help me!"

Mom reached over and put the cloth back onto my head, "Laurel, I am right here." I could not talk at that moment. My body kept shaking and unbearable pain took hold of me. I thought again that I was going to die with my mother by my side with this inconsiderate doctor deliberately letting me suffer like this. The doctor told the nurse. "Get the forceps and the suction cup now."

The nurse ran out of the room and quickly returned with the equipment he had ordered. I was delirious from the pain and looked up to notice the back wall was lined up with doctors and nurses watching me unsuccessfully trying to give birth. I was out of my mind in pain. When more doctors came in and filled up and lined along the back wall, I could care less if a TV crew was filming me "What is going on," I wondered? There were worried looks on the doctors' faces. Fear took hold of me. I needed help badly because things were not going well. I thought this is not what happened in the movie we watched in Lamas class.

I knew something was horribly wrong. I reached for Mom's hand and she looked frightened and worried, so I grabbed onto her hand to try and comfort her. We were both trying to comfort each other. Mom did, however, remain calm and just put her other hand onto my hand while I held on for dear life. I was feeling her love and support when Mom said, "Laurel, I am right here I won't leave your side."

I felt the suction cup go inside of me when the doctor said, "Push down." I laid back, holding in my breath and bore down again, and he placed the forceps deep inside of me. I lay back and a feeling that I was being ripped open came over my whole body—all the way up my back. I was being ripped apart like a gift on Christmas morning. I could feel the ripping and tearing of my flesh.

"Dear God! Dear God! Help me." I screamed out and I tore again as the flesh ripped open and tore apart my womb again. I thought to myself, "What are they doing to me? What are they doing to my baby? Is my baby, being ripped apart and feeling all this pain?" I thought. My mind could not think clearly because of the blinding pain, but I wanted this all to stop. I wanted this to be over. I wanted to be free from the pain and worry and I wanted my baby in my arms.

"Dear God," I screamed out and held my legs up in the air. The doctor pushed the forceps deeper inside of me and I bore down with all I had left in me. I felt the room spinnin, and I was losing control. "*Please let this be over,*"

I thought, "*I can't take it anymore*" when finally my prayers were answered and my baby boy Nicholas was born.

He was so big, but oddly enough, I did not hear him cry; only a little bit, more like a sorrowful whimper, nowhere like the two babies I had heard earlier being born. My baby Nicholas—did he cry? I tried desperately to keep an eye on my baby, but my view of him kept being blocked by the nurses that were cleaning him up. I wanted so badly to see my baby and have him in my arms. More and more medical staff kept blocking my view. I was being cleaned up and the doctor said to me, "You have torn from your vagina to just about an inch from your rectum and I have to stitch you back up. So please try to stay calm and relax." The doctor looked relieved when the baby was born. The medical staff then cleaned me up and the doctor began closing the tearing around my womb. There still was a number of medical staff in the room. I was searching for the baby. Mom had her head down and I could see was praying.

I said pleadingly to anyone that would listen, "I want to see my baby. What is going on?" My heart filled up with anguish but no one said a word of comfort back to me.

"Can I see my baby? I want to hold my baby," I begged.

I said again, "I want to hold my baby."

I held out my arms and finally my baby boy, Nicholas, was brought over to me. I held my baby in my arms, but he felt swollen and like a water balloon.

He looked beautiful, with a full head of dark hair and a round baby face. Nicholas looked to be everything I could have hoped for and then our eyes met. I reached to touch his baby face when the nurse said, "Sorry, we need to run tests," and she pulled my son out of my arms.

I held Nicholas tightly in my arms and tried to push the nurse away, but she took him from me and ran out of the birthing room, with the medical staff following right along with her.

"Why are you taking away my baby?" I yelled out. I held out my arms and was crying so hard I could not see out of them.

"We need to run a few tests on your baby," The doctor said.

"What is wrong with my baby?" I cried out.

I lay back not able to move and I could see I still had an audience lined up against the wall with grim-looking faces watching me, when finally a doctor said, "Your son has a lot of fluid on his lungs and we need to check on him. You had a very large baby. He was twenty-three inches long and weighed thirteen pounds. That is why you had a hard time pushing him out. We believe some of the weight is fluid. So we need to check on him, so please relax. I need to finish sewing you back up."

I laid back and a concerned feeling washed over me as my wounds were being closed back up, but my heart was cut open bleeding in pain wanting to hold my baby longer. I wanted to take a longer look at my son. I thought to myself and tried to remember, "Did I hear my baby crying? Did my baby cry?" This thought invaded my mind. I turned to my mom, who looked to be still praying. "Mom, what is going on? Is my baby all right? Did you hear him cry?"

Mom was thinking how to answer me and the doctor heard what I had said to Mom.

"Laurel, relax. Please relax. Your baby will be fine. I need to stitch you up. I only have a few more to go." He ordered me in a firm manner.

I closed my eyes, "Dear God, please let my baby be healthy. Please God." I lay back and could feel Mom hold onto my hand when another group of doctors came into the birthing room and stood around my bed.

At that moment, time stopped. I shook my head and kept saying "No! No!" over and over again. The doctors were at a loss for words.

"What is going on with my baby?" I cried out. An older doctor touched my shoulder softly. He then started telling me that, "Your poor baby is extremely ill and we want to life flight him to Rainbows Babies and Children's Hospital in a helicopter, but he was connected to too much equipment, and we would have to take him by ambulance."

I cried out, "What are you telling me? I do not understand?"

"We need you to sign these release papers, so your baby can get help at Rainbows Babies and Children's Hospital. I am sorry to tell you this sad news, but there is a chance that he may not make it to Rainbows."

"No! No!" I begged. "Please don't let that happen!"

He said in a comforting voice, "I assure you. Nicholas will get our best attention that we have to offer and Rainbows is the best place for him right now."

I composed myself as best as I could and said, "Yes I will sign, but what is wrong with Nicholas?"

Looking worried, one doctor said, "Nicholas has multiple defects. Your son has only two chambers in his heart and his pulmonary artery is not pumping enough blood through his system. He has only one lung and his heart is on the wrong side. He has a hole in his heart too."

"Oh, god," I cried out over and over again. "Why are my poor sweet baby's insides all messed up?" Mom was standing beside me and touched my hair pulling it back from my face. "Laurel, do you want me to call Dad? He will take me to Rainbow Hospital."

"Yes, Mom, go and tell my baby that his Mommy loves him, and to hold on and I will see him soon." Mom kissed my head and told me she loved me and asked me to rest. I watched Mom walk out of the room and I could see the fear ravaging through my mother's heart—a fear no mother wants after giving birth or a Grandmother who stayed by my side. One by one the doctors walked out and everyone was leaving me.

I lay back and life that had been inside me, my baby, was now in great need; in need of somehow holding onto his life. I felt vulnerable and worry ran though my head. I closed my eyes and prayed. I had never prayed like this before. "God help my baby be OK. We need your help. Please help us. Keep your strong arms around him and make Nicholas strong and healthy." I lay back in bed and felt lost and alone.

I was moved to a new floor where all the women had their new born babies with them. The medical staff put me in a private room and closed the door. The closing of the door did not stop my mind or separate my need for my baby.

The unbearable pain of not having my baby with me shot though my heart with a longing that I have never felt before. I laid back and let the tears pour out of me. I had never known such sorrow and had never cried like this before in my life. My body shook and trembled uncontrollably and a deep, intense sorrow filled up my heart. Then there was a tap on the door and a doctor walked in. "You have not eaten in over two days. We ordered you a tray. And Laurel, I know you are very upset, but try to eat and rest and maybe we could release you tomorrow." After the doctor had walked out of the room, I had the urge to go to the bathroom. I stood up and blood burst down my legs like a bucket of water hitting the floor. My legs felt weak, as I tried to go to the bathroom to clean up and get paper towels to clean up the mess I had made on the floor.

I moved blood from one puddle on the floor making a bigger mess of things, and looking out of sorts when a nurse walked in and saw me trying to clean up the blood I had lost, "Honey, go back to bed. I can clean this up. You need your rest. You had a long and hard labor and you are bleeding badly from it." She walked over to me and helped me back into bed.

When I started to cry she said in a caring, understanding way, "Cry all you want, don't hold it back. You need to get things out."

"I'm sorry for the mess," I said apologetically.

"Girl, don't be sorry. I see things like this all the time. I am going to clean you up and the floor. Now you listen to me. You take care and eat and cry whenever you need to cry."

I started crying again and said, "Please let me go to see my baby." I watched the floor get cleaned and the nurse then helped me out of bed and changed my sheets and gown.

I lay back in bed and ice was placed down on my vagina. She explained that the ice wound help the traumatized area that was torn. I kept moving my head, begging and crying for my baby, "Try to relax and I'll get the doctor to order you something to relax." The nurse walked out, closing the door.

The nurse came back with a pill and said, "Take this. The doctor said it will help you sleep and relax." I took the pill, but what would have made me relax would be to see my baby again. I laid back and prayed myself to sleep. I slept fitfully throughout the night. I woke to the sound of a crying baby. *Was it my baby crying?* I need to take care of him. I got up and my breasts were hurting because they had filled up with baby's milk. My whole body ached and my vagina was swollen and sore. It felt like it was swollen down around to my knees. I looked around the room for Nicholas; he was not with me. I came out of my disturbed sleep. What I was hearing were babies in rooms around me in need of feeding.

I walked back and got into my bed, turned over, and tried to sleep as the sound of the babies around me filled my heart with a deep longing. I prayed to God, "Stay by my sweet baby boy's side, until I can be with him. I prayed and cried all night long, tuning over and over, hoping I could see him soon.

Chapter 23

Reawaken

I reawakened early the next morning and lay back as I felt the warm light shining through my hospital window. I pulled the covers over my eyes and turned over onto my side. My whole body ached all over and my head was pounding fiercely. I covered my whole head with my covers, but that did not stop the grief and deep sadness that had a hold on my heart. I was all cried out and wanting badly to put on my clothes and run out of my hospital room to be with my baby. I heard my door open and an older woman walked in and dropped off my food tray onto my table and wheeled it over to me. She had a warm smile and said, "Good morning." Then she turned and hurried, walking out, closing the door behind her. I turned over in my bed, not wanting to look at food or even think about eating. I was emotionally drained, hoping that if I closed my eyes hard enough it may only be a dream. All in one moment how things can change—wanting to have my baby in my arms only to have him be rushed out of my arms and away from his mother.

I got up and slowly walked into the bathroom. I looked at myself in the mirror. I looked horrible and my eyes were swollen. I felt older than my twenty-one-year-old body actually was. I felt my stomach. It had gone down from being so huge that I could hardly move these last few months.

My stomach was now a swollen, little ball. I opened my gown to see the stretch marks that had covered my stomach and in between my legs. There was all the evidence right before my eyes of a life that was once inside of me. I took a good look at my breasts. They were bigger, and filled up with milk, calling out for my baby to be feeding on them. My body had changed overnight and the reminders of my pregnancy filled my mind. What a labor I had. I felt like

I was hit by a truck and my body felt turned inside out. I was lost and wanted my baby near me.

I needed to wash up and get it together, so I could get to my baby. I was given special pads that had dry ice in the middle. I sat down on the toilet and by now my bleeding had slowed a little bit from pouring out of me last night. I had piles of hemorrhoids and my vagina was swollen; it felt like the size of a small watermelon. I was given a donut to sit on when I sat down. I was told I needed to give myself a sitz bath every few hours to help me heal. I filled up the bag with cold water, then sat down letting out a holler as the cold water hit all around the swollen areas. I held my breath and closed my eyes just hoping for a little relief. I tried to relax. I replayed the day before in my mind step by step. Oh, my sweet baby is very ill; I am his mother and I need to go see him, look at him, and touch my baby, and take care of his needs. A guilty feeling passed though me.

I needed to be with my baby and not fussing over myself.

I began to fill up with tears, just wanting and needing my son. I put on my dry ice pad on a clean pair of underwear. I was pulling my underwear up when the phone rang. I ran out of the bathroom and almost tripped over my food tray, while I grabbed for the phone.

"Hello"

"Laurel, how are you? I am worried. Did you sleep or eat?" Mom said.

"Mom, I am OK. Did you go last night to Rainbows to see Nicholas?"

"Yes, I saw Nicholas and I told him you love him and will be with him soon."

"Thanks, Mom," I said and began to cry uncontrollably.

"Laurel, please listen to me. You need to eat, sleep, and take care of yourself. There is going to be long days ahead. I do not want to scare you, but Nicholas is in ICU and Honey, he is very sick. Nicholas was put onto a lot of machines that are pumping medicines to keep him alive." Mom paused. "Oh, Laurel, he is so beautiful and a blessing to us. He has your beautiful greens eyes. You had a big baby boy." As I listened, I heard Mom's voice break up with emotions. "Mom, I am hoping to be able to leave today. I don't think I can take another day in here," I said while I sat back on my bed. Just then the door opened and the doctor and nurse walked in.

"Mom, the doctor is here. I'll call you right back."

I hung up the phone and the doctor was studying me.

He came over to me in a caring manner, almost like he was sorry for what had happened last night, with his horrible bedside manner. He then opened the lid of my food tray, and he seemed worried. He placed the lid back down and said, "Laurel, I need to check on you to see if your bleeding is better and how your swelling is doing." I lay back while he examined me down below with a nurse, standing by my side.

In a consoling voice the doctor said, "Miss Wessel, you are badly swollen and your hemorrhoids are all pushed out. The good news is your bleeding seemed better. I am going to order something for your hemorrhoids, and keep putting on the dry ice pads. It will take time before all the swelling goes down and your body will heal. You had one of the hardest labors I have ever seen. But Laurel, you did great. I have never seen such bravery in the delivery room before. I am sorry that I did not make it easier for you when I could have. But please listen to me. You need to eat, so I can get your discharge papers going. You have a baby waiting for you." For the first time in a long time, I had a smile on my face. "Thank you, Doctor."

"I need to order Motrin for the pain and Ibuprofen to help you with the swelling, and Laurel, you need to wear a bra a size smaller so your milk will dry up. I am sorry to tell you this, but you will not be breast feeding your baby."

I nodded at him that I understood all that he was instructing me to do. Then he went to the door, followed by the nurse. He stopped and looked back at me.

Then he said, "Laurel, I am praying for both you and your baby."

I filled up again with strong emotions and said, "Thank you."

I reached for the phone and hit in my home number, "Mom I am going to be released. Tell Dad and come and get me."

I got dressed and ate half of my cold eggs and toast, but nothing tasted good. I was feeling like I needed something in me and cold food had to do at that moment. I sat waiting in my room with the door closed and waited for the discharge papers. I kept hearing babies crying in other rooms, and hope came to my mind. *There is always hope*, I thought. Just maybe, I might have my baby crying in my arms soon.

I was wheeled down the halls to the elevator and again my mom was walking beside me—this time we were walking out of the hospital. I looked in the hospital rooms as we passed and saw women in their rooms holding their newborn. I was happy for them, while pleasure filled my heart and put a smile on my face. I wanted to sing out, "I am going to see my baby too!"

Once we were outside, it was a bright January day, but very cold. We had no new snow on the ground. I was glad for that because the drive would then be easy to get across town. Dad was waiting in the driver's seat of my car. I wanted to drive because I knew how to get to Rainbows faster.

"Hi, Dad," I said pleadingly, "I'm fine and I want to drive."

Dad gave me a look then said, "No, Laurel you are in no condition to drive."

I got into the back seat and Mom sat with me. I knew that if I sat in front I would drive Dad crazy telling him to speed up. I sat back as Dad pulled off and every light we came too seemed longer than normal. Everything seemed slower when you are in a hurry. Everything seemed to be holding us up as we tried to get away from Metro Hospital to Rainbows Babies and Children's Hospital where my baby was waiting for me. I wanted to scream out, "get out of the way." I wanted the road for myself. Mom broke my thoughts and said, "I packed you an overnight bag."

"Mom, you think of everything, thanks." I sat back feeling a little funny being back to my own body after nine long months of pregnancy. I felt different. I was also overly tired and on edge. I put my head back, happy that we were finally getting on the highway at last.

When out of nowhere a young man in a fiery red sports car, cut Dad off, and was going way to fast.

"Jerk!" I yelled out.

"In a hurry, for what? He is going to get someone killed if not himself." Dad shook his head in aggravation. I wanted to shout out more obscenities, but with Dad driving I kept quiet.

Mom looked over at me and said, "Laurel, close your eyes and get some rest."

"Mom, I am OK." I kept looking out of the car window while we drove on the highway. We bypassed downtown Cleveland and the Terminal Tower stood out over the cold, gray sky. Then I heard a voice, "Laurel," I closed my eyes and went back to sleep. Then I felt someone shake my arms and say, "Wake up." I kept my eyes closed and wanted to fall back to sleep; it took a few minutes for me to gather where we were.

"Laurel, wake up, we are here at Rainbow Hospital."

"Finally," I said with a yawn. Dad dropped Mom and me off while he parked the car. Mom then said, "Laurel, you need to go to the front desk to sign up for a parking pass because you have the baby in the ICU."

"Mom, you know the ropes already." I smiled at her. I walked over and gave my name to a woman while she gave me parking passes and a special tag to put around my neck, so that we all can get into ICU.

Then the lady said, "Go around to the next set of elevators and go to the third floor." I listened to what the lady was telling me, and by now Dad had caught up with us and we all walked together around to the elevator.

I felt relieved that I would soon see my baby. Once we were off the elevator, I saw the ICU sign pointing down the hall. There was a waiting room with fish tanks and a huge TV. I saw a large group of Amish people sitting down watching the TV, as laugher filled the waiting area.

"Mom, I thought that Amish don't watch TV?"

"I thought so too. They seem to be enjoying modern television." We both started laughing when we came up to a door, telling us to press the button and give your name.

A nurse answered and said, "Can I help you."

"I am Nicholas's mother, Laurel Wessel." After I said these words out loud, I liked the sound of them. She opened the doors and we walked in. I looked around to find my baby, but I did not see him.

We passed young children and babies all looking very ill and my heart went out to each one. Seeing such young lives sick and suffering hurt me badly. A few Mothers looked up as we walked in and no one said anything. There was a feeling of anguish and sorrow in some of their faces. And one woman looked over at me, and a small, soft, smile came over her face like there was hope for all of us. She was reading a book to her young boy lying in bed who looked to be around six years old. Then we came to the other area of the ICU department. This place was much too big and filled with children who were all in pain. I felt sadness rip through me and felt so helpless.

Children need space to run and play and not be lying in a bed fighting for their lives. A group of doctors and nurses were standing around a bed of a patient. I wanted to move them out of the way because I had a fearful feeling that it was my sick baby. A doctor pulled me aside and said, "Laurel Wessel, Mother of Nicholas?"

"Yes," I answered.

He then pulled up an office chair and said, "Please have a seat." Dad and Mom stood next to me. He went and came back with a number of doctors; everyone introduced themselves. I tried to remember their names, but there were too many doctors, and to be honest, I wanted to get to my baby. The head off ICU said, "Laurel, you know that your baby is very ill and we are going to do our best to help him." Another doctor started drawing a heart, telling me that that is how a heart was supposed to look like. And then he said, "Nicholas's heart is on the wrong side with a number of other problems as well."

I took in a few breaths and said, "What can you do to help my baby?"

"Well, Miss Wessel, there is hope, but we need you to understand that not only your baby's heart is bad but there are other problems as well. He has only one lung and the other is not fully developed or working well at all. Nicholas has no spleen. We are hoping in a few days from now to open Nicholas up and repair his pulmonary artery, and he will need a number of other surgeries after that as well. We will take this one step at a time."

I just looked down to the floor, letting everything they told me sink in. I was overwhelmed after hearing of my baby's condition.

"Is there hope for Nicholas?" I said sadly.

"Yes, Miss Wessel, we will do our very best for your baby. Do you have any questions for us?"

"No. You covered everything. But yes I do I want to see my baby."

"I'm sure you do." He smiled and pointed, "He is right over there in front of our main desk."

I saw Nicholas as a nurse was checking on one of the machines. I stopped to take in what I was seeing. There was my baby in the middle of ICU, right in front of the main desk area, where the doctors walked in and out, and where the medical staff could keep an eye on him.

I felt safe knowing that Nicholas was right in front. All around my baby were a number of different machines and tubes going in and out of him. He was lying naked under a bright, warm light. I wanted to hold him close to me. I stood looking at Nicholas; my heart stopped and I wanted to change places with him to take the pain away.

My sweet lovely baby lay out in the open area and I held on to the hope that he could be fixed. Mom and Dad stayed close. I looked over at Dad, as his mouth quivered and his voice cracked. He said, "I will wait in the waiting room."

"OK, Dad."

When he walked over to me he squeezed my shoulder, turned, and walked up to Nicholas and said, "Hi, little fella" and then walked out trying to hold back from crying in front of me. Mom held onto my hand and I walked over to my baby's side where there was one free hand from the tubes. I put my finger into his hand. "Hi, Nicholas, Mommy is here." He looked and opened only one eye, letting me know he heard me. Next, I dropped my head and whispered into his ear, "I missed not being here sooner, but happy to see you now my sweet baby boy." Nicholas moved his finger onto my hand and we rubbed each other's fingers over and over again. Mom stood next to me.

"He is all boy and looks to be one month old and not a newborn, but you have to admit he is so cute," I said.

"Yes, Laurel, he is a sweet baby boy and he looks like a little football player. He has his Mommy's eyes."

"He sure does, and with him being twenty-three inches long and weighing in over ten pounds after his swelling has gone down, he looks like he is going to be a football player and he is going to be tall," I spoke proudly.

"Like his Mommy," Mom said while we fussed over Nicholas. I watched my baby listen to us talk.

"Yes, Nicholas we are talking about how big and beautiful you are." I had an urge to hold him, to feed him. I wanted to cover and wrap his baby body in a sky blue blanket. With his dark head of hair, I knew blue would be a good color on him. But I only sat there holding his little hand and talking to my son.

This was all I was allowed to do. Then a nurse brought over another chair for Mom to sit down on in the tight area we were in. Together we sat with Nicholas.

"Dad has been outside in the waiting area a long time. Why don't you both go home? I'll call you in the morning, first thing I promise," I said. I wanted to be alone with Nicholas and Mom knew that as well.

"OK, Laurel. But get your rest tonight. I am worried about you. You look worn out."

"I will be fine." I walked Mom out to the waiting room to see that in the waiting area the Amish where still watching TV and Dad was reading a magazine in the far corner.

I was put on a list for Ronald McDonald's house for parents who had children and babies in ICU, but for now there were no openings. The house is like a little apartment with everything anyone would need. There was a room that had cots lined up along the wall with one bathroom. I could stay in ICU all day and night but there were a few hours that the doors were closed.

I spent the day just sitting near my baby and at times I would sing to him, but in a low voice so no one could hear me. We were lost in time just being together. It was getting around the time that the doors were to close. I needed to get some sleep. I said goodnight to my baby.

"Sleep well, my baby, and may an angel watch over you at all times, and God make you all better."

I kissed his head and walked out. I went to the room and one cot was open. I put my bag on it. I went to the bathroom, but someone was in there. I sat on the cot for five minutes and then went back. I opened the door, and there was a sink, and toilet, and a walk in shower. I was only in for a few minutes when someone knocked on the door. "A few minutes please I just got in here." I got out my donut, and sitz bath filled it with water and sat down. A knock hit the door again and someone said, "I need to use the bath room bad."

"OK," I said. I dumped out the cold water, dried off the donut and sitz bath putting it in the bag. Mom packed me a jogging suit and I put it on and brushed my teeth. And out the door I went. The person passed me in a blur and closed the door. I went to my cot and pulled the curtain around me and laid on it trying to sleep. I am six one on good day if I don't slouch and I was too long, so I pulled up my knees and tried to sleep. All night long people were in and out of the bathroom and kept opening the door to go out in the halls. I turned over and over on my small cot.

The man sleeping next to me got up and went into the bathroom. I heard him walk back; he was on the heavier side. He opened my curtain and almost lay on top of me.

"Sorry wrong cot," I said.

"Oh, my! I am so sorry dear," he said in a sleepy voice. He turned and went back to his cot and snored. That was it! I got up and sat in the waiting area for over an hour, and then I went to hit the button to see if they would let me in to see my baby. It was around three in the morning. By now I was feeling tried and very sore. Then the head doctor from ICU said, "Can I help you?"

"I am Nicholas's mommy and I can't sleep. Can I please come in and be with my baby?"

"Well, OK, but don't tell anyone." He opened the door and the lights were low. I could hear machines working and a few doctors and nurses were around. I pulled up a chair, and sat all night long next to my baby.

Chapter 24

Together

I must have dozed off sitting in the chair next to Nicholas when the ICU started to stir and the doctors gathered around going by the bedsides of the young patients looking over their charts. I had only gotten about two hours of sleep and I felt stiff and sore all over my body. My breasts were swollen up again from the bright warm light that shined over my baby. I stood up and stretched. I noticed that I had milk stains on the front of my sweater. I wanted to clean myself up, look a little better for my baby, and to handle the day at large.

I leaned over and got close to my son's ear, "Nicholas, how did you sleep? Mommy is so sorry I can't pick you up and hold you close to me. I am going to call your grandma and ask her to bring some books, so I can read to you." Nicholas opened his eyes as I talked to him, but he looked a little more swollen than yesterday. Then a buzzing sound went off on one of his machines. I was in a panic. I jumped up and said, "Oh, god, please help us." I was filled with worry while I looked for help, and before I knew it, a nurse came over and hit a button. She smiled and said reassuringly, "Don't worry, he is fine. One of his bags is getting low."

"Oh, thanks, I am a little jumpy these days," I said with a yawn.

"Oh, that's understandable, with just having a baby, and with him being sick."

"Yes, it is hard and thanks for taking good care of Nicholas." I smiled gratefully at her.

"No problem, Nicholas is a sweet baby." I watched her while she wrote in his chart.

"There is hot tea and coffee every morning in the waiting area if you would like a cup."

"Sounds good," I said, feeling like I needed something to get me going. Then a group of doctors came into the room and walked over to Nicholas. I stepped aside, not wanting to get in their way. There was a tight space around us and I said to my baby, "Nicholas, Mommy will be back soon, I love you."

I kissed my baby's hand gently and went back to the sleeping room where my bag was sitting on my small and uncomfortable cot. I took my bag and went to the bathroom, but someone was already in there. Feeling tired I lay back on the cot waiting for my turn. I stretched out and tried to relax. When the door opened I got up, but someone beat me to the bathroom before I reached the door. I heard the shower turn on. *"Oh, that's just great,"* I thought to myself. I knew it would be a while before I got a turn. I then took my overnight bag and went to use a public bathroom down around the hall corridor.

I changed back into the clothes I had on the day before, brushed my teeth, and pulled back my hair into a pony tail. I was having a hard time using the bathroom and had not had a bowel movement in four days.

Everything in my body felt out of "wack." I hurt and was very tender to the touch in that area from all of the torn flesh from the delivery. Every time I had to use the bathroom in the sleeping room someone was using it. I was holding it in for too long. Now I was feeling all blocked up, and uncomfortable. I took paper towels out of the dispenser and ran cold water over them in the sink. I then went into the bathroom stall and I placed the paper towels onto my swollen area. I let out a moan as I washed myself and placed a dried ice pad on the tender area. I held in my breath and tried not to scream from the pain. It hurt so badly.

I wish I could have soaked the bottom half of my body in a tub of ice water. I took out my Motrin for pain and drank water from the sink. I took a good look at myself in a mirror. What a mess! I was frightened at what I saw. I looked exhausted and like I did not sleep in weeks. Gosh, I have a grey hair already at age twenty-one! Oh, well in a month I will be twenty-two, but still ways to go before I should get any gray hair. I am too young for gray hair! I pulled out some of the strands of the gray hair and I was grateful for the distraction. Meanwhile, my stomach was screaming from hunger pains and I felt dizzy. I was having dry heaves and knew I was going on four days with little to no food or proper rest. Walking out I saw a black Lab wagging his tail, walking into rooms making visits and making people happy as Labs seemed to know how to do.

I saw a pay phone at the end of the hall. The one in the sleeping room was always busy with someone on it. The Amish were always talking on the phone and it surprised me because I thought they wanted no contact with the modern world. And to be honest, I wanted to get away from the group of people who always wanted to use the bathroom, or phone when I did too. At this point, I just simply needed a little more space.

I called home and it was so comforting to hear my mom's voice.

"Hi, Mom, It's me Laurel. How are you?" I said.

"Did you sleep?"

"Well, Mom, it's a long story. A man almost climbed onto my cot with me."

"What!" she said.

"Mom it's OK," I laughed. "Tell you all about it when you come up. Mom, can you bring up the baby's books so we can read to Nicholas?"

"Sure I can. Sounds like a good idea and how is the baby?" Mom asked.

"I was by Nicholas's side all night long. He seemed about the same, maybe a little more swollen," I replied sadly.

"Laurel, I am worried about you. You need your rest. And remember, Nicholas is getting the best possible care. Is there a chapel there? Most hospitals have them. You need to take a break from the ICU. I know you want to be with Nicholas, but you need to get away from the ICU from time to time. And Laurel, I called the priest and he will stop in to visit Nicholas. I also have him on a few prayer list and I made calls to family and friends. They are going to keep us in their prayers too."

"Thanks, Mom, you think of everything. When do you plan to come up?"

"Dad will be dropping me off soon, and Billy and Veronica are coming up some time tomorrow," Mom said. "OK, Mom I'll see you soon," and I hung up the phone.

I glanced into the room and I saw the woman that was reading yesterday to a young boy. He was sitting up in bed watching a cartoon, while his Mom was reading a book next to him.

He looked better. I felt wonderful for them, seeing that they were out of ICU and into a regular hospital room. I thought that there might be hope for Nicholas and me. There has to be hope and I will keep it inside me. I then prayed for my sick baby and all the children in ICU. As the black Lab passed me, I stopped the owner and asked, "Do you mind if I pet your dog?"

"Please do. He would love it."

I got down and petted his soft fur. He kissed my face and his tail was moving in excitement. I felt better being able to touch a dog and the black Lab seemed to savor my touch.

"I come in here with Max monthly for visits to see the children. They just love him," the owner said proudly.

"I can see why. He is such a sweet-natured dog. He can put a smile on anyone's face." I was missing our dog back at home, but having a fuzzy face around helped pick up my mood even if it was only for a few minutes.

"Who do you have in there?"

"My baby, Nicholas. He is in the ICU," I said.

"Sorry to hear that. Can I say a prayer for him?"

"Sure," I said. I thought that she would say a prayer in private later in the day and move on with Max. Right in the hallway, she reached for my hands. She was a tall woman like me, with soft blue eyes and short, dark hair. It is always nice to look a person in the eye when you talk to them. Unexpectedly, this woman reached closer to me and Max stood by us very still.

She began saying, "Good Lord, help this young woman's son, Nicholas, and restore his health." I filled up with emotion and started to cry.

I tried to compose myself, but I got all choked up and tried to muffle a response and managed to say thank you through my tears. She squeezed my hand and said, "I will keep you both in my prayers. Come on, Max, we have a few more rooms to visit."

I watched them walk on, and Max turned back with his soft brown eyes giving me a loving and understanding look that only canines know how to give.

By now my stomach started to grumble. I turned to go down the elevator and headed into the cafeteria to eat. I ordered eggs, bacon, and toast, and a large mug of black coffee.

At that time I hated coffee, but thought it could get me going, as I heard it did helped you go to the bathroom. I ate the food and I sat back watching doctors, nurses, and people walking in and out, moving in a rush to get back to their workstations. The last few days hit me hard, as my mind continued to worry about my son Nicholas. I felt out of sync with my body from the overpowering fatigue. I closed my eyes to get some rest. All of a sudden, I felt something touching my leg. I opened my eyes and saw a young boy patting my leg.

"You are asleep," he said.

"Ho" I said, as his Mom pulled him away.

"Sorry he woke you."

"That's fine. I guess I was sleeping." I said as I sat up in the chair.

"You were snoring too," the boy said laughing.

"I was?" I felt my face turning red.

"Sorry that he bothered you." His Mother picked him up and walked away telling him that he should not have bothered me. Well, I snore in public and sleep in chairs. I am turning into an old woman over night. I was exhausted, when a lady cleaning tables came over to my table and asked, "Are you done with your tray?"

"Yes, thank you. Excuse me, do you have a chapel in the hospital?"

"Yes, go out and down the hall. Turn right. At the end, turn to the left about two doors down and you will see a sign that says chapel." I got a little lost and backtracked until I found it. It was a small chapel with a simple cross in front, not like the one I used to see when I went to my church. I kneeled down and prayed for my baby and was pleased that it was a small, cozy chapel and was empty. I went to the back pew and sat down and was enjoying my solitary time.

I almost fell off to sleep and looking at my watch I realized I had sat and prayed for over an hour. I felt better and refreshed, thinking I needed to get back to my baby. I was stretching and about to get up when an older man, walked in and smiled at me.

He sat down in a prayerful manner. I walked passed him quietly, not wanting to disturb him. He stopped me and said, "Sorry, but I think I saw you yesterday in the ICU.

"Yes, my baby is in there."

"My granddaughter is being moved as we speak."

"What a blessing," I said, "I'm happy to hear your good news."

"Yes, she is going to be fine, thanks to the good Lord. What is your baby's name?" he asked.

"Nicholas," I replied.

"Is he the one in front of the medical desk?"

"Yes, that's him," I said.

"Do you mind if I stop by and pray over your son?" he said in a heartfelt way. "No, please stop by anytime." He was a kind man, with a round older grandpa type of face. He seemed like the Grandfather I always wanted but never had. They both passed on before I was born. I wish I could have sat with him and talked longer, but I wanted to get back to Nicholas. He had white, thin hair and skin that looked weather beaten, like he worked out doors for a living. As I turned to walk out he asked, "What is your name?"

"Laurel," I said.

"That's a pretty name. I will pray for you too."

"Thank you," I smiled back and walked out.

It was comforting that there were still so many spiritual people in our harsh modern world.

When I got back there was a huge ultrasound machine taking pictures of my baby's heart. The young woman saw me and said, "I only need a few more minutes and I will be out of your way."

"Take your time," I said and as I looked over at my suffering son I noticed there was another tube in my baby. It was getting more and more difficult for me to cope.

To see Nicholas hurting and that I could not do anything about it tore me up. She backed up and wheeled her cart out of the room. I pulled up in the chair and whispered to my boy, "Well, Nicholas, you have a lot of people praying for you and we hope you are better soon."

I put my hand into his again and this time I felt a strength and a peaceful, loving, feeling that came over both of us. He actually was trying to rub his tiny little fingers over my hand. We were bonding and I sensed he was trying to comfort me. I saw that my baby's mouth looked dry, so I got up and asked his nurse, "Can I wet a cloth and put it around his face and can I give him some water? He looks so dry."

"No, sorry he can't have anything to drink and no cloth, because you might hit his tubes. But you can put lotion around his feet and one hand. I finally felt like I was doing something for my baby because feeling so helpless was the worst of it all.

"It's Mommy," I told him. I got lotion and began to rub his feet and one hand that were not bound to a wire and a machine. When Mom walked in, she had a picture of St. Jude, the patron saint of hopeless cases and a cross that we taped up on the crib near his head. Mom brought the books and more things packed into a bag to try and make my ordeal a little more comfortable. Mom pulled up a chair and read one story after the next. As I watched my mother, reading to her grandbaby, I knew we both were blessed to have such a gentle caring soul in our lives.

It was getting time for lunch and around the noon hour. They closed the doors in the ICU for a few hours before we could go back in.

"Well, Laurel, I packed a few sandwiches and let's take a look at what's in the cafeteria."

"Sounds, good to me, Mom."

We walked out and into the waiting area; on the small end tables pulled together was food and it smelled and looked great. The Amish had made huge amounts of food that could have probably fed the whole hospital. There was fried chicken, potatoes, corn, and every kind of fruit pie you could think of.

Mom and I were walking to the elevator when an older Amish woman stood up and said, "Please come and eat with us."

"Well, thank you," Mom said, "But we do not want to impose."

"No, we have enough food, please sit and eat."

"Everything looks and smells so wonderful. Thank you." Mom smiled over at me.

The Amish woman started putting food onto paper plates and handed them to us. I don't think we could have turned them down even if we wanted to. We sat and ate and we both enjoyed our meal and the good aura the Amish people had about them. We learned that her grandson had heart surgery four days ago and that if things kept looking up, she told us that he may be in a room by the end of the week. Looking around it seemed like the whole town came together to support the family who had someone sick. There were young, old, and middle-aged people. They all seemed close and somehow they all seemed to get along. I told her about my baby, as she listened sympathetically to me.

"We will pray for your baby," the older woman said.

"Thank you for your prayers and for the delicious meal," I said. Then they all got up immediately as though they were all of one mind. Everyone held hands in a big circle and the Amish woman began talking to God with Mom and me quietly praying for Nicholas and asking God to heal him and bring comfort to his ailing little body and to his mommy during this ordeal. Mom and I thanked everyone and afterward Mom looked over at me, and said, "We had a good meal."

"Yes, Mom, and I ate too much. Can you believe it, Mom? There are so many people praying for Nicholas."

"Laurel, that's wonderful—the more the better," Mom said.

"Yes, Mom, the more the better." I felt love not only for me, but for my sweet baby laying in the ICU from others who were actually strangers to me.

As night was coming, Mom called Dad, to come and pick her up. I wanted Mom to stay with me, but we had to check to see if the sleeping room had space for us. Mom and I checked, but all the spaces were filled as more Amish were there taking up all the space with sleeping bags. I was tired, and they were so kind to me and Mom. Mom looked at me with a warm look of concern in her soft green eyes, "Laurel, we live only twenty-five minutes from Rainbows."

"I know, Mom, but I hate to leave Nicholas alone, or maybe a room at Ronald McDonald house will open up soon," I said to Mom.

"But until then Laurel, I am worried. You do not look too well and need a good night's sleep."

"Mom please don't be worried."

"But until a room is available Laurel, please come home and rest, and first thing in the morning you will be back to visit. Honey, there is not much you can do for him. Nicholas is in the best care possible," Mom said.

"I know, Mom, you are right."

"And you had a long, hard labor. If you don't take care of yourself, you will be no good for Nicholas."

"OK, Mom, you are right. I do need some sleep."

As the visiting hours were coming to an end, Nicholas slept most of the time and it made me sad that I never heard him cry ever, only that one moment when he was born; it was a soft, sad, hopeless cry. I know it was because of all the tubes that were going into him, but I would have loved to have heard him cry like every other baby I heard in the hospital.

"Goodnight, my baby boy. Mommy loves you and may God's angels watch you close all night long and keep you safe. I will be back before the doors in the ICU open up, I promise."

As I held onto his hand, the ICU was getting quiet as people were leaving out for the night. Only doctor and nurses were around. A nurse walked over and said, "The visiting hours are coming to an end. You can stay a little longer if you like. We make exceptions for the rules for the parents."

"Thank you," my hand stayed entwined in Nicholas's for another hour.

"See you in the morning. I love you my son," I finally said. Then I kissed him goodnight and walked out crying.

Chapter 25

Stay Positive

I was up bright and early and we were off driving the familiar roads toward Rainbows. I was thankful that there was no new snow on the roads. However, the chill of January weather was in full speed and Mom was worried that there was ice on the roads. Mom kept reminding me to slow down. I was driving too fast, but I had a feeling that each second away from my baby felt like days. What if he needs me and I am not there? "Stay positive," I kept telling myself; Nicholas is in the best of care. "Laurel, slow down," Mom said and broke my train of thought. "You know haste makes waste."

"All right, Mom, I'll slow down."

Together we walked into the ICU very anxiously. I glanced around and no little patients had been moved out of the ICU. I kept my eye out for all of the babies who were ill, knowing in my heart that this was everyone's prayer that their child would get better and move out of the ICU and into a regular room. We all have our little, private wishes throughout the day; you know the ones: I wish it would stop snowing, I wish I had more money, I wish Friday was here already. My wish for that day was that my baby be moved into a regular room very soon and get better.

Mom and I turned the corner and Nicholas had his one, little, free hand stretched out.

Mom and I hurried over to him and I placed my hand into his, holding on and spoke softly to him, "Good morning, my love. I missed you last night. Grandma, is with me," I said as Mom bent over and kissed Nicholas on the top off his forehead. Then we both pulled our chairs up close to him to sit down.

We were getting comfortable and I started reading to my baby when a nurse walked over and smiled saying, "Sorry, I need to change a few bags."

"Sure," I said and pulled my chair out of her way to make room. Nicholas moved his hand around looking and feeling for my hand to hold onto.

"Don't worry, Mommy is right next to you. I needed to move to make room for your nurse." When the nurse had finished changing his bags, I went back to the chair. Together my son and I both went back to holding hands and I continued to read out loud to my baby boy. This was our only way of being close and we both could hold hands for hours lost with what was happening all around us in the ICU. When I was near my son, I wanted to do more for him and to help him somehow but I was powerless. So I turned to my faith and kept praying all the time for him.

The group of doctors came over and told me that tomorrow Nicholas will be having his first of many surgeries. Hearing this from them made a horrible fear come over me, the kind that would turn any parent's stomach into knots, but I knew it was to come.

I leaned over to Nicholas's ear and said, "Sweetheart, you are going to have surgery tomorrow and Mommy is wishing that you did not have to, but the doctors here are the best and they want to fix your heart."

Mom kept her head down in silent prayer for my baby. "I'll be here too, my sweet grandson," Mom said and her heart filled up with empathy for her suffering grandson.

I know that in the last few days if Mom had not been there to help me though all that had happened, it would have been impossible to bear. The research has shown that by far the worst emotional trauma a person could go through is to be forced to watch his or her child suffer and not be able to do anything about it. This is what I was going through. Having Mom's love and support helped to keep me strong. The days are long and time wears on a person when sitting back watching the one you love suffer in the ICU. To see my baby suffer weighed heavily upon my heart and beat me down, but with the help of Mom, I stayed positive somehow through the madness of it all. Nicholas opened his eyes from time to time and looked over to me in a loving manner and his love went right to my soul, and hope filled me up every time with his simple acknowledgment of me.

There was one rule that we needed to be follow——only two people back around the little patients at a time in the ICU.

Mom stepped out, while Billy walked back for the first time; he looked tired from a long, hard work day.

He had on his work clothes and his work boots. Billy painfully walked over to Nicholas's little crib and I could see that his emotions were getting the best of him. "Billy, do you want to sit down?"

"No, thanks I'm fine." Billy said sadly. "Mom told me that tomorrow Nicholas is having surgery which is the first of many." He looked down into his hands and placed them into his pockets.

"Yes, Billy, he is" I said sadly. Then Billy walked a little closer to the crib, bowed his weary head in grief and was quiet.

"Well, I guess, I'll go get Veronica. She is waiting." Billy said looking sad.

"OK, thanks for coming and visiting."

"Sure, I just wish there was something I could do." Before he walked out, he pulled out some money and handed it to me. "What this for?" I asked.

"Food, it gets expensive eating in a hospital." Billy glanced around the ICU and said, "Sad place for all these little babies and kids. It almost seems unfair."

"Yes, you can say that again. No way, that any child should spend any time here."

"Well, I'll go get Veronica," Billy said.

"OK, thanks for the money, Billy." I watched Billy walk out of the ICU with a heavy heart. Veronica walked back and walked up close to Nicholas and kissed him on the head. She then pulled up another chair up and sat down. "Laurel, he is a sweet baby, very cute, but big, he is going to be a big boy when he gets older."

"Yes, Nicholas is a sweet baby. Would you like to hold his hand?"

"Sure, I'd love to." I got up and moved out of my chair and Veronica sat down as I stood next to her. Veronica took his little hand so gentle and talked to Nicholas.

"Hi Nicholas, I am your Aunt Veronica. You are one good-looking baby. You took after your aunt I see." I smiled to myself and took a seat across from Veronica and watching her with my baby made me happy. It was nice to have her around because it helped to break up the day. The time can get long and dreary as the hours move by slowly. It's nice to have the visits by my family members who offer their support during this difficult time for me. Then a nurse walked over and said, "There is a dinner in the doctor's lounge today for all the parents and families in ICU. It's at six-o-clock."

"What do you think, Veronica?"

"It sounds like fun and why don't you go take a break and go get Mom. We can stay by Nicholas's side for a while." I looked over at Veronica and did not say a word. "Laurel, go take a break," she insisted.

"OK, Veronica. I guess it will be all right. Besides, I sure could use one."

I walked past a large water fountain with green plants around it that sat in the middle of the main lobby. I walked over pulling out change, closed my eyes, and made a wish. I sat down and watched the people go by. A few people pulled out change, made a wish, and then tossed it into the water. I love the sound of water. It helped me to relax. I watched the water go up and down in the fountain. I wanted to jump into the moving water, but just sat back. There is something about water that takes the stress away. While sitting there, I saw a young mother holding the hand of a little boy and she was very pregnant. She was around the time when one waddles from side to side when she walks.

"Mommy, can I have some change?"

"Hold on, Johnny," she opened up her bag and pulled out a wallet.

"Make a wish, then toss in the change."

"All right, Mommy." He closed his eyes and then tossed all the change into the water.

"Mommy, can I make another wish?"

"Johnny, sorry I have no more change you dropped all I had into the fountain."

"Excuse, me if you don't mind I have a penny he can have," I said.

He ran over to me with big hazel eyes, light brown hair, and moving his arms around excitedly.

"Remember to say thank you," his mother said. He took the penny and tossed it into the fountain.

"Johnny, did you say thank you?"

He ran back to me and said, "Thank you."

Before I got a word out, he was right next to his mommy, "He is all boy" his mother said.

"Oh, he is all boy filled with life. I bet he is keeping you busy."

"Yes, he is."

"When are you due?" I asked.

"In three weeks, but I am ready to have this baby now and get it over with," she said to me, as she took off running after her son.

"Sorry, he is always on the go."

"Nice talking to you."

I watched her catch up to her son and say to him, "Now remember to hold onto my hand. There are a lot of people around." She grabbed onto his hand and they walked out of my sight. I sat back hoping and praying that this young healthy boy could one day be my son, Nicholas, filled up with a zest for life and boundless energy.

I went back to the chapel, sat in the last pew, and prayed for Nicholas.

I started thinking maybe I should sit in the front pew. Maybe God listens to people up there better than people sitting in the back like me. No, God picks no favorite or how or where one prays. He likes for you to talk to him like a friend, so that is what I did. The next time I will sit in the first pew to see how that feels as I pray. One never knows until you try. I looked down at my watch; it was getting time for the dinner party, and I needed to get back to ICU.

All three of us were walking down to the doctor's lounge for dinner. We were a little early. We walked in and the tables were all covered in white table cloths and fresh flowers were in the center of each table. Soon, the group of Amish walked in and every time I saw them they seemed to have grown more in numbers as they filled up many of the tables. The Amish grandmother and her daughter sat down with us and other faces that I saw in the ICU came in and sat down with their families. Then an older doctor stood up and thanked everyone for coming and said grace. When the food started coming out, we ate salad and dinner rolls followed by roast beef, sweet potatoes, and mixed vegetables. Everyone seemed to enjoy their dinner; it was delicious. Then the sweets came out with trays of cookies and cakes. I felt like I was at a wedding as voices filled the room with laughter and a brief sense of hope renewed in my heart. I could see that Veronica and Mom were having a nice time.

Mom got to know the Amish way of living better, and Veronica was asking questions as well. Mom told the Amish woman that Nicholas was having surgery the next day.

"We will keep him and your family in our prayers," she said.

I thanked her and replied, "Well, it's getting late. I want to get back to Nicholas's side."

"I'm ready," Mom said.

Veronica said in a teasing way, "Do you want to race?"

"Sure." I took off running and Veronica started laughing out loud.

"I was only kidding." Then Veronica took off running, followed by Mom running down the hall.

"I will beat you both," Mom said a little out of breath.

"We need to stop acting like this or we will end up in the psych ward of the hospital," I said laughing out loud. We all came to a stop and walked the rest of the way like normal people. That little bit of spontaneous foolishness was very therapeutic. Once we were in the ICU area, Veronica said, "I'll wait out in the waiting room."

Together Mom and I walked back to Nicholas's side. "Hi there, I missed you," I said then put my finger back into his hand. A nurse walked over and handed me a note. A nun from our church had come for a visit with Nicholas and prayed over him. The note read, "Laurel, sorry I missed you, if you need anything please call. Love, Sister."

"Thank you for the note," I said to the nurse.

"Nicholas had another visit tonight."

"Oh, he did? Who had stopped by to visit?" I was curious to know.

"He said to tell you, the man from the chapel from the other day."

"Oh, thanks for telling me."

"Well, Nicholas, you have a lot of people that love you and are praying for you," I said and took his hand into mine. The time was moving fast and the doors were about to close for the night. I leaned over to my baby and said, "I will be back tomorrow first thing before you wake up. Nicholas, I am wishing so much that you did not need this surgery, but remember Mommy loves you. Sleep well and may the angels watch over you while I'm not here." I kissed Nicholas goodnight and I wished that I could just stop the tears from flowing every time I had to leave him. I walked out and Veronica came over to me, "Laurel, it is going to be OK."

"I hope so," I said.

"Just believe and it will. Can I drive your car home?"

I started laughing to myself. "Sure, why not? Did you bring your temporary license with you?"

"Yes." Veronica pulled it out of her pocket, and the three of us walked out. It was always hard to leave Nicholas's side. But in my heart, I was in the room still holding his sweet little hand.

Chapter 26

Too Much

Veronica pulled in the front of our home. It was late, around nine o'clock, and no one was out on this first day of February. I sat next to Veronica as she drove and the whole day hung heavily upon me. Worry imprisoned my mind as to what was going to happen the next day when my sweet baby Nicholas would undergo a major life-threatening surgery. We all walked into the house; Dad smiled warmly to greet us and was looking glad to see us. I knew that Dad was missing Mom because she was at the hospital all the time with me. I walked right into my bedroom and picked up Nicholas's stuffed bear with a blue ribbon on it and held it close to me, feeling the soft fur against my face. I then walked the small bear over and placed it into the baby's crib.

I broke down and let the tears fall. I was not able to move from the side of the crib. Mom slowly walked into my room and sat on my bed and said, "Laurel, will you pray with me?"

I started to cry again and I was not able to say a word.

"It's so hard to see a little baby go through what Nicholas is going through," Mom said.

"It's so hard to see him sick. Why, Mom? Why Nicholas?" I begged for an answer.

Mom held me close, "Good Lord, we know you know our needs. We are asking you to guide the doctor's hands tomorrow and help restore Nicholas's health. Please be near Nicholas's mommy as well. May your will be done." I was holding onto my mother feeling her loving words wash over me and soothe some of my pain.

Dad knocked lightly on my door. "Come in," I said.

Dad looked worried and forced a smile, "Maybe we all can watch a movie." It was wonderful how Dad in his quiet way was trying to be helpful. At first he was very upset about me having a baby. However, Dad came around and he was being very protective of his troubled daughter. He was stepping in and trying to do his best to help us in his own quiet manner.

"Sure, Dad." I said.

"I'll make the popcorn," Dad offered. Together sitting in the living room as a family, felt very comforting to me. I realized I wasn't alone in this ordeal and that made all the difference in the world. Veronica picked out the movie to watch. Dad walked in with a big bowl of popcorn and put it down onto the coffee table. I looked around and realized that I hadn't watched television in over a week. I would occasionally peek in to see what the weather was going to be, but most of the time my mind was preoccupied on the health of my baby.

I sat back and as the movie flashed before our eyes, I woke up to Mom tapping me. "Laurel, it is time to get ready to go back to Rainbows."

"What time is it?" I asked. I was feeling a little achy from sleeping on the couch all night. I moved slowly to sit up and saw that Mom and Veronica were dressed and ready to go. I jumped up startled and in a panic said again.

"What time is it?"

"Laurel, we are fine. We have plenty of time," Mom said in a clam voice.

I washed up vigorously and hurriedly got dressed. Walking out of the bathroom I noticed that Mom had made us breakfast sandwiches with eggs and bacon.

"Laurel, sit down and eat," Mom insisted.

"All right, Mom," I said while keeping an eye on the clock. I ate half of the sandwich and wanted badly to get going. I watched while Mom was putting snack containers into a shopping bag to carry along with us for the long day ahead. Mom then turned to me and said, "Well, I'm ready. How about you?"

"I'm ready. Hey, Veronica, do you feel like driving?"

Veronica said in an excited voice, "Sure."

I handed over the car keys to Veronica and she took over driving us to the hospital. She handled the car well for a new driver. I could see that she enjoyed the freedom of driving, and my little sister was growing up right before my eyes. Together we all went up to the ICU. Mom had called our priest and he was coming to meet us. Together we all held hands and prayed over Nicholas.

I watched my baby receive his Holy Baptism right in the ICU and not in a church wearing a white gown but here in the ICU unit. Father pulled out the holy water and said, "I bless you Nicholas in the name of the Holy Father, and of the Son, and of the Holy Spirit." Nicholas opened his eyes as the priest touched his head with the holy water. Then he offered up the blessing; it was beautiful and peaceful. The priest then anointed his head with holy oil. I held his hand listening to every prayer and blessing that my son received; it helped me as well.

These last few days Nicholas was blessed by so many different people praying over him from different faiths. I thought maybe God will be a little more aware of his needs, in the hope that somebody's prayers reached him. You know that everyone thinks they are practicing the "right religion," but I wonder if that in the end of one's life we all wind up together and realize we can learn from the gifts of praying to one God no matter what language or prayer we use. And that no one religion is right or wrong, but they all just teach us how to live a better life. All the prayers helped and I knew deep in my heart that Nicholas and I were in this together, as my baby is a part of me. We all got settled sitting in the surgery waiting room and there was a couple in the far corner watching the TV.

I did not feel like watching TV or reading. Mom had her rosary beads and she was quietly whispering, "Our Fathers" and "Hail Marys." Veronica pulled the magazines off the table in the waiting room, picking out things that she liked to wear, or furniture for her dream home one day.

I joined in as we both went through the magazines together. It was getting time for lunch as the hours were passing by slowly. We went down to the cafeteria on the main floor and sat down together and ate lunch. Mom pulled out the snacks that she brought from home.

The grandfather that I had met earlier in the week in the chapel came over to our table. "How is Nicholas doing?" he asked.

"He is having surgery right now to repair his heart, which is one of many that needs to be done," I said sadly.

"I have Nicholas on my daily pray list."

"Thank you. I really appreciate your prayers. You know what? I don't even know your name," I said to him a little embarrassed.

"Call me Mr. Granddad Bob."

"OK, Granddad Bob," I laughed. "This is my sister Veronica, and my mom Doris Wessel."

He said, "Nice to meet you" and extended his hand to greet us.

"How is your granddaughter doing?" I asked.

"Good news, Amanda is coming home tomorrow." As he talked, he grinned from ear to ear.

"I am happy to hear your good news, and thank you for stopping by the other day and praying over Nicholas. I'm sorry that I missed you," I said.

"It was my pleasure to pray over Nicholas. Well, I'll let you finish your lunch."

"Thanks again," I said, as I watched him get in line to order his food. Mom turned to me and said, "Laurel, you have met kind people in here."

"Yes, I have, and each one seems to have a story to tell." After we finished our lunch, we took a little walk around the hospital; I could get around by now without stopping and asking people for directions. This hospital became too familiar to me.

Veronica said, "Let's take a look in the gift shop."

"Fine by me," I said. We all looked around the little shop and everything was too pricey. Mom picked up a set of three little books for a newborn baby. "Mom, everything is too high in here."

"No, Laurel, I want to buy this so we all can take turns reading to Nicholas."

"All right, Mom, I said smiling." I was getting antsy and wanted to get back to the waiting room. "Well," Mom said, "Time to get back."

"Yes, I am ready," I said, feeling a little uneasy and wanting to be near Nicholas. Back in the waiting room we all sat waiting and I noticed that the couple that was there had left the room. I thought maybe they took a break.

Veronica opened the baby books and looked them over. Mom went back to praying the rosary for my baby.

I sat back closed my eyes and prayed as well, as the time went to a slow, painful, crawl.

When the couple walked back in, I smiled over at them. But they hurried back to their corner and watched the TV. I looked up at the clock and we were in the fifth hour of the surgery by now. It felt longer to me as the room came, closing in on me. I got up and moved around the front of the waiting room a few times and then sat back down again.

A young doctor came in and walked over to the couple in the corner and said, "You can come back now." I could not overhear what was being said but both looked relieved as they hugged each other and then they walked past us going into the room to see their child. After looking at the clock several times, I realized that another hour had passed by. As each minute passed by, worry overwhelmed me and I got up and paced the floor and stepped out into the halls and walked up and down the corridor with a heavy heart. Then I went back to sit and wait in my chair and the waiting started all over again.

I hate waiting, especially in a situation like this where the well-being of my son was not known. The not knowing was driving me crazy. Veronica wanted something to drink and asked Mom for a dollar. Mom pulled out a dollar and handed it to her.

Veronica got up and asked, "Do you want anything?"

"No thanks, I'm fine."

"I'll be right back," Veronica said.

"Veronica, maybe I should go with you," Mom said.

"Mom, please, I am a big girl. I'll be right back," Veronica said walking out of the door. Mom sat back putting her rosary into her purse and she sat back looking over at the clock ticking away. I walked and paced around the room again this time in restless circles.

I turned the TV on and chased through a few channels and then turned it off. Nothing was able to distract me from my baby's welfare.

Veronica was back, and she said, "Laurel, let's take a little walk. This room is getting to you I can tell."

"OK, I need to move my legs anyway." I said.

"Go ahead, girls, I will wait in here," Mom said as she reached for the rosary in her purse. I think Mom was relieved to get me out of there because I was pacing back and forth and making things more nerve-racking. Veronica and I walked the halls for over twenty minutes or so. I kept my eyes on my watch looking at it every few minutes. "Veronica," I said nervously, "let's get back."

"All right," said Veronica.

We walked back in and the seventh hour was passing by too slowly since Nicholas had gone into surgery when finally an older doctor from the team of surgeons came out to talk to us.

"Miss Wessel, we are pleased with what we have gotten accomplished so far, but we need to tell you that we need to stop for today. We had some problems with keeping Nicholas's blood pressure up to a normal rate. It keeps dropping lower and lower every hour. We will be going back in to finish up tomorrow and sewing Nicholas back up. We want to tell you that there is a medical plastic covering over his chest cavity. It may be hard to look at, so I want to prepare you as well as your family. However, we are all hopeful that Nicholas will get though this first step in his series of operations. Do you have any questions for us?"

"No, I just want to see him."

"Fine, just remember that it may be an upsetting sight to see your son in this condition," he said in a sorrowful tone.

Together we walked in and my baby lay there with his chest cavity wide open and we could see inside his little heart fighting away and beating as strong as his tiny will would allow. I held in my breath and let it out and walked over to his bedside and held onto his tiny hand. "Hi, Nicholas, Mommy is here. I am so sorry about what you are going through."

My knees started to buckle from the grief that gripped my heart. I steadied myself to make sure I didn't lose my balance. I closed my eyes for a minute and tried to compose myself.

I looked at my baby boy with his chest painfully cut open and his brave, little heart beating away, hanging onto life as best as he could. He was fighting with every ounce of courage his infant body could muster up.

There was my Nicholas, with his heart exposed waiting to be fixed. It looked painful beyond words and seemed so unfair that my little baby son, only a week old, should suffer this way. It seemed so unfair that I had to helplessly stand by and not be able to do anything to help my baby boy.

Mom and Veronica were strong as they both talked to him softly telling Nicholas that, "Everything is going to be fine." Mom pulled out the children's books and began reading. I had to work hard at not snatching up my baby and running out of the hospital screaming, "No! No! This cannot be happening," and somehow run away from all this madness. I just wanted to run him to safety somewhere or anywhere but in this hospital; run him away from all the pain; run him away from all the hurting. I wanted my baby to be healthy and not go through all this. I kept asking myself the same question over and over again, "Why is this happening?" But I could never get an answer. I started to panic and my breathing became heavier and more strained when I looked at his little chest again.

I then asked my son, "Why you? Why is this happening to you? You didn't do anything wrong to deserve this!"

All of these irrational and illogical thoughts flooded my fatigued brain. Mom could tell right away that I was in trouble. She looked over at me with concerned eyes and said, "Laurel, are you all right? Go and take a break. Go get some fresh air. We will be right here watching over Nicholas."

I turned away and hurried, getting out of there. I hit the button of the elevator to go down to the main lobby looking down and staring at my shoes because I was too weary to lift my head up. I felt like I couldn't catch my breath as my body was trembling. "Why?" was the question that kept running through my head. "Why? Why? Why?" I just wanted an answer—"Why?" When the door opened, I ran out of the hospital and into the February light snow that was falling and started crying uncontrollably. I was angry with God. I was mad at God. I paced up and down the street. I mumbled to myself like a crazy woman.

"Why? Why? Why is my baby suffering like this? What did I do? What did he do? I never drink. I never smoked. I never did drugs." I thought to myself, "There are women who party all the time throughout their pregnancies and their babies are fine. Why is my baby lying in the hospital with his chest cut open?" I was so overcome with emotion and physical anguish that I needed to throw up. I went next to the hospital building and lost the little I was able to eat that day.

Just then a bunch of college students were walking by and two of the girls started making fun of me, pointing over to me laughing out loud while I bent down to vomit. I overheard one of the girls saying,

"She must have had a hard night partying last night," followed by laughter while I threw up again. Rainbows Babies and Children Hospital sat in the middle of a Case Western Reserve College, as well as many museums that are around University Circle. I stood next to the hospital and sobbed out in pain. A young, male student came running over to me. He stopped and looked me right in the eyes and asked. "Are you OK?" He was tall with soft brown eyes, and looked concerned. He then reached into his book bag and pulled out a plastic container with Kleenex tissue in it and handed it to me. I took the tissue and tried to calm myself down. I was getting cold without my coat on. Then I looked down at all of the food I threw up that covered the snowy ground and got sick all over again.

"Hold on there! Do you go to college here?" He asked.

"No" I said taking in a deep breath to try and calm myself down.

He looked puzzled and said, "Can I do anything to help you?"

"No, I'll be OK. I am not a college student here."

"You need a coat. It's cold out here," he said looking more confused than ever.

"No, I have a coat."

He reached over and touched my arm, "Are you OK? Can I get you help?"

"No thanks, I have a baby who is very sick in the hospital. It's been a long, hard day."

"Oh, I see, I am sorry."

"I am fine, and thanks for the Kleenex." I tried to smile at him.

"No problem." He stood by me, looking worried and not moving from my side.

"Are you sure that there isn't anything I can do to help?"

"No, thanks, I just need a few minutes alone please."

"OK," he said. Then I heard the girls yelling for him.

"Come on. It's cold out here." He walked on looking back at me as I tried to gather myself. I watched him catch up to the girls who were still laughing at me. He turned back and looked my way again with concern and compassion.

I went back into the hospital and went into the bathroom. I washed my face and looked at myself in the mirror. I was twenty-one years old, and in less then a few weeks I would be turning twenty-two. I was still young and naive in many ways but growing old in many other ways seeing all that was happening to Nicholas and me over this past year. Seeing these young women my age laughing and making fun of me, not knowing a thing about me or my misery, made me angry. They had no idea what my life was about.

Their life to me looked pretty carefree with only the worry of passing tests or writing papers, while I was trying to deal with life, and maybe death issues.

At that moment, I was hurt, as anger was filling me up and the frustration started to creep up on me all over again.

The "why," questions continued to cross my mind again.

The notion that life was not fair to me or the baby lying up in the hospital filled my mind. I went back to the chapel, and no one was in there, thank God. I don't think I could bear to talk to anyone just yet. I sat this time in the front pew. I did not feel any different sitting up front than sitting in the back pew.

I pulled my head down to pray like I had never before in my life. I let go of all my "Why me! Why my baby!" questions and gave them all to God. I simply could not carry this back-breaking load around anymore. That is when something came over me, pulling me out of my mood I was in, and I was filled with a warming, soothing, powerful strength. I went back to my baby to see that Mom and Veronica both were reading the newborn books over and over to Nicholas. I took my place next to Nicholas and took his hand. "Hi, Baby, Mommy is back. I am sorry that all this is happening to you. I truly am hoping for better days for you my love." I held onto his tiny fingers. Mom and Veronica gave me some space and stepped out going back into the waiting room. I sat for hours with my baby. I wanted to stay overnight to be close to him.

I just couldn't leave him tonight, especially after all Nicholas had been through so far.

Veronica took my keys as Mom went with her and packed my overnight bag and brought it back to me.

I did not worry about sleep or if there is room in the sleeping room. I needed to be close to Nicholas.

The doors were closed for the night. I put my coat on and walked in the dark, lonely night, up and down the streets bordering the hospital. It was a quiet, midweek night, and only a few college students were out walking. I saw that Severance Hall was all lit up in the cold dark night, as a concert was letting out and people were all dressed up and were talking about the concert they had just seen.

I walked a good two hours on the streets. Then I turned, walking back, into the hospital and sat by the water fountain and picked a table that sat to the side in the back by all the snack machines.

For hours I sat and finally dozed off and took a short nap. The fatigue finally overwhelmed me. I woke up and watched while a few people passed by. Then I put my head down, when all of a sudden junk food of every kind started raining on my table in front of me. There were peanut butter cups, Snickers bars, Fritos chips and Milky Way bars dropping onto my table. Looking up I recognized that it was one of the doctors from the surgical team that tried to help Nicholas. He was a little older, kind of heavy set with a Santa Clause type of belly from enjoying too many good meals.

The Doc had a cheerful round face with thick reddish grey hair that needed combing, all over his head. The Doc also had these 1950s thick "Pork Chop," reddish grey sideburns on his chubby, cheerful cheeks.

"Dine with me my bonnie lass. I would hate to eat all this gourmet food alone."

"No thanks," I said. I'm really exhausted and I'm not very hungry."

"Oh no my dear, eat with me you must!" he barked in a jovial tone.

"I just hate to eat alone. If you don't eat with me I'll just have to sing out loudly and serenade you to lift your spirits. And the trouble is, I can't sing. My wife reminds me of that every time I sing to her!" All of a sudden he started bellowing off key to me and singing,

"Oh, dine with me my darling, Dine with me tonight, I would just love for you to dine with me my pretty, Oh, just dine with me tonight!"

Boy he was right! He couldn't carry a tune in a bucket if he had to!

"OK, OK, I'll eat with you," and I picked up the Snickers bar and tore open the wrapper and took a bite. The good doctor sat down with me, opened a bag of chips, cracked open a can of Coke, and munched and sipped away.

"I know as a doctor I am supposed to eat better, but once in a while you just gotta break the rules. Ya, know what I mean? And after what you have been through my brave lady, it's time to break all of the rules. I took a small bite out of a chocolate chip cookie, but just enough to stop my stomach from growling.

All of a sudden, the good doctor jumped up started singing, "When Irish Eyes Are Smiling" and danced an Irish jig around the water fountain.

"Well, my pretty if you won't dine with me you'll have to dance with me."
He whooshed me out of the chair and began waltzing me around the floor
pretending he was Fred Astaire. At that point, I couldn't help it any more. I
started laughing out loud, which was his general intent all along.

"See that, it's a good thing I made it doctorin, cause I sure as hell can't
make a livin singin and dancing!"

"I gotta, tell you miss you've got a beautiful smile and a great laugh."

"Thanks," I said. "I needed that. I just haven't had much to smile about
lately."

"I know what you mean. I guess we all have blessings in our life to be
grateful for, but you've seen and had to go through a lot of heartache these last
few days and I think you've handled it well. I have to tell you miss. You are one
of the bravest people I have ever met."

"Well, thanks, but I don't think I'm all that you are saying."

"Please dear, I have to tell you, I see things everyday in this hospital—some
sad, some happy. And all I can tell you is this—hold on to hope as dearly as you
can. Sometimes, that is all we have left."

"OK doctor, I will. And thanks for the dining, dancing, and serenading.
It really helped me get a grip on things. Maybe laughter is the best medicine
after all."

After that day, I hung on to hope. I am so grateful that God sent me an
angel impersonating an Irish surgeon and a true friend when I really needed
one.

Chapter 27

Breathe

Rainbows Babies and Children's Hospital offered me a private waiting room while Nicholas was back in surgery. I was grateful for the quiet, to be able to close the door, and to have Mom and Veronica to keep me company. This seemed like a must needed luxury at this time. I was trying to keep hope alive and just breathe and relax, and not to let myself fall back into an endless battle of fear and worry. The small room was cozy and decorated in soft, earth-tone colors. There was a couch and three oversized chairs with a television that sat up on the wall in the corner, and we chose to keep the TV off. I was relieved to be able to stretch out on the couch and try to relax and regain some sanity.

I must have dozed off for a while when I heard Veronica open the door and walk back in. The days seemed to be running into each other, and my emotions were running all over to places I had never known to exist before. I was thinking that no matter how worried I was about my baby when we held our hands together, peace and happiness filled my heart. It is true that little things can bring the most joy in life, and that closeness brought me the most comfort. My mom, as usual, thought of everything. She had packed sandwiches and cut up fresh fruit. I watched while Mom pulled the items out of her bag. Mom had the fruit in three small containers and brought Oreo cookies along for desert.

I knew that money was getting tight with eating in the cafeteria, and it was nice to have a little luncheon together and away from the noise and bustle of the cafeteria. Mom placed the food out on the small round table saying, "All we need is something to drink."

"I'll go down to the cafeteria and see what they have," Veronica offered.

"Veronica, I only want water," I said.

"Get me a coffee and a cup of water," Mom said, then she reached into her purse for money.

"No, Mom," Veronica said, "It's my treat."

I observed how my little sister was growing up and becoming self-sufficient. She was getting independent and filled with life's energy and curiosity. I then studied Mom's face and the last few weeks were getting to her as well. I could see the strain around her soft, Irish green eyes, and she looked pale. I can see that having Nicholas sick in the ICU was affecting each one of my family members and I knew that I was truly blessed to have my family by my side during this ordeal; it had helped me enormously.

Looking over at my mother and having her love, support, and devotion, and she being by my side in the past years, and in my life in general, has helped me manage all of life's challenges that I have had to face. Veronica walked back into our little private room, closed the door, and put our drinks on the table. Together we all ate our lunch, and I tried not to watch the clock, but I was aware of each second that passed. When it is your child in an operating room, each second feels like hours as you wait for word on how things are going. I hoped that Nicholas would be on the road to recovery and I knew this was only one step to many more operations he would need in the near future. I just told myself, "Breathe." There is a time and place for everything, and right now Nicholas was doing his part as a little baby and fighting as much as his tiny body would let him. I could only hope that his body would respond and grow stronger so he can live as a baby should.

"Mom," I said, "thanks for making lunch. The sandwiches were good."

"Oh, you're welcome," she replied.

"Mom, thanks for everything, for all your help in these past days," I said realizing I needed Mom more now than when I was little.

"Laurel, I wish I could do more to help you and my grandson."

Veronica started cleaning up the table and said teasingly, "Mom would pack the whole house if we let her, and bring it into Rainbows."

I started laughing, "But Mom never forgets anything and you never know when we would need something."

"That's right," Mom said. She then opened her bag and pulled out the extra plastic spoon and put it onto the table.

"See, Veronica," I said "you forgot a spoon to mix the creamer into her coffee."

"That's our Mommy!" Veronica said and reached over toward mom playfully and grabbed the bag and said, "What else do you have in your bag?"

"Things that we might need."

"What's this?" Veronica pulled out a bath towel and wash cloth.

"Maybe we might need to wash up," Mom said, blushing and turning a little red.

Together our much needed therapeutic laughter was filling up the room, and then there was a knock on the door. A grim shudder came over all of us and Mom, Veronica, and I, immediately sensed something was terribly wrong.

A surgeon walked in and sat down. He had a professional manner about him, but we could all feel the concern he had in his heart for Nicholas and us.

"Miss Wessel, we are happy with how things are turning out. However, we need to keep a very close watch over your son because the next few days can be crucial, and Nicholas will have to remain in the ICU." He sat back, took his glasses off, rubbed his tired, bloodshot eyes, and I could tell he was searching for the right words to say at this difficult time. Then he said, "You need to remember that Nicholas has a long battle ahead of him, with more surgeries to come. However, he is a fighter and each one of the doctors can tell you that." He smiled, "Do you have any questions for me?"

I sat back and let out a sigh of relief and just wanted to see my baby.

Looking over at Mom, I could tell she was happy that this major surgery was over. I answered, "No, I can't think of any questions. I just want to see my baby. When can I go see him?"

The doctor stood up and said. "Well, you can all go back and see him now."

Walking back together I spotted Nicholas right away. He was wearing a light green grown, and this was the first time I saw him with clothes on. Seeing my baby lying there covered in a soft color instead of his chest cut open was a relief. The soft color on Nicholas's skin made him look radiant. Before this, I had always seen him naked with machines attached to him. It showed off his dark hair and baby face features. I was proud of my sweet baby boy lying there, looking like a newborn, and at the same time relieved that I did not have to see the long scar down his little chest. Nicholas looked peaceful, almost in a sweet dream state like he could see the heavens.

Together we all stood around his crib in wonder, adoring my brave baby. Veronica smiled and said sweetly, "Nicholas is too cute."

"Yes, he is." My lips widened into a big smile agreeing with what Veronica had said. Mom spoke up, "He is darling looking, so sweet. I always loved to watch sleeping babies. They look so peaceful."

"Yes, Mom, I just wish I could hold him close to me."

"Laurel, I know you do," Mom said sadly.

I sat down by his side and watched my baby boy sleep. I sat by him watchful and hopeful as his little chest went up and down. I found that watching Nicholas inspired me to live in the moment and to be happy with the small everyday blessings life gives us.

The doctor kept a close eye on him and I fell into a routine sitting by Nicholas's side. The days came and went by and together we grew in our love for each other in a comfortable manner as best as we could in the hospital. I had gotten pleasure in watching Nicholas open his one eye and then the next eye before he woke up. I took great pleasure in the little daily wonders. I was allowed to do little things for him, like rub lotion on the one hand, and around his face. I still was not allowed to hold him because he was connected to too many life-support machines. I wanted more than anything to hold my baby close to me, and it hurt me not to be able to pick him up. It's a shame that sometimes what we take for granted every day, like holding a baby, was such an important thing to me, and at that time I was still not able to do that one simple act, which really tore up my heart.

A few new patients came in, but more seemed to be moving out into regular rooms. I could almost read their parents' minds and feel their relief when their children were moved out of the ICU. Next to Nicholas was the Amish baby boy who was older than Nicholas.

This baby was around three months and could be held and fed in his mother's arms. He made enough progress to be moved out of the ICU. There was only Nicholas in the one side waiting for his turn to make that big step out of the ICU. The Amish Grandmother stopped by for a little visit and said, "Well, we are blessed that my grandson is being moved today." I watched her look over at Nicholas and back at me sympathetically, "I will miss seeing you and Nicholas."

"We will miss you too," I said, but I was happy for them that their baby was moving along nicely.

"Nicholas will be in my prayers." She gently walked over and kissed Nicholas's forehead, then turned to me and hugged me a forceful embrace that had a sincere care in it. I filled up with tears and said, "We both will miss his bed partner, but we are happy for you. May he have continuous good health and soon be able to go home."

"Take care of yourself," she said. The Amish lady and I stood for a moment, exchanged a look of empathy and encouragement, and then she turned and walked out.

The new space around the ICU seemed open and enormous to me with room to move. I desperately wanted to pick up Nicholas into my arms and dance around the room with him. When I took in the space again, I felt lonely and scared for my son. I listened to the noise all the machines made that were hooked up to him.

There were machines all around him and it seemed like every day some new machine was being connected to his frail body. Mom and I took turns giving each other a break from ICU. I went and rested at my usual spot by the water fountain and the chapel. Deep down in my heart I knew that there was something not right with my baby. I could feel it right down to my soul. Nicholas was not moving along like he should have. His overall condition was failing and there was pain that a little one at his age should not feel or know.

I watched closely and often became transfixed to his vital signs hoping beyond hope for a miracle. Unfortunately, what I saw was his blood pressure dropping lower and the machine hooked to him would go off again and again. Every time this would happen, it would send fear and panic through my entire being. Every time a machine went off there were doctors rushing over to him, while nurses pushed on buttons to stop the buzzing. I felt secure and blessed that the medical staff handled his care well.

It was getting close to two weeks that Nicholas was in the ICU and he was not looking well to me. His skin had a yellowing, ashy color, and he was retaining fluids and swelling up again. I sat back hoping and pleading to God to help my baby each day that he could make it, and I know that I was blessed for each day that I had with Nicholas.

I could tell he did not want pity and he was always searching for me with his sweet, innocent, free hand, offering me comfort during this impossible time.

Mom and I were sitting by Nicholas when the head doctor came over. "Miss Wessel, I would like to talk to you in my office so that we can have a private conversation please."

"Sure." I said. This is when my stomach dropped and fear took hold of me. I knew in my heart what was coming. I sensed that it was not going to be good news and reality was setting in about my baby's terrible condition.

Mom and I were walking together to go to his office, and I looked into a few doctors' faces, as well as the nurses. No one said anything as a few looked down, and dread and sorrow showed on their faces. I knew that the last few days Nicholas looked different and was holding onto life with everything he had. Together we walked in and the doctor said, "Sit down, please," and then the doctor pulled out two chairs for us.

"Thank you," Mom and I said together.

A few more doctors walked in, closing the door behind them. An eerie sense of doom came over me. Together we sat at a long table surrounded by the medical staff that had been doing everything they could to help my baby boy. I felt as though I was shrinking into the chair and was hoping that this was a nightmare and I could wake up.

Mom sat next to me and a doctor at the head of the table said, "Miss Wessel, this is never easy for me to say, but I have found out in my years to say it straight out may be the best way. I am sorry, but we have done everything we can for your baby. Nicholas went brain dead about an hour ago. Take some time to think, but we are asking your permission for us to pull Nicholas off his machines. That is the only thing keeping him here. I am so sorry."

I looked down at my hands and saw that they were trembling uncontrollably.

Mom let out a sob that came from the depths of her sweet soul, and she put her head on the table because she no longer had the strength to sit upright.

I knew I needed to be strong and help Mom like she had helped me so many times throughout my life.

"Mom," I said, "it's OK. We will get through this heartbreak together." I heard my voice, but it seemed detached and distant as though another person was talking to Mom and me.

We both tried unsuccessfully to comfort each other. I looked up at the doctors and nurses who were also overcome with emotion with tears in their eyes and sobs coming from their hearts for this brave little baby. I finally found the energy to speak after a moment and said, "I would like to call in my priest and family."

"Sure," the doctors said, "and take your time and think this over. You do not have to give us an answer today."

I looked at the time. It was little after 12:00 noon on February 7, 1992—a time and date that I could never forget in a hundred lifetimes. I closed my eyes, opened them up and said, "No, today pull everything off Nicholas at seven o'clock and I would like for Nicholas to be an organ donor."

I wanted something good to come out of his short life, and maybe Nicholas could help someone in need. We all got up and I could feel the doctors' disappointment overflowing throughout the room at losing Nicholas. They all worked so hard to keep Nicholas going. At that moment, I felt that if God wanted my son to live, he would live when all the machines were pulled off, and if God's will was for Nicholas to go home to the heavens with him, I couldn't really stop it from happening. I had to let my baby go. Letting go was the hardest thing that I have ever had to do in my life, but I know that his life will live in my heart forever and that would never change.

Together Mom and I walked out. Mom made phone calls. I sat down next to my baby as I filled up with tears and cried, "Nicholas, Mommy loves you and your family does as well. You showed us all what strength and courage really means. I have grown a great deal in these last two weeks, my sweet baby. You are going home with Jesus. Hold a place there for your mommy and I will try to be good so I can someday be with you again." I could not take it anymore. I held his hand and dropped my head down. I no longer had the emotional or physical strength to hold it up. Mom walked back with the priest and he prayed over him, anointing him with holy oil over his little head. Mom sat down looking overwhelmed and filled with grief.

"Mom, I'll be back. Stay with Nicholas please."

"Yes, I will." I walked all the familiar halls again past the cafeteria, water fountain, and went back into the chapel. No one was there. I got down on my knees and prayed to God. "Thank you for my baby. We both knew that he has suffered enough. I know that he is going into heaven very soon. I need you to hold him for me please Jesus, until I can see him again." I sat back in the little chapel for a little while. I thought how many different people talked to God in this tiny non-denominational chapel, begging and pleading for his help. They were probably from all nationalities and creeds: Christian, Muslim, Jewish, or Amish, all with pains and hurts that really only God understands.

I know that there is a number and a time for us all, but I couldn't figure out why Nicholas and why now? It just didn't make sense. It seems that it's not what you are; it's how you loved others around you that really counts in the end. I felt a love so great for my son and in return a love flowed from him to us. I knew in my heart that this love that I had for my child is everlasting and will stay in me until we meet again. I slowly walked back and saw that Veronica, Billy, and Dad made it up as well as other family members and friends.

They each were in to see my son and said good-bye to my baby boy. They all looked sad and had red swollen eyes, and were in the private room each dealing with their sorrow the best that they could. As I was walking back in the ICU, I saw the fear in each parent's eye. I saw their worry; I saw their pain as they were hoping that their child was not next. I walked back to his side, he looked more swollen, and his fingers were turning red. I touched him carefully and sat down next to my baby. When the social worker came over and said,

"Miss Wessel, there is good news. We have a room for you at Ronald McDonald's house."

I started to cry, "I will not need it anymore. Thank you." When the head doctor saw what had happened, he raced over and said, "I am sorry. She did not know our situation."

He pulled the social worker over and talked to her. She looked sad when she walked back. "Miss Wessel, I am so sorry. I should have checked first on your baby's status, but I was so excited about being able to help you."

I looked at her and said, "It's OK. It's not your fault."

She excused herself and walked out in a regretful manner.

I looked over and it was seven o'clock when the nurse came over telling Mom and me "Take your time."

The nurse explained to us that they would remove the machinery from Nicholas and then come and get us so we could have our last good-byes.

"No," I said, "we are ready to say our good-byes now."

I just did not want the suffering to continue. Mom kissed Nicholas good-bye and said, "See you, my sweet grandson; go now and be with the angels." I kissed Nicholas on his head and said sadly, "I love you always." I looked at Nicholas one last time before Mom and I walked out together hand in hand. I wanted so badly to comfort Mom, but I couldn't get any words to come out of my mouth; I was speechless because grief had me in its grasp. I just held Mom's hand and she helped me walk out of the ICU.

We sat in the private room and twenty minutes later, a doctor walked in to get us.

The curtain had been pulled around his crib and all of the people were asked to step out of the ICU while the removal of the machinery was done. Together Mom and I left the private room and went to Nicholas's bedside. The nurse pulled open the curtain and all his machines were gone.

Nicholas was wearing a newborn blue hat and a baby blanket was wrapped around him. Nicholas took my breath away and I gazed at his little body. He looked so beautiful and so peaceful; he was lying still and already home with God. I picked him up and I finally held my son close to me——like a baby should be held by his mother.

Chapter 28

Preparations

The next few days were filled with getting the arrangements in order. There were phone calls to be made, flowers to be picked out, and a trip to the funeral home to make arrangements. My head seemed to spin just thinking over what needed to be done and set into place. To me everything felt like an obstacle course. Finally, when it came to making everything fit together, whom to call, and what to do, Mom stepped in and really pulled things into shape. I was grateful for her help because it was too much for me to think about, especially when it came to what small casket to pick out for my lost child. I was overwhelmed at times with a deep sadness and it seemed like I was missing something. I would make a list of things that needed to be done, only to lose the list, and wrote out several other ones—only to lose them too. When I was home, the phone was ringing off the hook with family and friends offering support, stopping by, and dropping off food. These kind offers did help, but I found out that it was only temporary.

What stops the pain that leaves a deep hole in your heart? I found that really nothing but time. When the house slowed down at night, I walked around the house feeling like I was missing something that was a part of me and there was a huge void that could not be replaced. Every time I walked into my room and saw the baby's crib, I would simply break down.

Who was there to listen? As always, my mom was there to listen even when she was busy working to get the house together because we were having the people stop over to eat after the funeral. There was the expense of paying for a funeral and some of the hospital costs. Because of my low income, welfare had helped pay a little of the expense, and my father took care of the rest of the cost. To my surprise, my little sister, Veronica, took her paycheck from her part-time job and helped pay for some of the flowers.

Veronica walked into my room and saw me looking sad. She sat on my bed and pulled out a little box. "I got you something." Then Veronica sat the box on the bed.

"What this?" I said as I reached for the box.

"Open it," said Veronica.

I sat up in bed and opened the box. I pulled out a lovely gold necklace engraved with Nicholas's name on it.

"Wow!" I said looking over the necklace.

Veronica helped me put it around my neck. What a caring gift coming from my sister that did not make a lot of money. I was speechless.

"Veronica, thank you for everything you have done. You have done so much."

"I hope you like the heart necklace," Veronica said.

"I love it! It's beautiful! I feel bad because you have done too much already, and I know you don't make a lot of money."

"Laurel, I wanted to buy you something and Nicholas is my nephew too, and with Valentine's Day coming up I just thought it was perfect."

"It is a perfect gift." I got up and went to my bedroom mirror to admire it more.

The heart necklace gave me an idea. I wanted Nicholas laid out to rest with a little heart-shaped pillow with one red rose on it and have one made for me. Red roses are my favorite as they are bright in color and when they are in full bloom, they send out a loving message and they truly are the symbol of love but sadly die young like my little boy. I felt like I was doing something to show how much I appreciated our short life we shared together and the heart-shaped pillow was a small symbol that helped to show our love. With Mom taking care of the ins and outs of the funeral, I collapsed into bed that night still wearing the necklace Veronica had given to me. I slept well, but I woke up early looking up at my ceiling relieved with how all the special requests had been set into place. I got up looking at my dresses.

I was not in the mood to wear black and I thought to myself, *"Is there some kind of a rule that had to be followed that says 'wear black'?"* If I did not wear black, was I disrespecting how one is to mourn?

Is there a hard and fast rule? I wondered. I had a little more weight on me and most of my dresses were feeling tight around the middle on me. I had a long sleeve cranberry dress that I had worn only once to a play in downtown Cleveland. I put it on and it fit me, and went past my knees respectably. I pulled out my black shoes and put them on and took a look into the mirror. I was pleased. Well, I decided that would be the dress I will wear to celebrate my love and life of my baby Nicholas. Now that I got the dress out of the way, I lay back in bed and tried to sleep only to toss and turn for the next few hours.

When the clock finally went off, my family members were all getting up and ready to go. We had only one bathroom and each member took a turn to get ready. I took a fast hot shower earlier in the morning and was back in my room, taking my time to dress. I put on a little makeup and curled my hair. I walked out as my family members were all waiting for me.

I noticed Mom smiled at me and said, "Laurel, you look lovely!"

"Mom," I said, "What do you think with my dress not being black? I hope it will be OK. Will I go to hell for not wearing black?"

"No, you have a nice subtle color on and it is appropriate," she said looking me over.

"Are you sure? I am worried that I broke a fashion rule for funerals," I said.

"There is no rule and it is a dark enough color, and with Valentine's Day coming up, it seems fine."

"Yes, Mom, and Nicholas is my little Valentine," I said with a hurting heart.

"Yes, Laurel, he always will be."

Together we entered into the funeral home. We were early so we could have a little quiet time before all of the people arrived. I walked in and a little, white casket was sitting in the middle of the back wall. White carnations and red roses were placed in colorful arrangements throughout the whole back area of the room. I walked over, and Nicholas looked peaceful all dressed in a white, little tuxedo. There were two heart-shaped pillows one next to his head and the other was laid at the end of the casket—one for him and one for me and both had a red rose on them. I kneeled down, looking at my baby whom I had only gotten to know for a short time, but it felt like a lifetime in a way. My heart went out to him and I touched him.

"Mommy will love you always. I will miss you, Nicholas, but you will remain in my heart forever." I got up and Mom, with Veronica kneeled down, and Billy stood next to Dad. I saw that Billy had a bag in his hand and he handed it to me. I pulled out two stuffed animals. They were Donald Duck and Bugs Bunny; I placed them on the ends of Nicholas's casket.

"Thank you, Billy. You put the finishing touch on my boy's resting place. It helps to soften up the mood of the casket."

Billy gave me his warm boyish grin and said, "Aw it's nothin really. I just thought it would be nice in there."

We sat together as a family in the first row of chairs. I took in everything. All of the flowers that came from my family and friends showed me that my little baby touched many lives. My brother's gifts were special and somehow made the situation more bearable.

"Billy, I am going to keep the Donald Duck and Bugs Bunny."

"They are yours to keep," he replied sadly.

The people started walking in about that time. I noticed that there is something about a small baby at rest with the Lord that makes even big, strong men cry. People offered up their sympathies by stopping over to me and said, "How nice and beautiful the flowers look," and everybody loved the stuffed animals. It was really a nice touch for such a grim situation. There were people whom I did not expect to be there who came to help us grieve our loss, and some of the ones I expected didn't make it.

When I was younger, I did a little volunteer work at Metro Hospital, in a children's play center. I would play games and watch movies with sick children in the hospital.

I had done this for a little while in my late teen years. I loved every minute that I had helped out with these suffering children.

Being with the children in the hospital always put a smile on my face to see their courageous love for life in spite of their illnesses. The director must have seen my last name in the obituary section of the paper and she came to pay her respects. While I had volunteered there, I had gotten close to a young, sweet girl whom had been born with AIDS as a baby and we would play the card game "Go Fish" and board games together.

She always had her hair pulled back in a pony tail and her big, brown eyes that danced with joy when she beat me in these games and her face would light up with a childish giggle. Well, I was saddened to hear that she had passed away a few months back. I learned that her body had been laid out in the same room that my Nicholas's body was in right now.

Wow! The world is small, and the spirits of these two souls somehow were together in heaven. I thought to myself, "*I'll bet that she is up in heaven telling Nicholas, I know your mom. We liked to play cards and board games together, and guess what, I beat her a lot.*" I could see her up in heaven making a fuss over Nicholas. The thought put a smile onto my face. The service was coming to an end when the priest came up to the front and we had a little prayer session for my baby. As the people were lining up to leave, I could hear and see people stand over Nicholas's body and cry, and many came over to me and said with a voice cracking and wavering, "We are so sorry for your loss." The next day, I wore a long, black skirt and a white sweater with my only black dress shoes.

It was a cold February day and I had on a long, black coat that was not warm enough to keep the chill out. Together we arrived early again at the funeral home and sat down in the first row. I looked at my baby's small body, and it was too painful to think that I would never see him grow up and go to school, play baseball, or even go to his high school prom.

I was sad knowing that I would never play with him or hold him. But then at the same time, I knew that he was with God, there was no more suffering for him, and no more operations to go through. This was a great sense of relief to me. I knew in my heart that he was free to play up in the heavens.

Then people started to come in and fill the room. It was around 9:00 a.m. The funeral director came to the front and we said a "Hail Mary" and an "Our Father," while each person took one final walk up to the casket for their last good-bye. The funeral director then closed the doors so our immediate family could have our last moments alone with our lost, baby boy. Together we walked up as a grieving family to the casket to say our final farewells. Only sadness filled my heart and I reached into the casket and took out my heart-shaped pillow and placed his near to this heart.

"Bye, my love, you have Mommy's heart!"

I felt a little shaky and started to tremble, so Mom held onto me and as usual, steadied me emotionally and physically, and we stood motionless and shared our grief in silence. Then we all followed the funeral van to the cemetery. It was good old Cleveland weather, cold out, with a strong breeze in the air that nipped at our cheeks.

We all came to a stop and got out in the children's section of the cemetery. There were names of small children and babies who had gone to heaven on all of the head stones in front of us. Seeing all these children's names on all of the head stones seemed to reflect a sadness that said that these innocent children were lost too soon.

I pictured that their souls were all in heaven playing and laughing in the best playground ever, and the babies were being watched over by the angels. The priest walked to the front of the mourners that attended and read out of the Bible. After the prayers ended, each of us received a white carnation to put onto his little casket that sat on the cold ground. I knew that my memory of Nicholas would never grow cold. I would keep the memory alive in my heart forever. I watched as the last person placed the carnation down, and that is when it hit me hard. This is the final good-bye. I know that I would never see Nicholas again. Time stopped for me a while.

I cried out in pain and Mom put her arm around my shoulder to comfort me. I looked up and tears were falling down from my family members' faces as well.

Finally, we were heading home. Mom had worked hard, cooking and cleaning the house, moving furniture, and putting out folding tables and chairs. I was happy that only half of the people came back to our home to eat. I wanted to go to my room and close the door and sleep.

I could see that each person who stopped over offered up good intentions with kind words, but inside I wanted desperately to be alone. I was pleased when the last person walked out of the door. I was helping Mom fold up the chairs and pick up plastic plates and cups that were scattered about the house. Mom came over to me and said,

"Laurel, please go to bed."

I did not argue. "Thanks Mom, and for all that you have done to pull this together. The house looked great and the food was delicious." I went to my room with my heart pillow, Donald Duck, and Bugs Bunny. I put them onto my bed.

I put on my pajamas and went to bed, only to see the crib in the corner calling out to me. I turned over and reached for my heart-shaped pillow, turned away from the crib, and tried to sleep. Sleep was not coming to me easily and I lay turning back looking at the crib; I was feeling a deep depression that had overcome me.

Chapter 29

Dear Message

The days that followed were like a blur. The grief from losing my baby was unbearable. I either slept endless hours or walked around the house aimlessly numb to what was around me and the outside world. I was ravaged by grief and I had an overwhelming sense of loss, like I was missing a part of me. I had fallen into depression as a deep longing for my baby had a hold on me. There was not much that I could do to distract my mind from thinking of my sweet son. I could have easily stayed right there on my island of self-pity and let the grief take me as a prisoner, but life had other plans for me. Time is supposed to heal all wounds and time did pass, but it did not bring hope back into my soul. I was living and staying stuck in the past. If I had not got myself up and started moving about, I could have lost myself forever in my sorrowful state of mind.

I knew I had things to do, but getting up the energy to do them was hard and seemed at times impossible because my grief robbed me of all of my energy. Fortunately for me, Mom had always showed no judgment toward me. Mom only would guide me and she would always listen to all my hurts and pains over and over again. I think back and wonder if I would have had that kind of patience like Mom? To tell the truth, I hope so, but I know I would come up short compared to Mom's unending patience.

She offered endless love and support during this difficult time in my life. Mom kept a close eye on me and I know that she prayed for me daily. I knew I had to get it together soon because life would leave me in the dust if I did not get myself going somehow. That was the hard part getting myself up and going when it was too easy to feel down and blue.

Then one day after a restless night of missing my baby, I thought to myself, *"No more of this feeling down! Get up and get going!"* I just got up, showered, and dressed, and was hoping to start off my day right. I kept up the fight only a little while until I walked into my room and saw the baby's crib and Nicholas's things and sadness set in again. My baby was gone.

I had to come face-to-face with the harsh reality that I would never see him again. Whenever this would happen, Mom would gently pull me back into the present. She had a way that never gave up on me no matter what and she knew how to get me going. Mom walked into my room and opened up my blinds, letting the sunlight fill my room. "What a nice day," Mom said while she picked up a pillow that fell onto the floor putting it back onto the bed. I could tell that she was starting to make a plan for the day. She looked at me lying back in bed and said, "I am thinking about making vegetable soup. I know it is one of your favorites."

I lay back in bed, not saying too much, and I only wished I could turn back over and sleep and close myself off from the world.

"Sure, Mom, vegetable soup sounds good."

Then Mom picked up the card on my dresser, that I had just gotten the other day in the mail, and started to read it out loud.

"Laurel, you have gotten a lot of cards and gifts. Maybe you can make a scrapbook." I watched while Mom put the card back down on my dresser.

"You are good at making things. Why not put a scrapbook together?"

"Maybe, Mom," I answered, but I was really not in the mood to get things started or making anything. I would rather drop back into my bed and sleep the whole day away. What a life! If my bed could talk, it would have said, "Get off me already and let me breathe." But Mom was not letting me off the hook that easily. She walked out of my room only to come back into my room, carrying a shoe box. She brought the box over to me and sat on my bed. Mom pulled out the cards that I received and began reading each one out loud.

"Laurel, I like this card the best, what do you think?"

I reached for the card and looked it over, and before I knew it, I was sitting up in bed, and together we both passed the time, pulling cards from their envelopes and looking at them fondly.

One of my favorite ones read, "There really are no words of comfort, at the loss of a baby, but know God already knows your pain." I sat on my bed and Mom pulled out other cards and spread them out on my bed. If I wanted to sleep, I needed to get the sympathy cards off my bed and kick Mom out of my room. I knew that both things were not going to happen.

"Laurel," Mom said kindly, "making a scrapbook helps you to remember and celebrate Nicholas's life, and you need to remember that he wants you to be happy and live your life. You know that when a loved one dies, they don't want you unhappy."

"I know, Mom," I said, looking down at the cards that were spread across my bed. "Why not put something together to remember Nicholas?" With hearing Mom's words, I felt like doing something constructive, and to be honest, my body was tired of not moving from the bed of self-pity. I was tired of being tired. I was worn out of feeling down. I was tired of myself feeling this pathetic way.

"Mom, you are right. I am going to make a special scrapbook to remember Nicholas," I said in a more upbeat voice that surprised me.

I got out my supplies, markers, colored pencils, and went to work. I started to feel better just by getting out my supplies. Mom seemed relieved to see me up and moving around, and working on the scrapbook.

I spent the whole day making the book, and when I was finished, I felt a sense of achievement and a momentary relief from the heartache. I was feeling better and I almost had forgotten how it felt to feel good again. I showed the scrapbook to Mom and we both sat down together looking it over.

"Laurel, you did a nice job, and now you are able to pull the scrapbook out and look it over anytime you want."

"You were right, Mom. I am feeling better just by working on my book, and to know that it is finished." I held the scrapbook close to me and began to feel better.

"Laurel, I was hoping it would make you feel better.

It hurts me to see you so down and you know positive actions go a long way."

"I know you are worried about me, Mom, but I am going to be fine," I said. Mom only had hopes for the best for me and I understood the feeling that all moms only want the best for their children.

Taking the book back into my room, I looked it over again, and then I put it into my night stand.

I thought, *"No way am I going back to bed. I need to get back on my feet and get back to work,"* so I pulled out a notebook and wrote out a number of options that seemed to be open to me. I would start tomorrow looking for work.

I had a renewed spirit about my life and knew I needed to work and get back to working on my GED, and setting goals are a good way to bring one back to reality.

I had steps to make in my life and I hoped that I would choose them rightly by thinking things over before I acted. I looked over what I had written down as potential jobs that I was interested in trying. Next, I wrote out a wish list, followed by my goals. One of the things on my wish list was to one day be able to buy a new car, and second, to get married to a wonderful, caring, and loving man. I did not care what came first, but I wanted both. I thought to myself, *"Don't just jump out there and try to run a marathon, but take that first step toward your wishes."* I wrote that out in red ink next to my wishes. I stopped myself. I needed to first work on me to improve myself and get my GED, and make my own money. So in red ink, I wrote in big printed words, "WORK ON YOURSELF!" I took my sheet of paper and placed it into my scrapbook.

The next day, I was up and dressed early and getting ready to walk out the door with the newspaper ads in my hand. I had circled about seven places I wanted to apply. I could see that Mom looked pleased with me and said, "I made breakfast."

"No thanks, Mom," I said. "I am fine. I will make myself some toast for the road." Then the phone rang, stopping me from buttering my toast.

I picked up the phone and said, "Hello."

Someone on the other side said, "Can I speak to a Laurel Wessel?"

"Speaking," I said and wondered who this could be.

"This is Section Eight calling and we have an opening for a one-bedroom apartment in Lakewood. You need to stop by at the main office, so I can give you your certificate."

I was taken back and stunned for a minute because that would have been my baby's new home and our new home together. I listened to her and did my best to compose myself.

"Thank you. However, I will not need the certificate anymore. My baby has passed away, and please offer it to the next person on your list."

"Oh, I am sorry to hear of your sad news."

"Thank you and thanks for calling."

"Certainly," she said and hung up.

I stood holding onto the phone, thinking that if Nicholas had lived we would be living in Lakewood together in a small apartment. It would have been our life together. Our life together would not have been easy I'm sure, with me being a single mom. Would I have been a good mother? These thoughts filled my head. I tried to pull myself together and back at the task at hand. What was it?—Buttering toast and getting a job. Mom walked into the kitchen and asked, "Who was on the phone?"

"Mom, remember the government program that I had signed up for an apartment?

They just called, telling me that I had an apartment that opened in Lakewood, but now that Nicholas has passed, I am no longer eligible for the program."

"Well, Laurel, maybe the next person needed a place, and you know this will always be your home."

"I know, Mom, and thanks for putting up with me these past few weeks. I know I have not been easy to live with and this is just as tough on you as it is on me."

"Well, Laurel, this being the first time I have ever lost a grandson, it has been really hard for me, but we can get through this together."

"Thanks, Mom. I knew I could count on you for help. The best thing right now for me is to go get a job."

"Good luck." I started out the front door when Mom stopped me and handed me my toast.

"Thanks, Mom, for always looking out for me."

I never liked going out and applying for work and going to interviews, but it needed to be done. We all know the questions that we ask ourselves after the interview is over. "Did I answer them right, or did I talk too much?" I am the type of person who goes over and over an interview in my head after it is done and over with.

However, by the end of the day, I had gotten a job working in a bingo factory full time.

The interview was on the spot. "Can you start tomorrow?" a middle-aged man with a sour face said.

"Sure," I said.

"Be here at 6:30 a.m. tomorrow, and we pay minimum wage." I held out my hand to shake his and said, "Thank you," thinking do you ask for more money or just keep quiet and be thankful for the job?

It was a job, and I felt better getting back on my feet again. The only thing was the long hours that the job demanded. I would pull out my GED book at night to study and I would fall off to sleep with the book still open. I was up and dressed for work by 5:30 a.m. to start my workday. I knew I needed to get back to my studies but finding the time was really hard.

Every night at around bedtime, a sad feeling would just come over me. I yearned for Nicholas and I lay awake looking over at the empty crib still unable to pack it away. By now a month had passed by when Dad walked into my room. He walked over and put his hand onto the baby's crib thinking over what he wanted to say. I think the empty crib was ripping out my family's hearts as much as mine.

Dad said sadly, "Laurel, if you like, I can help you fold up the crib today." I did not say a word. I could only be still and quiet.

I know that Dad meant well and he was right. I knew that in my heart, Nicholas's soul would live forever, and the material things were of no use to me. The time was right. I needed to take his baby things out of my room. But the crib, I don't really know why, but it just hurt to see it go. It would be hard enough to pack his things up, but then is there a right time really to let personal things go? There are no written rules to follow; only when one is ready can it happen. Why do I keep thinking there is some sense of order to these matters?

Mom sensed that I was maybe trying to move too fast to get things in order and said, "Laurel, if you are not ready."

I stopped Mom from talking, "No Mom, Dad is right. Do you have any boxes?" There was a young woman across the street that was pregnant and could surely use some of the baby's clothes. Mom helped me pack the baby clothes and toys into boxes. I kept a few things and set them aside, not wanting to part with everything. Dad worked quietly and was busy taking down the baby crib.

Then he took it out of my room and placed it up into the attic. I watched him. I wanted so badly to stop him from taking away all that had belonged to Nicholas. I wanted the crib to stay longer, but deep down inside I knew it needed to come down. I sat on my bed, not moving. Mom took the boxes over to our neighbor and I got up and closed my door, looking over at the bare space. I sat down where the crib was and cried.

I heard a knock on my door and Billy walked in. He was holding a cross that he had made out of oak wood. There in big, engraved letters was Nicholas's name on the cross. I had heard Billy outside working with the saw, but I had no idea what he was up to. He always had the saw going, working on something around the house.

I got off the floor and stood up. Billy walked over to me and said, "I know you would need this out in the cemetery and to buy it can be expensive. I know you only got back to work and your money is low."

He brushed his strong, working man's hands around Nicholas's name and said,

"The "O" in his name is a little off. I messed up a little."

"No, Billy, it's beautiful. Thank you. You did a wonderful job on it. You would have been a great uncle."

Billy stood quietly for a minute. Then he handed me the cross and I took it feeling proud of his work. Billy walked out, closing my bedroom door. I held onto the cross and thought I have a good twin brother, and how blessed I am to have my family's support. However, all through the day I missed Nicholas and my heart ached for him. There was a longing for him that is too hard to put into words. I missed him more now than ever, now that his crib was out of my room. I had a heavy, gloomy, sorrowful heart, and kept looking over at the empty space where the crib had been.

I had this impulse to fill the space with something or anything so that I would not have to stare at the emptiness. I decided to pull my writing and study desk into the corner. Mom, hearing me in my room moving furniture around walked in, and began helping me move my room around. We worked together throughout the evening getting my room back into shape.

When we were finished, Mom lay down in my bed with me and we stared at the ceiling and talked with each other about everything and anything, late into the night. We finally both fell off into a deep, restful sleep. All of a sudden, I just woke up out of the blue, with a bright light that filled up my room, and inside the light was a red rose, and a young woman spoke to me in a gentle, soothing voice.

"Why are you so troubled? Nicholas is at peace. Live your life worthy and you will see him again." The warm light came over to me, and the red rose appeared to be moving in a light wind. I was reaching for the red rose but could not get into the warm light; however, the warm light filled up my troubled heart with a peace that I did not have before. At that moment, the hurt and pain in my heart left. I sat up in bed not moving. I rubbed my eyes and wondered what had just happened?

I reached over and shook Mom, and in my frenzy said, "Mom, did you see the light?——that bright light, that filled the whole room? Did you see the rose? Mom, did you hear the young woman talking to me and comforting me?"

Mom raised up in bed and said, "No, Laurel, I didn't hear or see anything," Mom answered groggily. I told Mom what had happened as we both sat up in bed. Mom very calmly, in a reassuring tone, said to me, "Laurel, I believe you were blessed with a message from heaven."

"Yes I was, and the warm, bright light, the love, the understanding is too hard to put into words, but Mom it was right here in my room."

I got up searching for the light and the woman in my room. I went to my window to see if the light was outside. There was no light, only the streetlight that hung down that offered light to the street. I turned and walked around my whole room and everything was the same. Although everything was the same, I was feeling a lot better and almost at ease for the first time in a long time.

"Mom, I can't believe it. What a message!" I said as I went back to bed and pulled the cover over my body.

"Yes, Laurel, it was. You are blessed to have an angel of God to come to you as a messenger. This can only mean that you are a special person in God's eyes. I know that people are skeptical about things of this matter and we have to be careful to whom we tell this to. Some mean people may say that you had a dream or your imagination, went wild from the grief with which you are dealing."

"No, what I saw happened and was real, so real that I wanted to go into the light where you feel safe and loved," I said. "I don't care what people think. I know what happened and what I saw."

"I know, Laurel, and what happened is compelling and very real."

I know now, deep in my heart that my baby is safe up in heaven, and I am grateful because I received a truly blessed message that offered me hope and motivated me to be strong to move on with my life.

I have never since then seen or heard other messages of that nature, and I thought I better not mess up so I can at "Judgment Day" see my son in heaven. But then again if I do mess up, that is just how life goes, right? There is more than just us and earth? There is more to life than this right?

As for me, I know after this incident that there is truly more. I will be forever grateful to God for granting me this blessing. It was a blessing that came at the right time in my life. Mom and I went back to sleep that night, and I, for the first time, in a long time, enjoyed the most peaceful and renewing sleep without my worried heart troubling me.

Chapter 30

Blunder

I had gotten back to myself with a regular working schedule and had saved up a little money. I was off to work early each morning around 5:30 a.m. The days were long, boring, and standing in one place on my feet made the day seem even longer. I packed one box to the next with bingo cards into larger boxes, and after three hours I was ready to go back home. The work was tedious and monotonous, day in and day out. I would sneak in books to work and do a little reading while I packed. But that did not last too long because I got into trouble,

"No reading while working," my supervisor said in a stern voice.

"Fine," I said. I put my book away hoping that maybe I would be able to sneak my book back out and do a little reading when he was not around just to pass the time. That was not going to happen with my supervisor keeping a close eye on me when he passed, making sure I kept the line moving. I did, however, liked to pull out my book at break time and read, rather than sit around and gossip. My supervisor could not stop me. When I was on break, it was my personal time and my book was always at hand. So, when my supervisor passed me throughout the day, I no longer had a book out and when he walked into my work area, I always picked up my pace, keeping up with my work.

I believed what my dad always said, "You put in a day's work when you are getting paid." The pay wasn't much, but it was an honest living and I was back out in the world earning my keep.

Each new day offered a renewed hope and I found that I started laughing more, and smiling as well, and my family looked to be recovering from the grief as well. Mom and I always enjoyed our time together as it seemed that our relationship had grown, especially after losing Nicholas. My mother had "mother's intuition," which is a wisdom or ability to pick up on or recognize when something was bothering me. She knew me better than I knew myself. I did not have to say a word; somehow Mom knew when I had something on my mind.

"Laurel, you are working a lot. I know you want to get your GED. Maybe, we can look at the book together."

"Sure, Mom, that will be great," I said. Mom understood my need to pass the GED test. Together we both tackled the *General Education Book*, and I worked on my studies independently as well. Together we were learning partners. Mom and I went through the GED book every night for about two weeks. We faithfully worked together on getting me ready for the test. However, there were days that passed that I never opened the book, and Mom would be busy with the housework. I needed more help in understanding all that I needed to learn to pass my GED test.

I had time. I knew that I could go back to Project Learn, and right down the street from my home was the Marrick House that offered Adult Education Classes. The hard part was finding the time, and with working a lot of overtime hours made it hard to fit GED classes into my schedule. There were a number of times I walked into the house after working, only to fall onto the couch and not move until the next morning when it was time to go back to work again the next day. I knew better than to complain. I needed to find a way to make it work and get myself into gear and refocusing my time on what needed to be done.

It was the end of the work week and I was driving home, thinking I needed to study, but with the weather breaking and spring being in the air, I thought to myself that I would like to get out and maybe see a movie with a girlfriend, and get out and live a little. I pulled up in front of my home, and it was a wonderful spring day. I could hear it in the young voices that ran up and down the street playing. Birds were singing and I was feeling great. I walked into the house, and Mom looked worried as she was holding a piece of paper in her hands.

Mom spoke up and said, "Laurel, there was a doctor from Metro Hospital who called for you today. He didn't say why he was calling." Mom handed over the piece of paper with a Metro phone number and his pager number on it. I did not recognize his name.

"Thanks, Mom." I said, "Don't worry. I'm sure he called to see how Nicholas or I am doing." I took the paper and shoved it into my pocket and never called him back.

"Mom, I'm going out."

"Fine, be careful."

"I am a big girl, Mom, see you later." The weekend went by too fast. I blinked my eyes and before I knew it, it was time to head back to work. So there I was, back at my bingo card factory standing and packing boxes again, and had gotten little accomplished over the weekend with my GED studies. I was not planning to set a date to take the test, but I needed to buckle down. Time was moving and racing past me and I was getting nowhere with my goals, or with my wish list. I knew there was a time and a place for everything, but it started with work and discipline. I needed to get to work on the studies if I was going to accomplish this.

After another long day at work, I was driving home with my window down and the radio tuned up loudly. The weather had warmed up and folks were out enjoying it.

I passed a young couple holding hands, walking side by side. Love, I thought, what magic when it is the right person and what a headache and heartache when it is not. When the song, "Summer Lovin," from the movie *Grease*, came on, I started singing along, thinking I would not mind walking hand in hand with John Travolta.

When I pulled in front of my home, I saw that Mom was outside working in the yard.

"Hi, Mom, it's a lovely day to be working in the yard." I watched while Mom pulled out some weeds and she had the rake lying next to her. I took the rake and started helping her rake the front yard.

"Finally, spring is here," Mom said. "I wish everyday in Cleveland could be like this," I said, and kept on raking vigorously. After another long punishing winter, this spring day was truly appreciated by all. Mom reached back into the ground and pulled out more weeds that lined the side of the flowerbed.

"Laurel, the doctor from Metro called again. Call him back to see what he wants." Mom pulled out his phone number out of her pocket and handed it to me.

I reached out for the number. "OK, Mom, I will call him back." I went into the house and picked up the phone and put in the number. I waited until an operator picked up and said "Please page this number." I held on waiting, until a foreign accent picked up the phone, "Hello, this is the Doctor who called you earlier."

"Hi, I am Laurel Wessel. Why have you been trying to reach me?" I said while opening up the refrigerator and pulling out cold ice tea.

He paused, "Yes, do you remember me?" he said a little flirtatiously.

"No, I am sorry, but I don't. I have met a lot of doctors over the past few months."

I was thinking of my sweet baby while I talked, and reached for a glass and poured the ice tea into the glass.

"I was the one who first admitted you in the hospital when you were in labor." I tried to picture him but could not place him. I was thinking, why does he keep calling for me? What does he want?

"Sorry, I cannot picture you."

"How is your baby doing?" After he said that, my throat tightened up and I filled up with tears.

"Nicholas has passed away."

"Oh, I am truly sorry about your loss."

"Is this the reason for your call?" I wondered.

"No," he said with a little uneasiness in his voice.

"Oh, then why are you calling me?"

"I like to take you out to dinner sometime." I heard what he said, but I did not answer.

Then the doctor said, "I am finishing up my residency later this year, and very busy, but I would like to take you out to dinner if that is fine," he said in the best English he could come up with. I could not believe what I was hearing and I felt a little unsure about going out to dinner. I still needed time to myself. I needed time for my studies, for getting myself together, and had a tight schedule already.

"Well, Laurel, will you have dinner with me?" He said again in a playful manner.

"I guess so. Dinner will be fine as a friend." What did I just do? I picked up the glass of cold ice tea and drank it down.

"Great, I can pick you up tomorrow around 7:00 p.m." That soon I thought, and that was all I was thinking not sure what to think.

"Fine," I said.

"I need to know where you live so I can pick you up." I told him how to get from Metro to my home, which is close. I thought that it was too late to back out now.

Well, it's only a dinner date, and maybe getting out a little will not hurt.

"Fine, I'll see you tomorrow," he said.

"OK" I said. I felt anxious and uneasy for saying "yes" Why did I say yes? I don't really know this doctor.

I walked back outside, and Mom was taking a break, sitting on the front steps. She looked up at me and said. "What did the doctor want?"

"Mom, he wants to take me out to dinner."

Mom looked surprised and concerned and said, "Is that ethical or proper?"

"I don't know," I said. I then wondered how he got my number. I guess he got it off my records. Mom, still looking worried, and with concern in her eyes looked at me and said, "You have been through a lot. Take your time. You do not need to get into another emotionally taxing situation."

"Mom, it will be fine, I am a twenty-two-year-old woman, and we are having dinner as friends—that's it."

As I look back now, I know that Mom was right. I had my share of hurts and emotional trauma over the years. I did not need to get into a relationship at this moment of my life. I understood her worrying about me. Mom stood up and we both went back to working and shaping up the front yard.

The day came for the date and when the doctor came to the front door to pick me up, I remembered him right from the start. The doctor was very caring about me when I first went into the hospital—when I was in labor. He did seem however, shy and out of his element when he walked into my home to meet my parents. It was almost to the point that he was intimidated by our family, our home, and our neighborhood. I can sort of understand why he was afraid because the South Side had its share of problems at that time.

He was shorter than me, had dark curly hair, and had glasses on. Right from the start, I was not attracted to him, but I thought here I am a young woman from the city, and a doctor wants to take me out. I was a little flattered. I guess it would not hurt and I could just see what happened. In the back of my head, I was uneasy and I knew that I needed to take things slowly and proceed with caution.

Well, just maybe he would be good for me.

When I looked around at so many of the young men in my neighborhood, who were on drugs, or had drinking problems, and many simply did not want to work, I told myself, "Keep an open mind."

When we walked out of my house and toward his car, the doc turned to me and said in a low voice, "Is your neighborhood safe?"

"Yes, it is safe but we do have our problems. Why do you ask?" I said and was concerned that maybe someone had bothered him on the way over.

"No reason," he said, but he looked up and down my street with a worried look on his face while he opened my car door, and then ran nervously to his side getting in and pulling off as fast as he could.

After our first date, time went fast. I did not realize it but we had been dating each other for close to a year. I could tell that Mom or Dad did not like him, and were not happy with me seeing him. I can now understand why. We were two different people from two different worlds. There were little things like the fact that I loved dogs; he hated dogs and he would constantly remind me of that. He would say, "Dogs are dirty animals." I enjoyed the outdoors and riding my bike. He never learned how to ride a bike. He wanted to stay indoors most of the time with a medical book. I loved to laugh; he was serious and to the point of being gloomy.

I like to eat on the floor with a plate of food and watch TV. The Doc only ate at the table. We were two forces of energy that were constantly colliding. The list went on and on. We did, however, try to make the odd couple relationship work. There was a religious difference as well; however, he was of a Christian belief, but very different from our American concept of Christianity. There were other signs as well that I had turned my head away from what was really going on. When I would get overly critical of our relationship, I would ask myself, "What am I doing with this man?" But then I would wonder if in reality is there really a totally good relationship without troubles? I thought that, "Together you work on making it work, right?" Our time was drawing to a close. The doc was finishing up his residency and he wanted to move our relationship to the next level.

"Marry me," he said. "I will take you back home to where my family lives in California. Together we will be happy living out West." I thought maybe we could find happiness by moving somewhere different, but are you really the same person with the same values and ideals, no matter where you live?

So, together we flew to meet his mother and family in LA. When we were on the plane, he seemed very nervous and moody. He began to give orders. I just sat back a little shocked and glared back at him. I had a hard time controlling my anger.

I had nowhere to get up and run away from him because we were on a plane. He had the gall to tell me what I was allowed to talk about with his family, what I wasn't allowed to say in front of his family, and a list of instructions as to how I was supposed to act in front of them. He especially did not want his family to know that I was pregnant and lost my sweet baby. He treated me like I was his property and not his partner. I looked at him like you got to be kidding me and said, "Sorry to tell you this, but, I am a grown up woman, and I will talk about anything I want to talk about, to whoever I decide to talk to."

"Fine," he said angrily but looked scared to death. I could tell this really upset him. And the rest of the way on the airplane we did not say another word. I met his mother and from the start she did not like or approve of me being an "American woman." There was no love lost. Maybe I did not approve that she was a closed-minded individual, to the point that she thought that she was better then everyone she met. I know no one would be good enough for her son.

She had a hold over him so that he jumped up whenever she wanted something. When he was around her all I ever heard out of him was, "Yes, Mother."

"Oh, Mother." "You're right Mother." I wanted to yell out at the top of my lungs, "Stop kissing her ass!" I had some other Mother words for this lady but I held them in.

I wanted to be me, and I wanted to be liked, and accepted for being me. I did not feel comfortable at their home, but I tried to make the best of the uncomfortable situation I was in. Things were not going well in the city of angels. I could see that he was very different around his family and not the same person when we were together. The doc was more relaxed with me and much more uptight around his family. I knew I could never live up to their expectations of what they thought a wife should be, what he wanted me to be, or what his mother wanted, and if I tried, I would simply drive myself crazy. He came into my life at a bad time. I was getting back on my feet and not ready for a relationship.

While we were in California, the doc was going to interviews at different hospitals around the city, and I drove around with a realtor to look at huge, expensive homes in her Mercedes Benz. I did not care what car I was in and that it drove easy on the roads, to the point that we closed ourselves off from the outside world in a haunting silence. His world when it collided with mine was not a happy place for either one of us.

I wished I was back at home driving in my old car. Sure the homes were beautiful, the weather wonderful, and the ocean took my breath away, but I missed my rust-belt city of Cleveland, my home, my lake, and the famous Cuyahoga River that had caught on fire. But what I truly missed most was my mother.

I called her daily and could tell that the doc did not like that I was so close to my mom, with a bond that he would never be able to unravel. It bothered him terribly that Mom and I were so close and the best of friends.

After I was off the phone, he said almost like an order, "When we are married, you can only talk to her once a month."

"No, that is not going to happen; I will talk to her every day," I said and was hurt that things were not working out.

He wanted the wedding to be in LA. I wanted the wedding to be held in Cleveland. I was getting so angry my face was turning bright red and I was getting more furious by the minute. I got up and sat next to him and said, "What are we doing? I can't do this. It is not right for me or you."

We both were sad, but I was relieved that there was no wedding going to take place anywhere with him. Sure, he was a nice guy, had money, was a doctor, and I suppose he was every woman's dream—but not my dream guy. We were just not right for each other—plain and simple, and I think deep down the doc knew it too. We were two people filling a lonely void in our lives at that time.

We may have had a close fondness at times, but there truly was no love in my heart for this man. When I flew back into Cleveland I felt my sense of peace and well-being beginning to be reestablished. My sister, Veronica, and Mom picked me up.

"How did it go, meeting his parents?"

Mom said and wanted to know everything.

"Miserable, his mother hates me and in so many words said, I was not good enough for her son," I answered Mom and I immediately felt better getting her poisonous words out of my system.

"No, Laurel, the truth of the matter is that he is not good enough for you. I knew that on your first date. You two were just not a good match."

"Thanks, Mom," I said feeling like I was getting back to myself again.

Veronica said, "I've never liked him. You two did not look right together."

"We sure were the odd couple and I am sure that his family saw that too," I said. I felt mournfulness after losing our relationship, but at the same time, I felt a freedom that put me at ease. I am still living and learning, and I guess sometimes, the hard way. I realize people come and go in our lives; some for a season, some for a reason, and some for a lifetime.

However, sometimes we do have to make hard choices when it is our potential lifetime partner.

Veronica drove down I-71 and being back on my home turf, my life was coming back to me. It is true what Dorothy said, "There is no place like home," and home is where I needed to be.

I rolled down the back window and let the breeze wash over me and clean off all the negative vibes from LA. Mom reached for my hand and said, "Are you all right?"

"Never better. It's great to be back home, I could kiss the ground," I said with a big smile. I knew in my heart I would marry someone someday for true love and happiness. I would not settle for less.

Chapter 31

Perseverance

If you persevere you shall prevail.

—Sam Rutigliano Fellowship of Christian Athletes Dinner,
September 1978.

Time was passing and moving along much too swiftly and when I looked back on my life, I often wondered, "Why did things go the way they did?" Where did I go wrong in my life for it to turn out the way it did? Then I thought, *"Don't be too hard on yourself."* What if life came to me too easy and I did not mess up now and then? How would I learn or grow? What type of person would I be, someone different then me? Would I become a "Miss Know It All," and telling people how to live their lives, or a person that looked down on others, and their mistakes? Besides, we sure have enough of those types around. I knew I was far from that type of person. I stopped for a second and thought again and realized I was blessed to have survived all those misfortunes and lived through them and hopefully learned. I believed and understood that what helped me most to get through all that had happened to me was my mother.

We had a relationship that helped me find myself, and to believe that there is more to life than what we physically see or understand. My mom is and will always be that advisor, best friend, and strongest influence on me even as a grown woman and I was blessed to have her by my side.

With having my mother there to lean on when I messed up, which we all often do in our lives, was not only a lifesaver, but my strength. I am sure that I may mess up again, but maybe I became a little more aware of the signs when it came to bad relationships with men. I hoped.

I believe we all go through the "what if" questions at certain points in our lives. Isn't life meant to go in order, and we, or maybe only I, mess things up with our freewill and bad decisions? There was this one thing that was hovering over my head and that was why I wanted to show myself that I successfully earned my high school diploma.

I knew that my education was lacking from not getting it while I was in school. However, deep down inside of me, I knew I was capable and bright enough to pass. Mom would tell me when I would get down or questioned myself, "Laurel, you can do anything you want. You are hard working, honest, and have a good heart."

"Mom, thanks for your words of confidence, but I need my diploma in my hands to feel more able to handle the working world," I said.

Mom would listen to me and offer her words of wisdom. "With time, patience, and persistence, you will have your high school diploma in your hands. Just keep working toward that goal." Having Mom as the one person I could talk to about anything, helped me over the years, as she cheered me on and helped me to get through whatever predicament I had gotten myself into.

I listened to her and always found encouragement in her words. It was great to have someone believing in you, when at times it was too easy to stop believing in myself.

"You can make it or do anything you want. All it takes is a little dedication and patience," Mom said frequently to me.

"Mom," I said, "why do you keep telling me to have patience?"

"Well, I have found that when the time is right, and with a little patience things in life seemed to come together."

I had the GED test weighing heavily over my head. Why not take the test again? What was it that I feared? I was looking over the book for over three years now. "*Go and take it,*" I thought. So finally, I took the GED test thinking I did better this time around, and maybe I even passed the test. Now the waiting to see the results come in the mail was difficult. I wanted to know on the spot if I had passed or not. I still was working full time in the bingo card factory and I liked getting a steady paycheck, but I knew that I wanted to do something else with my life someday. I had really envied people who knew what their career paths were right out of high school. Everyone knows the type of people I am talking about.

These folks seem to know what schools they were going to attend and where they wanted to work and live.

Some people just, "have it together," from the start—wonderful grades in school, great in sports, and a great job.

Deep down I wished that I could be that way and know what I wanted in life. For me when I started to think of a career choice, I would write out a list and a number of things would appear onto the paper. I thought, "You cannot do everything," and I knew I needed to narrow it down. There were always a few things that popped onto the sheet when I was writing different things down. They were working with children, animals, or food service, and of course, I always loved to read and write. I had options that held my interest; I would go to Mom and we would talk them over.

"Mom, I am not sure what I want to be, but I know I like children, animals, or maybe working with food, and I also like to journal and write."

Mom would listen to me go on and on about what I should do in life and trying to pick a career.

I know I must have made her "nuts" with all my confusion and indecision.

But then again, how do you really know what to do, and if it's the right fit or not until you are in it? Not being sure on anything, kept me wondering and dreaming.

I showed Mom my list that I came up with.

Mom always reassured me, "Making a list is great and maybe you will have tried a number of things until you find out what you really like to do."

"Mom, is it really OK to just find out as you go along?"

"Sure it is, but keep it legal," Mom said in a playful voice.

There is not one thing wrong in finding what makes you happy. I thought about how many people want more and more and then louse it up when they get what they thought they wanted, and the people who have that great career, but in the long run hurt others in the process to get what they want. Money and career were everything to them, but what about life, love, and happiness?

Thoughts like these filled my mind when I was in my twenties. At that time in our lives, we all want our own identities, and most of us are trying to figure out where we fit in, in this world that moves along with or without us.

Each day after work I walked in the house and looked to see if the GED test scores came in the mail. Then the day came and Mom had the envelope in her hand and handed it to me. I opened it up quickly, reading down my scores. I stopped after reading each score.

Well, there they were; my scores were right there in my hands. I smiled to myself pleased that I stayed the same and was very close but did not pass the test. I felt disappointment, but I was not going to punish myself. I did not feel great about my scores, but I had no choice but to accept them. I knew that I had my work cut out for me if I was going to get that passing score.

Mom stood next to me saying, "What does it say?"

"Mom, I did not pass the test, but there is good news. I am close and I scored the same as last time I took the test."

I laughed at myself and put the test results down onto the table. Mom picked it up looked the paper over and I know she was wishing she had the power to change what I had already read. Mom looked over at me kindly and said, "You will get it next time. Look how close you are, you're only a few points away."

"Mom, I hope so. The number three is my lucky number." I was not sad or depressed from not passing. I knew that I needed more help than working on my GED alone or with Mom's help.

"You will get it next time, I am sure," Mom said, giving me her support as always.

I knew I had to make some changes in my life to get that diploma. I needed more quality study time, and the eight hours, and with the overtime I worked, I was too exhausted to study and fully concentrate on my GED work. I hated the job anyway and I was ready to move on. So, I went out looking for a job. I found a part-time job working nights in a hospital dietary department. I liked the job. I was running the front cash register and sometimes passing out the food trays to the patients. There were enough hours each week to help me live on, and living at home, I knew Mom never would kick me out for not giving her enough rent money which I never had to pay anyway. Mom's kindness was a big relief to me.

After all, I really did not have any more daunting financial pressures on me. We were simply working-class folks just getting by as a family.

Another benefit was that my new schedule allowed me to go to Project Learn during the day. The program offered small classes going over a number of subjects. I had gotten close to a number of volunteer workers there who were offering their time to help me learn, but there was this one special lady who always sat down and helped me out no matter what the question was. Nora was dedicated and she taught me many different things that I had missed out on by dropping out of school. I felt very comfortable and at ease with going to her for help. Nora never made me feel bad no matter what mistake I made, and I know I had made many.

"Laurel, let's go over this again," Nora would say. Then she would pull up a chair and go over step by step on what I had done wrong and why. I attended each class and took all that the program had to offer and I was feeling more and more confident; finally, "I was getting it."

The people at Project Learn became my second family as I was faithfully going to the center four days a week. When a class would get up to go, Nora would check to see if anyone had questions, and she would sit down and go over the material again if needed. She had a special way with the students.

I never held back from going to her for help and watched how my education was making vast improvements with the gift of her freely sharing her knowledge had helped me more than I could ever say.

Every day in the late afternoons, I would come home to change into my uniform and go to work. Every time I ran into our home to change into my work uniform after a day of learning at Project Learn, Mom liked to look over what I was doing as well. We both were learning as Mom would go through my work and pick up on the different subjects that we were covering. I knew Mom never graduated from high school and she was learning right along with me. Mom and I had this one little thing that we liked to do. Together, we would look up different words in the old dictionary, pick out words, and then we would both write them out over and over again until we got the word spelled out right. That's not to say that we said the word right to begin with, but we learned to spell it. Who cares?

The important thing was that we were learning at our own pace, and what really made it special was that as a mother and daughter, we were in this learning process together. I know that I was ready to take the test again but kept putting it off. I was worried that I would not pass. I had taken the practice test and passed.

The folks at Project Learn and Mom knew I was ready to try again. "Laurel, go take the test because you are ready," Mom would say reassuringly.

"Mom, I don't know. I am worried. What if I don't pass again?"

"Laurel, go and take the test and see. What harm is it in taking it again?"

"Mom," I smiled, "I think that I am ready, but I'm worried that I won't pass again and I am afraid that I am just too dumb to make it."

"Laurel, never say you are dumb. You are an intelligent person," Mom said with reassuring confidence. When it came to test taking, I got very nervous to the point that I would not eat; I did not eat because I was afraid I would throw up right on the test. There a word for it—"Test Anxiety." I had that to the maximum. I knew it was time to take the test and I prayed that this would be the last time I would be tackling this exam.

On the day that I took the test, I only drank water and took antacid because my stomach was always messed up from the anxiety. I tried hard to relax with breathing slowly in and out of my mouth. After I looked the test over and I turned the test in, I had the feeling that was the end of me trying to pass my GED. I hoped and prayed that I was ready to move on to Community College, but that old question kept popping into my head, "What do I want to do in life?" I still to this very day ponder this thought.

I pulled out the paper again that I used to try and shape my future and wrote out things I like to do: kids, food, animals, and I liked working with people. Maybe I could figure it out before I die and if not I decided to just do my best in whatever job that I ended up in.

I walked into the house after taking the test and Mom said, "How did it go today?"

"I think I blew it again."

"What, did you say?" Mom said coming over to comfort me. I burst out laughing, "No, Mom, I think this time I passed the test and no one can say I haven't worked hard and tried."

"That's what I like to hear. Keep working, keep believing, and good things will come your way." I loved to listen to Mom's kind and heartfelt words of encouragement. At those times I knew in my heart that Mom really cared for me and was concerned for my future.

When my GED test results came in the mail, and I opened the envelope up again, hoping for the last time, I closed my eyes for a minute, composed myself, took a deep breath, let the air out slowly, and read the results. I had passed the test! I guess three was my lucky number, that's not to say all the hard work I put into it finally paid off. I was jumping up and down and our family dog, Star, was jumping around in circles and barking triumphantly. I cried out in victory, "I made it! I made it!"

"That's wonderful," Mom said. Together we both were filled with happiness. Not only did I pass, I was asked to make a commercial for Project Learn to motivate other people to build up their reading and writing skills—you know the commercials that come on late at night when everyone is sleeping.

I was proud of how far I had come and there I was, a high school dropout and on my way to the doors of Community College. I hoped that maybe someone might late at night see my commercial and go get help because learning truly is freedom. I saved many of my school papers and knew I had come from a very low reading level that had improved, and now I was ready to try and read college level books. Mom was ecstatic that I passed and I could see that Dad was a proud papa as well. Mom made my favorite dinner to celebrate my passing and my commercial. She had cooked cabbage rolls, or more like cabbage rolls soup with warm bread that soaked up the juice. I was feeling good about life and having my GED, my confidence level was at a new high. There are turning points in one's life, and mine just turned. The future was out there and I made a huge step into it. I started to get up to get more cabbage rolls. Mom stopped me and took my bowl and filled in up for me.

"Thanks, Mom, for dinner." I said while putting a spoon full of food into my mouth.

"Sure anytime. I'm glad you are enjoying dinner. Laurel, you are the only one that likes my cabbage rolls."

"More like cabbage roll soup," I teased back at my mother.

Pointing her server spoon at me, Mom said playfully, "Watch yourself young lady."

Chapter 32

Good Intentions

I started attending Community College and I made sure that I spaced out my classes, so I could keep up. I knew more than anyone that I could fall right on my face if I overextended myself with too busy of a schedule. I discovered that there was a new freedom in my life—taking classes during the day and working at night in the hospital was more than enough to fill up my schedule and expend all of my energy. I got to meet different people while in school. They were keeping tight schedules while attending classes and many were single mothers. The single moms, I could see, had it hard, but were out there working and going to school doing their best for their children. When I saw these single mothers, I felt for them because that would have been me, but things do change in life with no warning and without our approval.

I still was not sure what I wanted to take but thought about getting a general Associate of Arts and took classes toward an early childhood special needs assisting degree. I kept in my mind what Mom always said, "Do what you enjoy and do your best to your ability at any job, and try different things until you find your place in this world." I stopped thinking that I immediately needed to pick out a career. I relaxed and relished in the moments while attending classes knowing that what I wanted to do will come to me, and if not that was fine too.

I stopped in the school cafeteria and saw pamphlets for the March of Dimes Walk for healthy babies. Many times we ignore things we see every day like charity events or fundraisers until we can personally relate to the cause. I took a few minutes to read it over and filled out the application. I had never walked for a charity event and thought this will be a great way to volunteer and to give back, for Nicholas, and other little ones in need. I thought about it for a minute and realized that there were a number of little ones out there that needed a helping hand. We all need to get out there and do something to help one another, so that's what I did.

I had gotten a few sponsors and had my calendar marked in a bright red circle waiting with anticipation for the day to come. Mom was delighted to see me walking for March of Dimes, and finally functioning among the living. When the day arrived I put on my sweat pants, running shoes, and a light jacket, and I was feeling great to be doing my part. I opened the front door and looked up at the sky. The weather felt to be around sixty degrees, but there was a chance of a rain shower. I hoped that the bad weather would hold off until the walk was over. Mom came and stood next to me and said, "Laurel, take an umbrella with you today."

"Maybe the rain will hold off until after the walk," I said to Mom looking up at the sky in a wishful manner.

"Maybe," Mom said, "but take the umbrella to be safe."

"OK, Mom, I'll see you later."

I reached downtown Cleveland, but it took me time to find a parking space that did not cost me a fortune. I finally found a cheap lot; however, I had a little walking to do before I reached public square. There is something I like about walking in downtown Cleveland. With the wind whipping in and out from between all the tall buildings and being so close to the lake, you can really feel the weather deep down to your bones. It was a cloudy morning, but the sun was peeking out from the rain clouds and I had hoped that the sun would stick around faithfully throughout the day.

When I finally reached Public Square, there was a huge crowd of people, and many were from companies wearing t-shirts that supported the March of Dimes. I walked up to the middle of the crowd alone, and volunteers were giving out bottled water. I took one and noticed that there was an instructor up front showing the crowd how to stretch out before the walk. It was hard to see while people were moving in and out of the group blocking my view. When I missed something, or could not see what the instructor was doing, I did my best to stretch out my legs on my own. I noticed that next to me was a middle-aged woman that seemed to be alone. She smiled at me and said, "Hi, I am Anna."

I introduced myself and said, "Hi, I am Laurel."

Anna asked me, "Are you here to walk for a child you know?"

I was stretching and stood up and said, "Yes, my son Nicholas. He passed away from heart complications not too long ago."

"Oh, I am so sorry." Anna had warm round face, brown eyes, and was very soft spoken and had a slight Spanish accent. I thought it would to nice to pair up with someone and walk together.

"Anna, do you mind walking with me?"

"Sure I'll walk with you. I would love to have a partner."

"Great, Anna why are you walking? Is there someone in your family that has a sick baby?"

"Yes, I have a niece that had a hole in her heart when she was a baby, but the good news is she getting big and better now." Anna's face lit up in a warm, bright smile.

"We all have our reason for walking today and every little bit helps and benefits a child in need."

"Yes it does," Anna said. I looked down at my watch and noticed that we should be running or walking soon. The starting bell rang out, we were off walking, and many people around me were running. I was satisfied with a fast walking pace and Anna was keeping up. We did not talk or comment on anything during the walk. I was happy for that—I wanted to have it quiet and keep up my pace.

While many women loved to talk and walk, I preferred to keep my mind on my walking and thinking my own thoughts. Having Anna for companionship helped because she had competed in a number of these walks and was in great shape. I had a hard time keeping up so Anna slowed down a little so that I wouldn't get too far behind. Anna had mentioned earlier that she had hoped that the weather would hold off until after the walk.

To our surprise it was a bright sunny day with plenty of sunshine, keeping everyone dry and happy. When we reached the point where we needed to turn back toward the finish line, I opened my water bottle and drank it down. I was feeling great thinking I needed to get back to walking daily again. Like most women, I felt like I could lose a few pounds, and found that walking had a way of relaxing me.

I looked up to the sky and the storm clouds were coming in and we were getting close to the finish point; just our luck. I wanted to curse at the skies. I watched as many people were pulling out rain jackets, and Anna had put on a light weight yellow jacket that was folded up in a little bag that she had carried. I had on my jacket, but it was not water proof. Unfortunately, I had forgotten the umbrella, and left it in the car. I pleaded this time out loud to the cloudy skies above us, "Mother Nature please be kind and hold off the stormy weather. We are almost there."

Anna turned and said to me, "Did you bring any protection against the rain."

"Yes, I got an umbrella sitting in my car, but it's not too helpful lying in my back seat," I laughed out loud and felt the rain drops hit the top of my head.

"Sorry, but this yellow jacket is all I got," Anna said while pulling the plastic hood over her head.

"That's OK. I guess a little rain water never killed anyone."

"No. But it looks like it's going to pour down any minute."

I looked up, "Here it comes." Anna and I picked up our pace and walked a little faster. I saw that the storm clouds above us were moving next to the lake and the sun had disappeared from the horizon. The rain came down, drenching the crowd from their head to their shoes. Anna said, "We got about eight minutes to go before we are finished." We both let out a silly laugh.

"Well, remember we are out for a good cause," I said while I pulled back my wet bangs from my face.

"That's right, now let's get moving," Anna said. We both were moving swiftly and then we reached the finish line. I saw that there were a number of companies that had buses waiting to pick up their employees. I envied them for the fact that they had a warm bus to take them back to their cars at their company parking lots. I did, however, felt great and almost renewed for my efforts to help sick babies, but I felt waterlogged straight down to my running shoes.

Anna smiled at me and said, "Nice to walk with you."

I held out my hand, "Me too." I watched while she pulled out a bus schedule from her pocket and looked it over.

I thought to myself, *No way. I can't let her wait in this rain for a bus.* "Anna," I said, "where do you live?"

"I live off West 44th and Bridge, but I am fine. My bus will be here soon."

"No please, I want to give you a ride. I live not too far from your home," I said.

"Thank you, I'll take you up on that offer," Anna said.

"But I parked a little ways down, so we may have a bit of a walk in this rain," I said apologetically.

"That's OK, we are already wet," We both were laughing to each other and I felt the water squishing in my shoes as we walked toward my car.

By now the rain was slowing down when we reached my car. I started it up and pulled off holding two hands on the wheel, as the rain came down hard again. I turned the heat on high, while my windshield wipers were making a sloshing sound as they went back and forth across my windshield. Anna told me the best way to get to her house.

"This is Cleveland weather for ya. Cold, windy, and rainy today and in a few days, we will not be happy with the heat," I said, "Good old Cleveland."

We both were agreeing and laughing when Anna said, "I'll take the heat over this mess any day."

Anna said, "Turn right, I am in the apartment building on the right hand side." I pulled over and dropped her off.

"I am really grateful for the ride. Thank you and God bless."

"Thank you too for "buddying" up with me on the walk. Take care," I said. I watched as Anna ran up the stairs to her building. When I pulled off, I was thinking that I should have given her my phone number. But it was nice to have met someone to walk with who knew about what a struggle it was to have a child that is close to you suffer. I figured I would see her again at the next walk.

Now the rain slowed down, but the day was dreary and dismal outside. I wanted to get home to shower and eat because by then I was starving. I got to a one-way corner that came off to a one-way exit ramp. I stopped at the red light and moved up a little to see if I could turn. All of a sudden, WHAM! I heard the screeching sound of metal fenders tearing at each other. I tried to hold on to my steering wheel as tight as I could, and I caught a glimpse of large, silver, four door sedan, that seemed to come out of nowhere. I got smashed into real hard and my body was jerked around in my car seat.

I realized then that I was half turned around facing the street and side walk. I took in a long, deep, breath, and felt around over my body and realized I was fine. I got out checking on my car.

The bumper had been half taken off, but everything else seemed fine. I looked down the road and the car that hit me was about twenty-five feet up the road and the silvery metal flake custom-paint job seemed to glisten in the rain.

I ran to the car and could see the passenger side front fender was hit and the tire was blown out. I went up to the window to check on the driver; he looked to be without any injuries. His car stereo was blaring loud with Latin music.

I stood out in the rain, and said as loud as I could, "Are you OK?"

He looked at me and said, "Yeah, I'm OK." That is when I heard the police coming. I ran and got back into my car and waited. There were two police cars that came; one cop was moving the traffic by while the other officer took our personal information. He took both of our driver's licenses and auto insurance cards. I handed over my driver's license, and said, "I had auto insurance all through my driving years, but it lapsed four days ago. I have an appointment tomorrow to get new coverage first thing at nine in the morning." At that time the insurance laws were not so strictly enforced like they are today.

The police officer looked pleased with what I had to say. Then he went back to his car. My insurance rates were sky high because of where I lived in

Cleveland. It seemed that the rates were getting out of hand and had doubled from when I first had gotten it years before.

I ran out of money with my last payment due, and was all ready to renew my coverage with a new auto insurance plan, the day after the race when my next paycheck came in. What terrible luck! "Luck," I thought, is there really a true meaning with this word for me?

Mom told me, "Keep your auto insurance until you get a new policy with lower rates."

How come moms are always right? Well, I thought, *I am going to jail and eat old hard bread and drink stale water.* The policeman came back and said, "You have never had a moving violation for all of the years you have been driving and I have seen a number of accidents at this corner. I believe fault wise, that it is fifty-fifty. He was going too fast and not paying close enough attention and that is why he hit you. You edged out a little too far trying to see if you were clear to turn. We need to change the light here and put up a sign that says, *No Turn On Red.*"

I only nodded my head and agreed with what he said. I waited while he went back to the other driver, and he came back saying that the other driver would like an ambulance. The police man looked at me and said, "Do you need to go to the hospital?"

"No, I'm a little rattled but I'll be fine. He hit me pretty hard, but I had my belt on and I think I am OK." I kept thinking, what is this guy up to? He seemed fine and I hoped he was not hurt.

I dropped my head down and prayed "Oh, God, I hope he is not hurt. Help me please. I am sorry I drove four days with no auto insurance."

When the ambulance came, the paramedics took him to the nearest hospital. I watched as they checked him out. I was soaking wet and the policeman asked me with a curious look on his face, "Why are you all wet?"

"I just came from walking The March of Dimes for healthy babies.

"Oh," he said, "that's a great cause to support." The officer called a tow truck to move the other driver's car out of the way. He turned back to me and said, "Do you think you can drive your car home?"

"Yeah, these old Chevys are hard to kill," I said.

"You are right. They seem to want to run for a long time.

I'll show in my report that you had a valid operator's license, and that you normally drive with auto insurance and the date you called to make an appointment to get new auto insurance." I thanked him for his kind words; however, I knew that I would be getting sued. That's what people do today; most are sue happy and are looking for an easy buck.

The policeman stopped traffic as I pulled out, and I drove home felling my bumper scrape against the road as I drove along and darkness seemed to have fallen over the sky and the rain hit my car with forceful anger.

When I pulled in front of the house, I sat in my beat-up old Chevy and looked to the gloomy skies and cried out, "Why? I was doing something good, now this."

Mom come out and ran up to the car, opened the passenger door and climbed in next to me. She noticed the damaged bumper and fender and said, "What happened? Are you OK?"

"Mom, I had a car accident and the man that hit me is fine, but he took an ambulance to the hospital and I think I will be sued." "Laurel, thank God that you are fine and I am sure he is fine. Now let's get in the house and I can open up a can of soup so you can warm up."

"But, Mom, what am I gonna do? I know that I will be sued and I barely earn enough money to get by now. How am I going to pay for a lawyer and a law suit?"

"Well, so what? The important thing is that no one was seriously hurt. I know that you can get past this. I just thank God that your guardian angel made sure you didn't get seriously hurt. I know you. You will pay your debt fairly and honestly. That's how I raised you." I understood that there was not going to be any government buyouts or financial rescue for me. I knew that this was my mess and I needed to take care of it. And yes, I got sued. I found out that little weasel was fine but all the costs of the hospital, the ambulance, and the damage that he caused to his car came onto me because I had no insurance company to fight his insurance company.

I learned the hard way to follow the law of the roads and stay insured no matter what. I had saved a little money for a rainy day, and I had one. I got a lawyer who took the case and helped take a little off what the insurance company wanted for a settlement. I really got a raw deal.

I guess you live and learn, and money is only a number in a bank account, and the world does not come to an end when you lose a clump of it.

Mom was right again and she graciously never once gave me a, "I told you so." when the incident was over; it was over and we just moved on to the business of everyday living. Mom comforted me as usual and got me through another mishap. It took me some time, but I did pay off my debt. I didn't file bankruptcy like the lawyer wanted. I knew that I would someday need to keep a good credit rating; I had to do what was right the way Mom had raised me to do, and follow that thin straight narrow line and keep my moral compass pointing north.

Chapter 33

Restlessness

I had a number of woman to woman talks with my mom over the years about men, and the same old question always popped up—Is there a Mr. Right out there for me? I knew that, for the lucky ones, there is true love out there, and it really does happen, and I hoped it would happen to me someday. I often asked myself, "Do you believe in fate?" I am someone that hoped and truly prayed for a loving partner to come my way, but where can I find him, I wondered—at a bar or club? No, that's not a place where I wanted to find love, or where I had any luck finding the right guy. Maybe walking though a book store I could meet somebody headed in my direction, and maybe I could offer him a flirty smile. I once heard supermarkets were a good place. You could look into a guy's shopping cart to see if he had more beer than groceries filling up his cart. But then I thought maybe "Mr. Right Guy" will come around when I'm not looking at all.

I suppose it's possible that fate would bring two people together and when they meet they would just know that they were meant to be. I still believed that this could happen; call me a romantic fool, but maybe, just maybe, it could happen. I wished that I would fall deeply in love and one day live happily ever after together with my special guy. My only hope was it would happen to me someday.

It's wonderful when I see couples walking hand in hand moving in the same beat and synchronized rhythm; it's called love. Sure I had my relationships in my life and learned sometimes the hard way what incompatibility really means and also what it means to be close and appreciate each other. I knew that I never had truly fallen deeply in love with anyone so far. No, I deeply cared for a few men, but not really deeply loved anyone so far, not the way that I need to love and be loved back. I also knew that I was part of the problem, so I worked on myself so that I could be a better catch for someone and hoped that one day that I could fall in love.

I wanted one day to be a wife and maybe have children again with the right man. I always turned to Mom for advice and I would listen to her answer all of my questions about relationships with men. Mom understood many of my feelings because she had had her share of heartaches from men, and with years behind her came the wisdom. Mom's main response every time we had this talk was, "Find a man that respects you and takes time out to attend weekly church."

"Where do I find a man like that in Cleveland that's not a priest?" I loved to tease back at Mom when she told me this.

"Laurel, you have a lots of time. Do not worry. When the time is right and you least expect it, he will come your way. Remember to pray to God that he will guide you to the right mate." Mom would tell me in a confident manner almost like she herself saw it happening to me.

Well, I guess Mom had a point. Just maybe adding this into my daily prayer list won't hurt. Why not talk to God like a friend? He knows our needs anyway. I started praying this special prayer each night, "God, when it's your time, please send me someone that is a good positive man." In the back of my mind, I hoped that my prayers would get answered before I became an old maid. I knew there was a time and place for everything and I held on to the belief that love will come my way when the time was right; I guess I needed to let my restlessness take a back seat and just believe.

I can remember many Friday nights sitting at home with a bowl of popcorn watching the Cleveland Indians' games with my parents, and around the fifth inning I would fall off to sleep on the couch and dream in anticipation that my husband would walk right in my front door. I loved this dream, because my mom and family all seemed to love him as well. But then I would wake up to see that the game was still playing on the TV, and it was only a wishful dream. Mom would fill me in on what I missed while I was taking a nap. I knew that both of my parents liked having me around the house at night, and together we kept up on the Cleveland Indians and watched a lot of PG-rated movies.

However, when too many weekends came and went by I was still at home, I thought in my worried mind, "I'm twenty five years old! I am on my way to becoming an old maid!"

I am too comfortable being at home with my parents. I shared my fears with Mom and she said.

"Laurel, you have time, and you are better off at home. There is only trouble out there in the night clubs."

"You are right on that one Mom, but I need to get out a little and just meet new people," I said wishing that one day it would happen where I could meet that special someone and fall in love.

"Getting out is great, but the night cubs worry and bother me. There seems to be too many men on the make just looking for a good time," Mom said. I know that Mom was right, but being young, I liked to get out sometimes with a girlfriend and just hang out, listen to a little music, and be a part of the younger generation. I am not a drinking type person, or had the need to get high, which was a blessing. I saw enough people in my neighborhood ruin their lives with booze and drugs and found nothing but pain that brought pain in their families' lives from druggin and drinkin. For me, I felt that life has its ways of giving you enough highs and lows all by itself without any illegal substances involved. I had made plans with a girlfriend on a Saturday night in June, and I was getting dressed to go out. I put on a pretty blue blouse, new denim skirt, and a new pair of sandals that I never had worn before.

I fixed my hair and applied a little makeup to my face.

I knew that when I walked out of my room, I wondered if Mom would approve of what I had on.

Mom gave me a good look over and said, "Well, I like your blouse, and new sandals, but is the skirt too short?"

I laughed at Mom, "No it's at the knees, and believe me Mom, I picked out the longest denim skirt I could find at K-Mart."

Mom reached over and pulled on my skirt a little and said, "Well, I guess it's fine. You do look very nice. Have a good time tonight and be careful."

"I will, see you later." I walked out the door, looking down at my denim skirt and realized that Mom would have loved it if it could reach the floor. I realized that I could buy one shorter, but that was not me. With my long legs I knew I would only find trouble if I wore a shorter one and I did not want to send any message that I was looking for trouble.

In Cleveland, at that time, the place to be was called the flats. There were a number of bars and night clubs to go dancing.

Also in the flats you could see that downtown Cleveland was all lit up, and next to you was the Cuyahoga River. Cleveland looked bright and renewed at night with the downtown new and old buildings standing up in the sky.

I parked my car and together we got out and walked passing bar after bar with loud music and loud conversations blaring over each other as we walked on.

It was a warm summer night, and right now I would have loved an ice-cream cone and a quiet spot to enjoy it. I hated huge crowds, loud music, and drinking, and had to ask myself, "What am I doing here?"

Oh, then I remembered, maybe I'm here to meet a nice guy. Together we kept on walking, and by now I was ready to turn back and go home, get on the couch, and watch TV, with my parents setting in the quite calm of my living room. But then I thought again, I needed to relax and enjoy the summer night. That's what young people do. I needed to figure out how to settle down in big noisy crowds. I was starting to get a headache and my feet were killing me by now. I wished I could take off my sandals and walk bare footed.

I kept on walking along with my girlfriend and I knew that she loved every minute of this madness. It was in her eyes that I could tell she was having a good time. They became brighter as we walked along. She was a young pretty girl and got noticed by many men as we were walking through the summer time crowd. I guess most young people want the energy, the night life, the noise. To me it felt disturbing and it was starting to make me a little nauseous.

And again the question came up in my mind, "What am I doing here? Relax a little, try to enjoy yourself," I told myself. We continued walking when Janet broke my thoughts, "Let's stop in here. This place is new and looks like fun." I was trying to not be a party pooper and said, "Sounds good to me." When we walked in, the music was loud and there were wall-to-wall people crammed into a small smoke-filled place, with a dance floor in the middle.

Janet walked up to the bar and I followed beside her. She turned to me and said, "What do you want to drink?"

"Ginger Ale," I answered hoping it wound clam down my stomach and my headache that was overwhelming me by now.

"Aw, come on Laurel, you are no fun," she said. I knew better than anyone that I was no drinker and I liked to be aware of what was happening around me. Get more than two drinks in me, I'll become sleepy and then I'd be out like a light. I listened as she placed the order in, a light beer and a ginger ale. I was getting ready to hand her my money, when a nice-looking guy, came up and stood in between us pulling out his wallet smiling and looking over at Janet and said, "I got it," and he put the money down.

"Thanks," she moved in closer and smiled big at him. They both started talking and before I knew it, they were off on the dance floor. I took my ginger ale with me and tried to find a place to sit down.

I saw that there was a small round table open in the corner. I sat down and watched the people around me.

After I finished the ginger ale, my headache was getting worse and the people at the next table were smoking cigarettes and getting loud and all I heard were "F" bombs falling all over the place, followed by foolish laughter. I thought, "*Boy, I am getting too old for this mess*," so I got up and headed for the door.

I walked outside, headed over to the river, and watched the boats as they slowly moved by.

I took in a few deep breaths and just stood there enjoying the night air. I took a seat on a bench overlooking the Cuyahoga River and passed the time relaxing and just letting my thoughts drift to where ever they wanted to go. I looked down at my watch; I knew that I needed to get back into the bar because I was out to meet a nice guy and I knew it was not going to take place sitting out by myself staring at the Cuyahoga River.

I walked back into the bar, and the smell of cigarettes and spilled beer hit me like a ball bat in the head. I saw that Janet seemed to be hitting it off really well with the guy she met talking at the bar and he kept on buying her more light beers. I walked back to the corner table that was still open and sat down when out of nowhere a tall, nice-looking young man, come over and sat down next to me. He was not bad looking and had a tall, thick build, I thought while he sat down his beer bottle.

He turned to me and said, "Well, do you want to dance?" Before I could answer, he grabbed my hand and we were off to the dance floor.

He was on the dance floor banging his full head of hair up and down. He was moving fast and gyrating all over the place to his own sense of rhythm. I had a hard time keeping up with him. When I got a little closer to him, I smelled his breath, and could tell by his eyes that he was intoxicated. Just my luck! With all the guys in this club, I get the wild drunk one to ask me to dance. While he was jumping more than dancing he lost his balance, and fell right into me.

"Hold on there," I said and pushed him away from me. He only picked up speed and started jumping up and down on the floor like he was having an epileptic fit. I was getting tired, with only one dance, and wanted to get away from him. When the music stopped to a slow song I said, "Thank you, but I had enough dancing for tonight."

He moved up close to me and said, "No, baby, you haven't; we have only gotten started."

I turned away and started walking to find Janet when he stopped me and pulled me back to him. I couldn't get away and he kept moving me close to him while moving to the music. I wanted to not be anywhere near him let alone dance with him. He had a strong hold on me. I looked him in the face and tried again to get as far away from him as I could without causing a scene.

I looked right at him and said, "Thanks again, but I do not want to dance anymore." Then his hand went under my blouse and he cupped my breast in his hand. I pulled back pushing him away, "Stop that right now!"

He pulled me back to him and wrapped his arms around my waist and picked me off my feet telling me in his drunken slurring voice, "I want to be your superman."

I started yelling at him, "Put me down now! Put me down now!" His eyes turned dark and he dropped me down hard and my feet hit the dance floor with a loud thud. I immediately turned and ran away from him. He screamed at me and said, "Hey, bitch, what the hell is wrong with you?"

I ran into the bathroom, washed my hands, put cold water on my face, and then looked for an open stall to sit down and gather myself. I wanted to meet a nice man, not a man who is drunk, and thinks he can be my "Super Man." I wanted to meet a man who would be nice to me, but I think I'll pass on the Super Heroes part. He was strong and really frightened me; I hope that he was long gone. I sat back and tried to calm myself down when I heard Janet call into the bathroom, "Laurel, are you in there?"

"Yah, I'm here." I opened up the stall and walked out.

"Are you OK?"

"Not really, but I will be once I calm myself down. Thanks for checking up on me. That guy was such a creep! I hope that he is gone."

"No, he is setting at the corner table, half falling off to sleep," Janet said.

"I am going for a walk by the river. How about meeting me in an hour by my car, and we can go home?" I asked.

"Sure, I'll meet you in an hour by your car."

"Great, see you then," I said. I quickly walked out of the bathroom and did my best to dart out the door before "Clark Kent" woke up.

Before I cleared the door of the night club I noticed my friend was next to the new guy she met getting cozy. There was not anything for me here at this night club. I wanted to go, but I felt it was only fair to give my friend a little more time because she seemed all smiles sitting there talking to this guy she met.

I started walking toward the car. By now there was more traffic and it was moving by slowly passing by the bars. There were a number of people out and couples holding hands, and I felt safe walking back to the car.

The night air felt good walking along the river and I was thinking I might stop and get something to eat. All of a sudden, a group of young guys driving in a car called out to me. "Hey, you, sweetheart, do you want a ride?"

"No, thanks I'm fine," I said.

"Yes, you sure are fine baby," One guy yelled back at me.

Great! Here we go again. I wondered what the heck was going on tonight. This surely is not my night.

Do I have something on my back that said, "If you are a creep, please bother me?" I picked up my pace and tried to ignore them. I could hear them getting louder with rude and crude remarks; so I just looked straight ahead and walked on. They slowed down again and one guy in the front seat hung out the window and said, "Come on already, just get in; we only want to give you a ride."

"No thanks," I said getting annoyed. I thought maybe if I could catch the group of people walking ahead of me these goons would leave me alone. I walked faster, but each time I started to get some distance on them, they would catch up and yell vulgar things at me out of the car window. Then out of nowhere a beer bottle hit the ground around my sandals, and beer and glass splashed up around my feet and legs. I could hear the boys laughing at me. I needed to get away from these jerks.

"Come on, get in, we don't bite," I heard one of the creeps in the car say. I was thinking hard about what the heck can I do to get rid of these bums? So I started to run across the street to the other side to get away from them when an older black man with a strong physique got out of a newly polished long, black, limousine wearing a black suit. He called out to me in a non-threatening manner,

"Get in and I'll drive you away from those deadheads."

He had a fatherly looking way about him and I felt safe. He stood up tall and turned to the car full of jerks, gave them a menacing look that would back down a pro wrestler and spoke slowly and deliberately, "That's enough. You guys had your sick fun. Now go home and grow up." I watched while they did not say a word and looked like little boys out driving around not knowing what to do with their time.

Cowards that they were, they did just that and slinked down the street. The limo driver opened the back door. I smiled at him and got in the back seat. I saw the drunken hoodlums turn and pull off in the opposite direction. It was clear that they wanted no part of the large man with the grim-looking face that had an expression that said, "Mess with me chump and I'll snap your neck." I closed my eyes and said to myself, "Thank God, he stepped in and helped." I was relieved to see that they were gone. I sat back for the first time ever in a limo.

I was sitting back in luxury with the air on. The limousine was impressive. It had cushioned wrap around black leather seats, a TV, and little wet bar. The driver got in the front, and the line of cars cruising through the night scene followed slowly behind us. He turned to me and said, "You need to be careful. There is trouble out here at night when it gets later. Next time walk with a friend."

"I will," I said.

"Where are you headed?" he asked.

"Up to the main parking lot," I said. I wanted to turn on the TV, but kept my hands to myself.

"Fine, I'll drop you off, and here are some wet wipes so you can wash off the beer."

He handed them back to me with a caring manner.

I took them and said, "Thank you."

"Sure, you seem to be too nice of a young woman to be treated like that. I've got two girls of my own around your age. I would hate to see them get treated like that. It seems like the more beer in some young men the more trouble. They forget how to act."

"Yeah, you can say that again." He pulled over, I looked out the window and realized that we were at the parking lot and I said." Thank you for your help and the ride."

He got out and opened my door, "My pleasure," he said and tipped his hat.

I could hardly wait to tell Mom all about my night, and how it was a night from hell, but a Good Samaritan with an imposing physique took the time to interfere and rescued me. I started walking toward my car when I heard Janet call out, "Wait up, Laurel." I turned back and watched her get out of a blue Ford truck and run over to me. Once she reached me, she grabbed me tightly and gave me a tight hug, then I listened to her go on and on about her new guy and could see that she had one too many drinks as she kept on babbling on about what a great night she had.

We both got in my car and headed home. When I pulled up and parked my car, I saw that Mom was letting our dog Star outside. She was older and always had to go the bathroom in the middle of the night. "Hi, Star, how's my old girl?" She came over to me and started sniffing and licking my legs and enjoying the spilled beer that was all over my legs and new sandals.

I reached down and patted her head, "Stop that," I said and pulled her from my leg. Mom called her back into the house and looked up at me and could tell automatically I needed to talk.

"Laurel, looks like you had a bad night."

"Mom, I sure did." Together we walked into the house and once again I had my best friend to confide in, and like always, I had plenty of tears and laughter on my night out to share with her.

Chapter 34

The Date

Mom was out in the kitchen rolling out dough getting ready to make dumplings. I sat on the kitchen chair and helped Mom cut the dough into small squares. I got up and dropped each dumpling into hot chicken broth that was simmering on top of the stove. Mom had made one of my favorite meals—chicken and stuffing topped off with homemade dumplings. My mouth was starting to water, so I helped myself to a small plate and ate. "Wow, Mom, you out did yourself. These dumplings are delicious."

"Glad you like them," Mom said while working tirelessly making more dumplings for the rest of the family. I sat back watching her prepare the last of the meal. I know that Mom had worked hard making the dinner even if she was not feeling her best; she looked like she was catching a cold, but it did not slow her down. Mom sprinkled more flour into a large bowl that had the dough in it, and then started kneading it together, running her hands into the dough, working the flour, oil, and sprinkles of water until they turned into a smooth texture of dough ready to be made into dumplings. Mom looked over at me as I was getting seconds on the hot dumplings, and she could tell that something was bewildering me and said, "What's on your mind?"

"There is a man at school that I am attracted to. He is my English tutor, and I really feel comfortable around him. I don't know why but I keep thinking about him constantly," I said while shoving more dumplings into my mouth. Mom was paying close attention to what I was saying and said, "Well, Laurel, what do you like about him?"

I felt my face turning a little red and answered, "I like everything about him." I started to laugh. Then I said, "He is kind, understanding, and helps anyone who comes to him for help, and he listens and he really helps to bring out the best in the student's papers. What it is, I see in him, is that he takes the time to care. Oh, Mom, I really like him."

Mom let out a sigh, "He sounds like he enjoys his work. How old is he and is he married?"

"No, I don't think he is married, but he acts kinda distant like he is married. If I even thought he was, I would have nothing to do with him and stay clear of him, I guarantee you of that Mom. He has no ring on his finger and yes he is older than me, and he has pictures of kids of all ages all over his office walls."

"Well, today some married men do not wear their rings," Mom said in a way that told me to be careful. I knew Mom was right, but he seemed the type of man that would keep a ring on his finger if he was married.

I know that every time I was around him, I had a warm feeling inside that I never had with anyone.

"Mom, the other day I needed to break my appointment. I walked into his office, and he was taking time out to read the Bible. We both looked at each other and there was something that connected between us." Mom listened to me, but before she spoke, went to the sink to wash her hands, and collect her thoughts. I wanted her to give me the answers that I needed. "Laurel, take your time and if he is interested, he will make the first move, but you can let him know that you like him. Smile a little more and give him a look that says I am interested."

"Well, Mom, that is all I do around him. I smile like a kid on Christmas morning, and Mom I think he likes me too, but it is awkward maybe because he is my English tutor." I was twenty-six years old by now, and at times I felt fifty-six with what had happened in my life because of my past relationships that had failed. However, I knew one thing for sure; I wanted to be near him if only to listen to his voice. He had a way of putting me at ease and feeling safe like no one else before has done. I kept smiling to myself when Mom broke my thoughts. "Laurel, what is his name?"

"His name is Mr. Nick Salupo," I said smiling. "Mom, we have been working together for a few months and we are becoming more than teacher and student—we are becoming friends. Not to mention, Nick is tall, strong, with kind, light green eyes that seem to call out to me when we are together."

Mom, while getting the dinner plates ready said, "If it is meant to be, somehow you will get together but remember, take your time."

"I will," I said in a reassuring tone.

Spring break was coming and for some reason I could not shake Nick from my mind. I kept up with my studies and had deliberately kept men out of my life for a few years and only wanted to concentrate on my degree without any emotional distractions. Deep down, I really wanted to work on improving myself first. Nick had mentioned to me that he was going to see his sister in Dallas, Texas, and Mom and I were taking a little trip to Amish Country. I had him on my mind day and night. *"What is going on?"* I thought to myself. I could sense that there were feelings going on inside of me that I never had experienced before in my life. It seemed like no one could break the mood I was in. I wondered if it could really be love or was I getting ahead of myself?

Mom and I were heading to Sugar Creek in Southern Ohio, and we both were enjoying the view of the open country roads.

"A penny, for your thoughts?" Mom asked.

I laughed, "Mom, I keep thinking about that Nick guy."

"Laurel, you seem different, more relaxed, and there is a glow about you."

"I don't know why. We haven't even gone out together."

"Laurel, does Nick, show you any signs, that he likes you?"

"Yes, Mom he does. I can tell it in the way we talk to each other, and there is something between us like I said before that I never had with anyone. Mom, I am falling hard for this man."

Mom leaned over and gently brushed back my hair off my forehead, with her familiar, gentle touch and said, "Go to Nick and ask him how his Spring break went, and tell him about our little trip to Amish Country as well. I think it is fine to let a man know you are interested, but he should make the initial move. I guess I'm old fashioned."

"That's a great idea. I'll do that."

Mom and I had a good time together on our one-tank-trip. We went through small shops, ate out, and enjoyed an old-fashioned, homemade meal in a cozy Amish-style restaurant. I could not get enough of the homemade mashed potatoes. At the end of the day we topped off our trip with homemade strawberry shortcake ice cream, in a cozy and charming ice-cream parlor that overlooked the rolling farmlands of Amish Country. I was thinking how beautiful my state of Ohio looked to me driving back up 77 North in the spring in the early evening. Everywhere we looked along the highway was lush, green colors that were coming alive after another long winter.

I wanted the Spring break to be over. I had a few days before going back to Tri-C. I wanted to get my pictures of our Amish trip developed to show to Nick and a much-needed haircut.

Spring was in the air, but I was questioning myself if I was putting too much attention on my feelings and getting way ahead of myself. I could tell he was interested, but I could not tell for sure. I had to wait and see.

I woke up the next day getting my books ready with my class schedule in hand. I checked myself out in the mirror and added a little makeup. I never did this before. I always went to school and work makeup free. I headed out the door a little early, so I would be able to stop and visit Nick. Mom stopped me before I reached the door reminding me, "Laurel, remember to be you, and if it is meant it will happen, and if not, there is someone special out there for you somewhere."

"Thanks, Mom," I said walking out the door, but something inside me told me that he just might be the one. I took in a long breath before I walked into his office, and there he was, sitting at his desk.

Nick looked up and saw me and we both smiled widely at each other, and it seemed that we couldn't stop gazing into each other's eyes; I walked over and sat down, and asked Nick, "How was your visit with your sister?"

"I had a good time visiting with her. I really miss her. I wish she wasn't so far away."

He smiled at me and asked, "How was your break? You mentioned that you might be going to Amish Country."

"Yeah, we made it there, and it was great. Mom and I both had a nice time, but Mom is more of a traveler than me. I think she would still love being in the car and drive through each state across America if she could," I said.

"Do you like to travel?" Nick asked.

"Well, yes, but I like to be in my own bed at night. I guess I am not one to travel too much."

Then I reached into my book bag, pulled out my pictures, looked at Nick, and I said, "What about you, do you like to travel?"

"Not too much, I am happy just being at home. I traveled when I was in the Army, and then I went to college in a small Pennsylvania town. That was enough for me. But a little road trip now and then to get away is nice." I was thinking we both have one thing in common; we both are not travelers. I thought to myself, "*What can I say next?*" then I looked down at my pictures.

"Oh, I took some pictures of our trip in Amish Country," I said. Nick looked at the pictures and asked me a few questions. When he handed them back to me, our hands touched and I let my hands stay with his for a brief moment. There was a special moment when we both stopped and looked into each other's eyes.

I had it bad for Nick and I finally understood what it meant to have chemistry between a man and a woman. I thought to myself that if that is what is happening between us, I can live with this feeling for a long time. Then a student came over to his desk pulling us both back to the present moment. I was truly lost in time.

Wow! I liked that feeling. I got up to leave and Nick excused himself and walked me out the door.

Nick looked like he wanted to say something, and I had hoped he would ask me out. I knew what I would say, "Yes, I'd love to," but I waited to see what Nick was about to say. He nervously cleared his throat and finally asked, "When are you coming in to see me for an appointment to work on your paper?"

"Oh," I said trying not to look disappointed, "This coming Thursday."

"Oh, that's good. I'll see you on Thursday," Nick said and turned back walking back into his office. I had a few days to go before our next appointment and I was not sure what to think. Was I too forward? No. I replayed our visit in my head, but I did feel the attraction between us that I knew for sure was real and not imagined. I had to get to work and I needed to get my mind off Nick and into the reality of life and responsibility. I was happy to go to work and be fast on my feet, hoping that I kept my mind busy as well. After a long night passing out the food trays to patients at the hospital, I was tired and looking forward to go home, climb into bed, and rest.

When I walked in the door, Veronica started teasing me. "Laurel, you had a call from someone today."

"Who called?"

"I know it is someone you've been talking about," Veronica said.

"Stop messin, with me. I'm tired. I've had a long day. Who called?"

Veronica had a devilish grin on her face and said, "It may be somebody you would love to have a call from."

"Veronica! You are really aggravating me! Now tell me right now who called."

"No one important," she said, "Just that Nick Salupo guy from Tri-C you have been 'goo-gooing' over for the past few weeks."

"No way! I don't believe you!" I said getting madder that Veronica was getting a rise out of me and teasing me.

"Yes he did. Check for yourself on the caller ID. His phone number is on it." It was funny because we just had the caller ID installed about a week ago and I was still learning how to use it which was quite easy after Veronica explained it to me.

"No, I don't believe you. Nick did not call. Veronica, stop teasing me."

Then Mom spoke up, "Yes, Laurel, he called about an hour ago." I went to look and there it was—Nick Salupo, name and phone number.

"Mom, I'm not sure what to do. Do you think I should call him back?"

"Sure, go ahead. Nick called you first. It's fine to return a call." I put in his number, sat down, and let the phone ring until Nick picked up and said, "Hello."

A smile filled my face because I knew as soon as I heard Nick answer the phone my life would change forever with that simple "Hello."

"Hi, Nick, this is Laurel Wessel. You called earlier?"

"Yes." Together we both talked on the phone for over two hours. I told him that I enjoyed our talk and Nick said he did as well.

Then, I said, "Maybe we can go out for coffee sometime," I had only asked one other man out for coffee, and put it on a piece of paper, and after I did that, I knew I was sorry, knowing he wasn't the one for me. I was a little perplexed and I was feeling a little bit of regret, and wondering if I did the right thing? Was I being too forward? I wondered what was getting into me. I was never like that before. It just spilled out of my mouth, and I couldn't believe I asked Nick out without thinking. I wanted to get to know him better. I am getting bolder with age, I thought. Well, it was already out of my mouth, and I could not take it back now. Nick broke my thought and said, "Thank you for asking. We will see. That sounds nice."

"We will see?" I felt rejected more than ever. I had made a fool out of myself. When I hung up the phone, I did not know what to think.

Mom could see that I was looking a little down as I walked into my bedroom closing the door behind me. I heard a tap on my door, and in walked Mom. Mom sat down onto my bed and said, "Laurel, you were on the phone a long time, and it seemed that you both enjoyed talking to each other."

"Yes, Mom, we had a great conversation."

"Well, then why are you looking so down?"

"Mom, I can't believe it, but I asked Nick out for coffee, and he said "we'll see." I don't know why I asked; it just came out."

"Laurel, maybe Nick is a little nervous too, but I have a feeling he will call you back."

"Really?" I said in a hopeful tone.

"And if not, you are going to be fine. Laurel, you have a lot to offer any man, and I am sure Nick knows that."

"Thanks, Mom." She always had a way to make me feel better, regardless of any situation that I was in, and even if I felt like I made a fool out of myself. The next day, I only had school and I did not have to go into work that night. I was hoping to get onto my bike and enjoy the warmer weather.

I was filling up my water bottle, when the phone rang. I looked on the caller ID, it was the call I had been hoping for. I let it ring three times and took a deep breath before picking it up.

"Hello," I said.

"Hi, Laurel, it is Nick, do you like plays?"

"Yes, I love going to live theater."

"Great! There is a play at the Beck Center in Lakewood about the long suffering fans of the Chicago Cubs. It sounds like it is a good one. Would you like to go with me?"

"Sure, I would love to," I said without hesitation, and gave Nick directions to my home.

"Great, I'll see you this Saturday at seven. See you then."

"I am looking forward to it," I said with a big beaming smile that seemed that it would never fade. Mom walked into the kitchen, and saw that I was grinning like I just won the lottery.

"Why so happy?"

"Guess who called and asked me out?"

"Let me guess, a guy named Nick Salupo," Mom said.

"Yes, we are going to see a play this Saturday," I said thinking about what I was going to wear.

"Laurel, that's great, I am looking forward to meeting Nick."

"You'll love him, Mom. I know it."

Saturday came, and it was a cool, April day. I decided to wear black pants with a soft, white sweater, and I played with my hair until it was just right, and put on a touch of makeup. Looking at the clock it was 6:25 p.m., and my date would be here soon. I went to the front window and looked out, hoping that the rain would hold off until later tonight when I saw Nick pass up my home.

With living on a one-way street, there was a car behind him that was driving way too fast, and I know Nick had missed my address. I stayed in my room, looking at myself one last time in the mirror. I needed a little something to finish off my outfit.

I took out my heart necklace, that had my baby's name engraved on it and put it on, and then I felt ready.

"Nicholas, my sweet baby, you would have loved Nick. I know it," I said out loud to myself.

I saw that Nick pulled up front and parked. I watched while he pulled out a comb and checked himself out in his rearview mirror. He then combed back his hair a few times, before getting out of the car.

Nick had on blue jeans and a light blue button down shirt, and he carried red roses in his hand. While I watched Nick, my heart took a few leaps. I cannot put it into words, but all I wanted to do was run into his strong arms and have him hold me close to him. Mom, walked into my room, and saw that I was starring out the window.

"What is out there that caught your eye Laurel?" Mom said knowing darn well that I had been glued to my window for the last few minutes.

Mom could not resist teasing me and said, "Hurry it up, fella! You got a young lady anxiously waiting on you!" Mom stood next to me and got a good look at Nick.

"Well, he is a nice-looking man, tall, and strong. I can see why you like him."

I let out a nervous laugh, "Yes, Mom, he is." Then there was a knock on the front door. I went to open it. "Come on in," I said. Nick smiled at me and handed me the roses.

"Thank you, red roses are my favorite."

"Laurel, you look nice."

"Thanks, you look nice yourself." Nick followed me into the living room. I introduced him, to my dad and Mom.

Nick shook both of their hands, sat down for a few minutes, and talked to both of my parents. I couldn't believe how well at ease Nick was with Mom and Dad on the first meeting. He seemed right at home. Nick looked over at me and said, "We better get going. Nice to meet you both, Mr. and Mrs. Wessel."

"You can call me Doris," Mom said.

Dad was quiet; he only nodded then said, "Nice to meet you." I could tell that Dad liked the way Nick had handled himself in a polished and respectful manner. He was a little old-school, which we all found to be very refreshing and very comfortable to my parents.

I simply relished the fact that my parents approved of Nick right away. Nick opened all the doors for me and off we went. I had the best date of my life. I felt comfortable and totally at ease—we laughed and talked together with effortlessness about a variety of subjects. We were hitting it off very well and there was no denying that we both had a very strong attraction to each other. I wanted to live this first day, over and over again.

Nick took me home after dinner and he walked me to the front door. "Do you think it is too late to stop in for a visit?" Nick asked.

"No, come on in. My parents stay up late." I did not want the evening to end either.

Nick sat down and talked to both of my parents, and I could tell that both of my parents liked and felt relaxed with him. Nick is a unique person in that he comes from a working-class family, loves the arts, sports, and is well educated. This combination makes him a pretty well-rounded guy, and just a plain, nice, loving man. Mom was one that took in everything around her. She had a good intuition about things of this nature. She was a good judge of people. I could tell by her manner that Mom was thinking, "Finally, Laurel found a nice guy, not like the other ones she had gotten involved with that disappointed her." The evening came to an end and I walked Nick outside, and all of a sudden I could tell that we were both very nervous.

"Now what?" I thought. Am I supposed to kiss him good night? What if I don't kiss him right? What if I kiss him, and we both could not stop each other? Will he get the wrong idea? God knows I wanted to kiss him. This is what makes dating so hard. In the middle of my thinking, I could tell that he was nervous too. All of a sudden, my hand jumped out in front of me and I grabbed his. He shook it nervously and said, "I had a wonderful time tonight." While Nick was holding onto my hand I said, "That makes two of us. I had a great time too." We stood there for a few minutes, locked in that handshake, and dumbfounded, stared into each other's eyes. All time stopped for that instant while we were looking at each other, holding onto each other's hands, and just cruised into nowhere for what seemed like the only place we were supposed to be.

Then Nick gently grasped my hand and placed a soft kiss on the middle of my palm. Nick came to his senses first and said, "How about going to see a movie tomorrow?"

"I'd love too!" I smiled at him.

"Great, I'll call you tomorrow afternoon and we can pick out a movie together."

"Fine, I am looking forward to hearing from you tomorrow, and a movie sounds like fun." I turned and walked back into my house.

Mom walked out of the living room, and said, "Laurel, you both look good together. How did your date go?"

"Mom, it was the best date of my life and we are going to see a movie tomorrow!"

"Well, Nick seemed like a gentleman with good manners. You two seemed very relaxed together."

"Mom, he is the one. I can feel it," I said walking into my room.

"Take it slow, but I have to say I feel good things are going to happen for you two," Mom said.

Somehow I just knew that there was going to be a beautiful relationship between us, and for the first time in my life I was falling in love. I could feel it each time our hands touched each other, and I know Nick felt it too. Love is truly a gift from God. I guess somehow if we can get through the heartaches and busted romances, and put it all on the line one more time, something really special can happen—and it did.

Chapter 35

Proposal

My family adored Nick. To my relief I was able to just be me. What a blessing to be loved without the controls of a self-absorbed, controlling man, like the mistakes I had made before I met Nick. Together there was simply an easy way that we enjoyed our company together and we were moving along in our relationship really well. I had never felt this way for anyone and was falling more and more in love every day. When we were apart, I had Nick on my mind all the time, and truly felt like I was walking down a street in "Happyville" because I knew I would be seeing him soon. I had a special kind of happiness about me, an inner glow that went down to my inner soul. I was learning that love is not a continuous series of drawn-out battles of endless who-is-right-or-wrong struggles, but more of what two people do to bring out the best in each other. I had fallen madly in love with Nick and I relished our time together. Mom knew that I had fallen in love because I talked about Nick all the time.

If I was not talking about Nick, I was walking around thinking about Nick with a smile that filled up my heart. Life seemed a little different to me when I had a partner I could trust and I knew I was safe with. Mom heard me speak highly about Nick all the time and Mom was happy to see my happiness and told me a number of times, "I can tell Nick is a good guy and you both make a great couple."

I agreed with Mom, "We do make a nice looking couple, but Mom do you think he will ask for my hand in marriage?"

Mom had a look like she knew that something was up, but said, "Maybe, it looks that way, and that will be the next step."

"Mom," I said, "do you know anything? Has Nick said anything to you?"

Mom looked down then back up at me and said, "No, Nick has not said anything to me, but I have a good feeling that something great might happen between the two of you."

Every Sunday, Nick and I would go with Mom to church together, and I was extremely happy that Nick took out the time for weekly mass. This helped to add to our growing relationship, and with each new day, I found another reason why I was so deeply in love with him. After mass we would go out for breakfast, and on this particular Sunday I was getting hungry and wanting to fill up my empty stomach with some hot cakes and scrambled eggs.

Nick asked me to stop with him at the side altar where there was a statue of St. Joseph the worker, for a prayer. We both kneeled down and made the sign of the cross. After a few minutes, I started to get up when Nick said, "Laurel, I am not done praying yet."

I looked at him and said, "OK." But I thought to myself, "*What is he praying about anyhow?*"

I wanted to get going, so I can get something to eat. God knows, I get moody when I go without food. I looked back down at Nick who was still kneeling and went back and kneeled down next to him.

Then Nick took my hand, and with his other hand pulled out a tiny box out of his jacket and opened it up—there was a sparkling diamond engagement ring inside! My stomach felt like butterflies were fluttering about inside of it. I looked at the ring, and all I wanted to do was jump right into his arms. I knew what was coming; Nick is getting ready to ask me the "let's get married" question. Nick looked into my eyes and cleared his throat searching for the right words and finally said, "Laurel, I hope to be a good husband to you, as St. Joseph was to Blessed Mary. I promise to love you more with every new day we have together. Will you be my wife?"

I filled up with tears and said, "Yes, I will be your wife."

Nick took my hand and placed the ring on my finger. I could never have asked for a better proposal. Together we both sealed our engagement with a gentle kiss. Happiness took a hold of me, while tears of joy continued to fall from my eyes and this joyous moment still warms my heart. I was running on high, extremely ecstatic emotion, and not anyone or anything could bring me down—so I thought.

Our next stop was to find out where we were to get married. Nick had mentioned maybe his church where he was baptized as a little baby because the church was in the middle of town, and both sides of the family east or west could attend easily. Together we both thought it could be a perfect spot for our wedding day. There was also a small inexpensive hall two blocks from the church, which would have really been convenient for our guests. Nick had called and made an appointment to talk with the priest and we were able to make an appointment only two days after the ring was placed on my finger. Love I thought? What can two people together do, but only bring each other up to greater heights. And the word unity came to my mind.

Life was meant to be shared and we both understood that we were companionship type of people that understood the term, "lifetime commitment." I know I was blessed to have Nick by my side to share our love, and hand in hand Nick and I walked in together, following the priest into his office.

The priest said, "Have a seat." I watched as he moved around to his desk and sat down on an oversized, large, black, leather chair. He acted as though it was his throne and two peasants were before him annoying him. I noticed his face, and he showed no emotion, as he looked up at the two of us. It seemed like his mind was somewhere else. Nick and I held hands and faced the priest sitting across from us. There was a moment of uneasy quietness between us. Then Nick spoke up and said, "Thank you for seeing us. Father, we both are happy to have each other. We both feel blessed." Nick squeezed my hand while he talked. "We would like to be married here."

The Father only looked down on his desk looking over at some papers in front of him. I could tell he seemed to be in a lousy mood. We all have a bad day from time to time and priests are only human. I only hoped he could see that what we had together was a blessing. I looked over his head to the wall and studied the cross of our Lord. He kept his eyes down and turned over a sheet and read the second sheet.

"We have an appointment," I thought and he just kept reading and paying no attention to us. How rude! All this reading should have been done before we got there. I was starting to get mad. He was outright ignoring us like we didn't really matter. Finally, he looked up at us and said in a little raspy voice like he was catching a cold, "How long have you both been dating each other?" I thought maybe that was why he looks to be in a bad mood. He may not be feeling well, and with a heavy work load that today's priests have, I could sort of understand why he was so indifferent to us.

Nick smiled big and said, "Laurel and I had been dating over a year." Father looked back down at his desk and was looking over paperwork again when he said, "Do you both go to weekly mass together?"

"Yes," Nick said, "We both go to weekly mass together."

"Your record shows that you have been through a divorce." He said to Nick. "Yes Father, it was the single most difficult thing I ever had to go through. She left me for another man and we got an annulment."

Nick sat up straight and asked, "Father, can we have another priest preside at the church service?" Nick had known Father O' Donnell for a number of years; he had worked in Cleveland for years doing missionary work and Nick worked with him in the prison ministry. The priest looked annoyed, "Only I will say the mass." Then he added, "Father O'Donnell can sit with the altar boys."

Nick seemed a little put off and said, "Why would it be an issue for Father O'Donnell to preside?"

"Like I said before, only I will say the mass." He looked bent out of shape, had a scowl on his face, and was irritated that Nick wanted an answer. That is when I gave him a look that said—who are you? Some joker on a power trip? And what authority does he hold over us anyway? I could feel myself getting angrier and angrier by the minute when he went back to reading his paperwork.

I was holding onto Nick's hand and I could feel him squeeze my hand in a way to relax me. Father asked, "How old are the two of you."

Nick said, "I am forty nine and Laurel is twenty seven."

Father took a minute, "No, I will not marry you because of your age difference and Nick has already had a failed marriage, a divorce, and an annulment." How rude. How ungodly. Nick was disappointed and in shock and was at a loss for words.

However, I was done with this fool and needed to let him know how ridiculous he really was. I tried to get my wits about me and cool off before I spoke. I calmed down a bit and said, "Excuse me, Father, but you will not marry us because of our age difference and those other foolish reasons? And will you please put your paperwork away? We do have an appointment, don't we?"

He looked back up from his paper looking irritated, and gave one of those looks that said, "How dare you contradict me." I knew at this point he was boiling mad because I questioned and challenged his authority. I just knew it and Nick was holding onto my hand letting me know we were fine. "There is too much of an age difference and Nick was married before and it did not work." Nick spoke up. "Yes, Father, I was married before. However, she left me and would not come back after I tried everything I could to get her to come home. She moved in with another man and would not have anything to do with me. I received a divorce from the state and an annulment from the church. I have a good woman next to me that I want to spend the rest of my life with. Why are you making a problem here when there is no problem?"

Father rolled up his sleeves and said, "Thank you both for coming in, but our meeting is over. Have a good day."

"Father," I said, "I'd like a few words before I call it a good day!"

I looked over at Nick who sat back, quietly, and was not sure what to say, but I could tell Nick was thinking over his next words. Like a good Catholic boy of twelve years of Catholic school, he did not want to upset Father anymore and had respect for his office but not his attitude. Not me, a jerk is a jerk whether they have a religious robe on or not. I could feel my blood pressure going up. I sat up looking at Father in the eyes and said, "If I walked in your office with a man my age, you would marry me right?"

"I might, but you have to understand your age difference is a huge factor here."

"Well, how about the man I dated eight years ago? He was my age and had a good job working construction. However, he drank, smoked dope, and knocked me around. Or how about the medical doctor that I dated, who wanted to control me and my life and tried to force me to give up seeing my family that he felt were beneath him? He was only nine years older than me. Would you marry me then? Let me tell you something Father. Nick and I are blessed to have found each other, and yes we had past relationships that did not work, and we both found a special love between us—one I have never known before. We love each other and you can't take that from us. We will be married somewhere in a church that still honors the love between two people, and does not reject them because of the problems of their past that have already been resolved." The priest looked down at the same old paper again.

I wanted to reach over onto his desk, rip up the papers, and throw them on his face. I kept my cool for Nick's sake. I could not sit back and let this guy push his weight around.

"But you do not understand, your age difference seems to not be an issue now but in your future you may end up being a caregiver to him."

"Yes, Father, Nick is older than me and God may call him to Heaven before me. But you know what, if I have ten years with Nick, they will probably be the best ten years of my life and God only knows who will go first. Besides that, what do you know about relationships anyway? When was the last time you were in one with a woman? Have you experienced the loss of a baby? Or walked away from bad relationships? Have you prayed to God each night that he will send you a good person, one that believes in the Lord, and takes the time out for church every week? No, thank you, but I do not want you to marry us, that is, our day with the Lord's blessing and not a day for your head trips. Father, now you have a good day."

I stormed out of the office and Nick followed closely behind me. Nick embraced me tenderly in the parking lot; whenever he holds me the world always seems to be a better place.

"I'm sorry, Nick and God forgive me for being rude to a man of the cloth, but that felt so good to tell him off."

Together we stood in the parking lot and held each other. Nick did not say a thing. He just gently held me in his arms.

It was just what I needed to calm my angry spirit. Nick pulled me close and said, "Well, there is a fire inside of you that I never saw before, and you, like your mom, have a keen sense for what is right and wrong. And boy was that guy wrong! I like that in you, Laurel. Don't worry; we will get someone else to marry us. I am really disappointed. I have never seen a Father like that. He took me completely by surprise. But that's OK. No one can ruin what we have together."

"Nick, did you see his sour face? Would you really want him presiding over our wedding?"

We both started laughing. "No, I can't. That's gonna be the happiest day of my life and I wouldn't want someone like that guy ruining it."

"All that heated conversation made me hungry. Let's stop for a bite to eat," I said leaning into Nick's strong arms.

"Great," that sounds good. The priest did not stop me from my love of the church or our love for each other. I know that when it comes to men of the cloth that there are just as many good ones as there are bad ones. And none of them will ever stop me from believing in my faith.

"Nick, let's call my priest. He knows me and he is nowhere close to that priest's personality."

So, there we were again, two weeks later, sitting across from another priest trying to get it right. Father McGonegal, gave us a grand Irish smile and said, "How's the good looking couple doing today?" I let out a breath, and smiled. Father asked a few questions and wanted to know what month we would like to get married. Father let us know that we had to attend Pre Cana classes and we would need to go to some counseling classes because of Nick's divorce and annulment. Nick asked, "Can we have Father O'Donnell preside at the wedding as well?"

"Sure, but I will have to be on my best behavior. He is a saint. His work with the homeless and his prison missionary has made him a legend in our town among people of all faiths. I would be honored to have him celebrate the mass with us." Father looked into his appointment book and told us the dates that were open. Together we choose February 8, 1997. Father thanked us, and told us both to have a blessed day.

He also told us how great it is to see a couple growing in faith and believing in marriage. Nick and I looked relieved and stood smiling. "Thank you Father, have a blessed day yourself."

Nick smiled at me and said, "Laurel, February 8, 1997, we will be husband and wife."

I took his hand, "Yes, we will." And then I kissed him.

Nick opened my front door and together we walked in. I called out to Mom, "Guess what Mom? February 8, 1997, is our wedding day."

Mom was beaming while walking out of the kitchen and said, "Oh, I am happy for you both."

"Thanks, Mom, I am blessed to find a good man."

"Yes, you are and Nick is blessed to find a good woman." Mom reached over and touched Nick's hand.

"You are right on that one, Mom. Laurel is everything to me," Nick spoke up.

"Mom, we are both blessed and soon we will be husband and wife." After I said the words out loud, it felt wonderful hearing them. The wedding would be here soon and I wanted to ask Mom a question.

Mom was sitting down putting her hair up in bobby pins, something I saw her do every night.

I walked over to her and sat down next to her.

"Mom," I said, "You know how they usually have only Dads walk the bride down the aisle in church? Well, I would like to have you both walk me down the aisle."

Mom smiled up at me, "I'd love to walk you down that aisle. Is it OK that we both walk you down? I have never seen that done before?"

"Yes," I asked Father and he said, "Sure, it will be nice to see both parents join in on our wedding march down the aisle."

"Well, Laurel with both Dad and I ushering you down the aisle, you won't have any chance at all to try and get away. No runnin down Lorain avenue for you young lady."

"No, Mom, I guess you're right. But I feel like this is the right person everyway and anyway I look at it."

"That's true, Laurel. He's the right guy for you. The two of you are going to have many years of happiness together."

I woke up on February 8, 1997, and looked out the window, and there was a light snow on the ground, and it looked windy.

I dressed in my wedding dress and made sure I covered all the requirements—something borrowed, something blue, something new, and something used. I borrowed a new pair of pantyhose from Mom. I had on a new dress. As for something used, I wore a pair of old earrings. I only needed something blue. I looked into my underwear drawer and I had a pair of blue panties, and I put them on.

Mom walked into my bedroom to check up on me, "Oh, Laurel, you look beautiful."

"Mom, I feel beautiful and ready to become Laurel Salupo." Once I was in church, I waited in the side Lady's room of the church because there was no bridal room. However, at St. Ignatius church in Cleveland, there is one of the longest church aisles a bride could walk down, and the church was huge with long pillars that reached the beautiful decorative ceiling. The weather was not exactly perfect outside; however, the church was lovely and I was anxiously waiting for our "I do." When the time was right, I had to walk outside to the front door. My Dad knocked on the ladies room door, "Laurel, it's time."

"OK, Dad." I smiled over at Mom sitting in the small room with me, "It's time." Once the three of us were outside, the cold air went right through me. Dad said, "Oh boy, it's cold and windy out here."

"Yes it is," I said as the three of us walked swiftly to reach the front door. All of a sudden, the wind went under my wedding gown and blew the gown over my face.

"Laurel, you are showing your underwear," Dad said. I heard a car horn blowing and a man yelled out. "Great legs! Nice underwear!"

Dad and Mom both pulled down my wedding dress and tried to hold it down. By now, my hair was a mess, and I knew my face was red from the cold.

We reached the front of the church and Mom straightened out my dress while I played with my hair. Dad was blowing into his hands to try and warm up.

I looked ahead and saw the wedding party line up, and the music began to play. Mom and Dad took their places on each side of me. Then our turn came, to walk down the aisle together arm in arm. I saw my soon-to-be husband, looking handsome, waiting for me at the altar.

I could see that Nick was filled up with joy that he could not contain. We reached the front of the altar and Mom stepped away while Dad took my hand and placed it into Nick's hands. Together Nick and I in front of God, family, and friends became man and wife. I looked out to see that Mom had cried with tears of joy in her eyes. Mom looked so happy for us; she dropped her head down and said a little prayer for her daughter and new son-in-law. At the end of the wedding ceremony, Father McGonagall looked over to Father O'Donnell and said, "Is it time, Jim?"

"Yes it is," he said. The two Irish priests came to us, face-to-face. Father O'Donnell put his hand on my shoulder, and Father McGonegal, put his hand on Nick's shoulder, and blessed us with the Irish blessing. The two Irish ministers took and their time took turns reciting each line of the blessing to us.

May the road rise up to meet you.

May the wind always be at your back.

May the sun shine warm upon your face,

And rains fall soft upon your fields.

And until we meet again,

May God hold you in the palm of His hand."

Chapter 36

Johnny Cash

Nick and I adapted well to married life and now that we both have each other we both agreed to talk things over, whatever came our way. There was easiness about our marriage, like a pair of comfortable, old shoes. We both realized that what we had together is special, and that we should never discourage each other from growing within our marriage. We both understood early on that we were in this thing together because we understood that we had was, "A Life Time Commitment." As a new couple, Nick and I seemed to be able to read each other's moods and were able to respect one other.

I was content for I only left my mother's home once in my twenty-seven-year-old life and I tried to make rent and other expense living in an apartment. But that only lasted for about three short months. I had to work around the clock to make it and lucky if I could feed myself. When I went back home to live, as a young adult, Mom or Dad never stepped in my way or tried to take away my personal freedom. I had responsibilities to take care of and contributed as best as I could to keep the household running, but having their support helped me make it, and it made life easier for all of us.

My relationship with Mom grew stronger with the passing of time. I found that I reached more for the phone when I had a question or no questions at all. I loved to call Mom and have our "girlie" chats.

I would pick up the phone more than once a day to check up on Mom, or to tell her something humorous I heard or saw. But more than a few times in my early years of marriage, I called Mom and asked her how to make a particular meal.

"Hi, Mom, It's Laurel"

"Hi, Laurel"

"Mom, Can you tell me how you made your vegetable soup?" I sat back and listened to Mom explaining step by step how to make her soup knowing that if I missed a step or forgotten to write something down that was fine. I could call Mom back and she would talk me through the whole process again. Every time we were talking, we would get off the subject, and Mom would tell me funny stories that she had remembered. One of my favorites was the one about the time a drunken husband came home hungry.

"Laurel this is a true story. I think you'll get a kick out of it," and then Mom started telling the story.

"A man came home hungry after drinking in the bar all night, wanting a sandwich to eat. His wife was tired of him coming in late, disturbing her sleep and wanting her to get him something to eat. One night she put her foot down and told him she would no longer make him a sandwich especially after he came home from drinking up the household budget, and told him to make his own dam sandwich." Mom paused a moment, and then chuckled, "Well, he opened up the refrigerator, and pulled out a Tupper Ware container and spread the contents onto his bread and ate his sandwich. The next day he asked his wife what was in the Tupper Ware container. It was pretty good." His wife opened up the refrigerator and saw what he ate, "Well, honey you ate the left over canned dog food."

There were times I dialed Mom's phone number and asked, "Well, Mom what do you think about this?" The good thing with Mom was you could take what she said or leave it. Mom had a way that never seemed to insist she was right; she only told me what she felt and it always came from her heart.

When I saw something disturbing on the news, I called Mom, and we both discussed what we thought on an issue. Or, there were times when there was no reason at all. I would call only to ask, "What are you doing? I was just thinking about you."

Before I know it, our conversation went on over an hour. Mom was the one person that I could turn to for anything, anytime of the day. It could be good or bad, and the two of us talked it over, and after each phone call I always somehow felt better and understood life a little better.

Nick would laugh and say, "Let me guess, you are talking to Mom, tell her Hi." Nick and Mom had grown closer in their relationship as well.

I saw that both Nick and Mom loved to laugh and joke with each other. And I thanked God that my mother was not the type of person that never interfered in our marriage, but supported our love as a husband and wife.

While driving in our car together, every time Nick turned on the radio, and when Mom was with us, he loved to tease me and say, "I am so old that my mother-in-law loves my music." And in a teasing way he would always remind me, "She is my mom too."

Nick understood my need to get Mom's opinion on things. What I appreciated most was, when I called Mom, and asked Mom not to tell anyone, I knew that Mom would keep her word. That made our relationship grow to new levels. These moments were one of the many times that I realized that Mom was my best friend and that Mom only cared and wanted the best for me.

Mom's love to me is like a bouquet of flowers because at each angle one can see a different part to the beauty of the bouquet. Mom was just like that because at every angle and point of her life, Mom poured out and gave endlessly each day, more beauty and love in the little things that she said or did. There are a number of us daughters out here that are like me, in that they feel the same way about their mothers as their best friends.

As women we learn as we grow how much our Moms really mean to us. Now that I am older and understand more, I realize that if we are honest we know that no mother is perfect, but they only do their best.

I watched how Mom handled situations and learned from her. I learned to embrace Mom's love, understood that I needed her in my life, and if it was only a phone call that brought Mom to me when I could not see her in person, I simply loved to just talk to her because it always brought joy to my being. While talking I could feel her love that reached down to the inner most part of my soul, that offered a comfort that no one can give to you, but a Mother's love.

"Hi, Mom," I said into the receiver. I could sense Mom smiling on the other end and she would ask, "What's on your mind?" And with that friendly response, I always felt so fortunate. Also, Mom was always the optimist believing in me and the future.

One of Mom's main pieces of advice was, "Take things that happen in life in stride." Another one of her pearls of wisdom that Mom gave me was turning things over to our Lord daily in prayer. I know that the love between daughters and Mothers is one of God's basic blessings. To take the good and loving moments in life and hold on to them and not dwell on the bad times is our best option.

In today's modern cynical world it is too easy to hold on to the bad. Too many adults complain about their childhood. They often say that their mother never said "I love you" enough, showed more love to my brothers and sisters, and not enough to me, and never hugged or kissed me enough. These are some of the common complaints made by grown people who have unhappy lives.

Too many troubled adults blame their past and their parents for their troubles that they are realistically creating now in their own future. Unfortunately, it is a sad truth that many children have to grow up in a negative bullying domineering household that stifles the growth of children.

On the other hand, I was one of the fortunate ones that, even though we had problems and challenges in our lives, I had a strong supportive Mom to see me through all of the bad times I faced. Therefore, all of the good things I have in my life and who I am are because of my mother. I am a believer that we as adults need to look at what our Mother's tried to do for us when we were younger, and then we will continue to grow in that Mother/Daughter love if we allow it to develop and grow.

One day while on the phone, I could hear in the background that Mom was listening to her Johnny Cash CD, one of Mom's favorite county singers. "I Walked the line," played on. "Well, Mom I can hear that you are listening to Johnny Cash."

"I get my days where I play his music all the time. He is one of my favorites."

"I like to listen to music when I clean the house," I said. "Well, Mom, I better get off the phone. I'll talk to you tomorrow, have a good night," I said.

"You too, Tell, Nick I said hello, and you both have a good night."

"I will."

I hung the phone up and saw Nick reading the paper on the dining room table.

And he asked me, "Laurel, did you say that Mom's was listening to Johnny Cash?"

"Why?"

"No reason, but he is one her favorite country singers right?" Nick asked looking like he was thinking of something. I saw that Nick had the Friday newspaper and was looking it over.

"Oh, yes, Mom gets her days were she plays Johnny Cash while she is cooking and working around the house." I smiled to myself because Mom could not hold a tune if she tried while singing along with the music. What would Johnny Cash think? He'd probably say, "Put a cork in it honey. You're killin my song darlin."

To my surprise a few days later Nick walked into the kitchen and handed me two tickets to the upcoming concert to see Johnny Cash. He kissed me and picked up an apple and started eating it.

"What's this for?" I said in wonder.

"For my two special ladies in my life," Nick said smiling, and I wanted to do something special for your mother."

"Really Nick, Mom will love it." I hugged Nick so hard and said, "I can't wait to tell Mom."

I ran to the phone, picked it up, and dialed Mom's number, "Guess what, Mom? Nick bought us two tickets to see Johnny Cash."

"Wow, you tell my son-in-law he went out of his way. I hope the tickets weren't too expensive. Put, Nick on the phone."

"Nick, Mom wants to talk to you." I said to Nick as he put the apple down on the counter and took the phone.

Nick belted out a Johnny Cash song and sang into the receiver. *"Because you're mine. I walk the line."* I stood next to Nick as he sang Johnny's big hit and Mom's favorite song, to my mother, and I couldn't help to fall even more in love with my husband. Mom asked Nick why only two tickets, and why he was not going.

"Well, Mom, I'll tell you, I wanted to do something for my two favorite ladies. So it's a special girl's night out for the two of you." Nick reached over and pulled me next to him. The day of the concert came and we were both so excited. I parked the car on a side street.

We were way too early getting to the concert, but I was fine with that because it was held at Cain Park, that was an outdoor open concert hall with a stage, and has half of the pavilion covered. The park is breathtaking within itself with its beautiful flowers and plants all around the grounds. I had been there before with Nick on a date to see a play. I know that Mom would love it there sitting in the middle of Cleveland Heights. Anytime Mom got out of the house, it was more than a ride to a new place; it was an outright thrill.

Mom loved taking rides and seeing different areas and became totally engrossed in whatever new place she saw.

We walked in on the side of the park and it started to rain a little. It was a soft light rain. The weather was just right for the early part of summer, without the hot heat and a gentle rain that hit the ground around us; it seemed to glisten in the approaching twilight. Mom opened up the umbrella that was big enough to hold two under it. Nick was right, it was nice for it to be only the two of us together going out enjoying the evening and looking forward to the concert.

All of a sudden, a big black bus pulled in only about ten feet from where we were walking. Mom said, "It might be Johnny Cash's bus."

"It might be, Mom," I said, and we both started waving our arms in the air at the bus, like two teenage girls. And then right by the side window we both saw June Carter. She smiled at both of us and waved back. "Laurel, that was June Carter. She waved at us. Can you believe that?"

"Wow, Mom, she sure did," I said. Together we both picked up our pace and waved back wanting to get a better look. We were like two giddy school girls both star struck.

When Johnny walked out on stage, the audience got up on their feet and cheered. He walked up to the microphone and said, "Hello, I'm Johnny Cash." That is when the audience let loose and roared with applause. I put my hand close to my mouth and yelled out, "Hi, Johnny Cash."

We had the time of our lives listening to Johnny Cash, and Mom was singing along and moving her feet.

That day sitting in Cain Park, Mother and daughter, left a tender moment in time for me. We had a ball, up on our feet, clapping, yelling, and singing in our off-tune voice with our favorite entertainer. What a gift my loving husband gave to us!

"Laurel, I am having such a good time," Mom said to me.

"Me too," I said. While looking at the expression of pure joy in my mother's face, I realized it was a moment in time that would stay with me for a long, long time, and I would cherish it forever.

Chapter 37

Timeless

To watch your parents grow older is never easy and their love seems almost timeless. It's almost like they are always going to be there your whole life and never leave. I realized that their love was more like building an endless bond of love that stays in my heart that will never leave with the passing of time. It seemed that only yesterday my father was up and dressed getting ready to walk out the front door and head off to work, and before Dad went out, a big grin would come over his face and he would say tenderly to Mom, "See you later, Miss America," and they would always give each other a quick peck on the cheek and then he would be on his way to whatever construction job he was on at the time. That was my father, a man of a few words, but his simple loving good-bye, always softened my mother's heart.

My father was an orphan from the early age of three and lived in many different foster homes while growing up. I can only imagine how rough his life had to be with all of that instability he had to endure. But I never heard my father complain about his childhood or offer up many past memories.

I however, asked my dad more than a few times, "Dad, how was your life growing up as a child?"

"Fine, I was taken care of," Dad would always answer with a few words and at times you could feel that he rather have it quiet and have no conversation at all.

"Dad, did you have a favorite place or home that you stayed in as a kid?"

I wanted to know more and I would push my dad a little by keeping questions coming his way, and he did his best to get me to stop asking questions by giving me short direct answers.

"Why all the questions? My childhood was nothing special or different from anybody else." Dad would not give me anymore than that as an answer and he turned away from the questions by picking up the newspaper and turning me out.

The years and time passed by and Dad had grown older, but he still worked around the house and yard and was always finding work to do. I always admired my father's work. No matter how large or small the task was, Dad would look it over and picked out the right tools and went to work on it and did his best to complete each project properly. He never cut corners or did anything half way. Dad's motto for work was this, "Do the job right the first time around, and you save money and time later." Dad was a sensible man and one can see that he took great pride in his work and it showed in every project he completed.

When Nick and I were first married, there were repairs that needed to be done with buying an older home, and with having dogs we wanted to fence the backyard. I went to my brother Billy and asked him for his help on the job. Sure enough Dad found out. Hard work was his passion, and working with his hands brought him great joy.

So when the fence project started, my father was working next to Billy and Nick, digging and pouring cement mix into the holes for the fence posts. Even with his age, Dad wanted to be a part of the work and there was no stopping him; he worked with the pain of an ailing body.

While growing up and when times were hard on the family, Dad and I worked together on a few side jobs to make ends meet by painting homes. I always had paint all over me, while Dad remained paint free. I don't know how he did it, but there was never a drop of paint on him. Dad would stop his work and come over to check on me and my work regularly. He would take his cap off and shake his head in disapproval.

He would then take my paint brush and would clean it off for the umpteenth time and would show me "the right way" to paint. I watched my father explain to me while he moved his steady hand and the brush over the wood of an old home. "Laurel, make nice and even strokes."

"OK, Dad, I got it," I would sigh and hope he would just leave me alone already. I took my brush, while Dad went back to his side of the house working.

Yes, I can say I can paint—that's about it when it comes to fixing things and my painting had improved, but in the end I still had paint all over myself, and as for my father, not a drop was on him.

Dad had a way about him that made work look effortless.

He somehow seemed to float through each project with the most natural ease I had ever seen.

What I most remember was his quiet love for my mother. When there was an argument between my parents, Dad would get up, put his hat on, and take a walk. He went to the corner bar for a beer and talked sports and politics with his softball buddies. Dad was a man that liked his beer after work and on the weekends. It only took a couple of cold Stroh's and Dad would open up and laugh telling jokes with a comfortable grin on his face.

However, back when I was fifteen years old, the after work beers caught up with Dad as he was showing symptoms that his liver was going bad.

Dad's stomach had swollen up and he went to Mom and said, "Looks like I am pregnant. How can that be?" I watched in wonder and thought how can his stomach get so big overnight? With my father always on the slim side, it worried me and a helpless sense of dread filled my heart.

"You need to go to the doctor," Mom told him. "You need to get checked. I'll call and make an appointment."

"OK, I'll go see what's going on with my stomach," Holding on to his stomach Dad said, "I better get checked out." However, like most men of his time he wasn't one to go to the doctor's office very often. He believed that no matter what he had it would pass and he would be better in a little while. But this time it was different, Dad knew there was something wrong. He went to the hospital to be checked out, and the news of his test was in. Dad was told that he had cirrhosis of the liver and that if he did not stop drinking he would die in six months.

Six months! Life would come to an end for my father if he did not change his lifestyle. My father listened to what the doctor had said, and stopped drinking, smoking, and gambling.

He was never much with the gambling. It was more or less five bucks on a football game, and a trip to see the horse races once or twice a year.

So I guess that part was easy to let go. But the alcohol—that was the hard part. It was a true battle for him, but somehow he pulled through it. I'm sure the grace from Mom's endless prayers helped get through this tough time.

I remember when I was a young teenage girl around thirteen years old, Dad and I took a bus ride together to go and watch the horse racing. I was happy to have the time alone with my father. That was the first time we rode the bus together, and I remember feeling special setting next to him even if we did not talk. When we arrived at the track, Dad handed me a racing form and said, "Pick a horse."

I looked over the names not really knowing who to pick or the odds. I was so worried, "What if I picked the wrong horse and we lose our money?" I said to my father. "Don't worry about it. Just pick out a horse." Dad grinned at me.

"OK, I pointed my finger to number three, *On to work she goes*," I said smiling back at my father. It was my favorite number and that name sat next to the list of horses, so I went with it.

I always liked that number and I crossed my fingers. Now I only wished it would come in and be a winner. Dad went up to the window and put a three-dollar bet on the horse I picked out. Together we went as close as we could and watched as the horses were lining up at the gate. I held my hands over my eyes and could not bear to look when the horses shot out of the gate. "Please, please let her be the winner," I said half watching with my hands over my eyes, but peeking from time to time when they rounded the corner of the race track.

"Keep going your almost there," I heard my dad yell out.

I moved my hands away from my eyes to see that number three was moving in closer and passed three horses around the bend.

I started yelling "Go! Go! Number three." I started jumping up and down and hit Dad on the back.

"I think she is going to win!" I screamed.

To my surprise, my horse did win and we won thirty dollars. I could not stop myself from jumping up and down and turned to my father, "Wow, Dad we won! Let's keep on betting. Maybe, we will get rich." A look of worried concern came over my dad's face, and he grabbed onto my hands and said, "We are leaving."

"Why Dad? Maybe we can pick out more horses and win more money. Look how easy that was."

"That's why—I should have never brought you here with me. Gambling is no good! And you never win money, you only lose in the long run, and you never get rich here."

Dad said to me in a stern voice.

"All right Dad," I said sadly following behind him as we quickly walked out of the race track.

As an adult, I understand now that Dad did not want me to get the gambling itch. I could tell that he silently regretted bringing me to the track and was beating himself up for taking me to the racetrack in the first place. However, I took the whole experience as a great way to bond with Dad. And of course the thrill of watching those beautiful animals gallop around the track was a thrill

I'll never forget. Dad was a sensible man and took care of the family first. For my father it was a social thing, to sit with the guys and have a beer or go with his construction buddies and watch the ponies run once in a while.

When I look back at that time, I wondered if my father could go without a drink for a day. Drinking beer was a big part of his life. *"Could my father make it?"* I thought this over and was very worried because I did not want my dad to die.

I knew my fear that I could lose my father when I needed him the most, and Mom was worried too. It was a time of stress, to think we could lose Dad in six months and that number always bothered me. Do doctors really know when your life is going to end? I only prayed that they were wrong, or that my father would listen to what the doctors told him.

To my family's relief, Dad took full responsibility for his health, and listened to the doctor's words and stopped drinking, and smoking cold turkey.

We as a family witnessed Dad's hand shaking and mood swings, and it was hard on the family to live with him during that time. But I also witnessed a personal strength that I never saw before in my father. He was driven to improve his health and live.

He did not want to die, he wanted to live, and be with his family. Dad turned to vitamins and health foods. Dad changed his life and his health improved; his doctors were pleased with his new outlook and how his body made vast improvements.

While many alcoholics turn to AA, my father chose his sobriety on his own terms. I often wondered, was my dad an alcoholic? Does he need to drink? The answers to those questions were difficult to face. There were days I could say, "Yes, he was," and other days I would say, "No, he was not." It could have been in denial on my part because of the love I had for my father. He knew he had a wife and children at home to tend to; so he took the challenge on his own will power and stopped drinking all together.

It might have been better for him to have an AA group, for the support. But my father by nature was more of a quiet man; he was not one for groups or to stand up and tell everyone his private affairs, or how long he has gone without a drink. He took all this upon himself and he made it work for him. I am forever thankful that my father chose to live and not continue drinking. Our heavenly father granted my dad twenty more years of good heath while the doctors gave him only a half a year if he did not stop the drinking. Life is worth the fight, and Dad was in it to live.

"Well, I have to stop drinking, it's no big thing," I heard my dad say to Mom. Mom also helped with his diet and took steps to cooking more nutritious meals, and they both went to reading labels on store bought foods. That was a first. I had never seen that happen before. It used to be that if it looked good, or the price was right, it went into our shopping cart. Now there was a change happing in the family. Dad also researched the benefits of herbal teas, vitamins, and mineral supplements to repair his body. Dad had books all about different herbals and how they benefit your heath. I watched him reading these books and mixing up different herbals into a tea holder, for a cup of tea.

When Dad was younger he was a tall strong man with thick broad shoulders, and rough calloused working man hands. There was this strength in my father that as an adult I wanted it to remain, and not leave my father with a fragile body. It was sad to see Mother Nature catch up to him and we watched him age and his strong body was broken down by Father Time. Dad's health started to decline and he had to return to the hospital where he had an obstruction in his lower intestines.

My two immediate siblings, Billy and Veronica, and I were around his bed a few days before he had to go into surgery. The TV was on and we were all watching the Cleveland Indians' baseball game. Dad turned to Billy and us when Mom stepped out of his room to go use the bathroom down the hall and said, "I need to talk to the three of you, I am having surgery, and not sure if I'll make it. The house is older and needs a lot of work. So Billy you are going to have to keep it up on your own. All of you are going to have to check up on your mother to make sure she has what she needs."

Billy leaned over in the chair and said, "Dad, don't worry, you will be fine. I will take care of the house and look in on Mom no matter what happens."

Dad only nodded. There was a moment of a strange and frightening feeling that passed right though me. I held back from crying. Then we all spoke up and told Dad not to worry about Mom, and he will be just fine. I kept thinking over my father's request and realized that he knew that his time is coming to end. I could see it in his words and expressions that he was worried about Mom. Do we know when our time is up? Or only God knows? I think it's a little of both and no one can hide from their time to leave this earth. Mom and I were sitting next to Dad's bedside the night before he was to have major surgery. I could tell he was in pain and his body was weakening because of the illness that was overwhelming him. I admired my dad for a lot of reasons. As I look back, I remember how upset he was when his roommate was in for a routine procedure and was moaning in pain so that everyone could hear. Dad rolled his eyes and stared up at the ceiling in disapproval. My father could tell I was worried about him and he looked at me and said, "Laurel, don't worry this operation is no big thing and if it is my time, then it's no big thing, it's my time."

"No big thing. That's what you always say Dad." I looked at him and wanted to talk more but I knew he wasn't much of a talker, so I just let him rest.

We all sat back and were quite, and I could see that Mom looked as worried as me. That was Dad's famous saying "It's no big thing." No matter what was going on, to Dad in his life he seemed to handle any impossible situation with a calm unassuming quiet dignity. Dad was always composed and clearheaded about everything. His heart was good and loving, and Dad seemed somehow at peace that he understood his time was coming to an end. I only prayed that God would give him his health and more days on earth with us.

After he came out of the surgery, things had only gotten worse. He remained in the ICU, and had slipped in and out of a comma. I remember just before we had to make the decision to take Dad off his life support he briefly came out of the comma. We all knew that Dad's wishes were not to live on machines. "Let me die than live like that," Dad would always say. When he momentarily came out of his comma, Dad's eyes searched the room for his wife. Somehow Mom, even though her back was to Dad because she was staring out of the window watching the sunset, sensed Dad needed her, and came over to Dad's bedside. There were no words exchanged, but we all could feel the silent conversation of appreciation they had for each other.

All of a sudden, those times of bickering and arguing over what seemed now trivial nonsense that married couples go through disappeared. With a loving look, they both gazed into each other's eyes and spoke those unspoken words of kindness and appreciation to each other. "Thanks for the years of taking care of me. Thanks for the birthday cakes, Christmas dinners, Easter hams, Thanksgiving turkeys, all of our beautiful children, and especially that peck on the cheek you gave me when I left for work in the morning. Thanks for being my Miss America." I watched in wonder while this was happening between my parents and knew that love is a timeless gift. And right before our eyes Dad closed his eyes again for the last time. Dad had suffered for days while waiting for the good Lord to take him home; it's a suffering that life and death have to work out together in their own time.

My father was a quiet man who endured many hardships in his life and still found a way to be a loving and caring father and husband. He is still remembered fondly to this day for his fine example he set for us, his responsible ways, and his caring loving nature for all of us. And Dad's famous words of wisdom, "It's no big thing," have helped me throughout my life to keep a realistic perspective on all of life's challenges.

Chapter 38

Devotion

Why do we wish time away, or cannot wait until an event takes place? I would often say to myself, "I can't wait to be finished with school. I can't wait to find that good paying job that I love to go to every morning. I can't wait to be married." We count down the days and events, and wish they were here already, and not wanting to wait until they naturally evolve in time and do get here. I wanted desperately to turn twenty one years old, and now time is moving cruelly fast and I wish for time to slow down and be kind. Time works in its own natural ways. I have been guilty of wanting it all right now. "Be patient," Mom would remind me. I planed and mapped out my life in the hopes that all would turn out just so, in a smooth uneventful order that would have no major mishaps. Well, I guess I was a dreamer with endless optimism. However, life is not that easy and I have found out that I can get myself into a tail-spin from being worried about this or that and as a result of all the stress I end up not sleeping or eating well. And for what?

Did my days of worrying and fretting over things I had no control over ever put me on the right path? Never! It only lay heavily on my heart and I got completely stressed out. I hated getting all emotionally and psychologically stressed, and when I did, that is when Mom would come to the rescue with her kind words of wisdom.

"Laurel, give it to God."

When I heard Mom soothingly and objectively talking things over with me, I could feel myself calming down and becoming more objective about my complications and feel myself relaxing.

"And remember turn all your worrying over to our Lord and move on. You insult the Lord when you start worrying about it again."

"It easier said than done," I will often remind Mom.

"Laurel, life is a long journey and along the way, we experience little glimpses of both heaven and hell. All we can do is try to help each other through the bad times and make sure we enjoy the good times." I know that Mom loved me, and truly wanted me to live, laugh, and enjoy life. After each talk I sometimes replayed Mom's words in my head, and it was like she was talking to me and guiding me through another difficult time.

The years and poor health are catching up on my mother and I find that I am worrying for Mom. But to be honest, my biggest dread is what will I do without Mom in my life? Mom's words of comfort, the phone calls, our shopping trips, and our road trips were always special. It's not easy to replace a good friend like that. I need my mother, and truly had her there for the most painful times in my life.

I wanted my mom and myself to have more time to enjoy what life had to offer, and maybe a little more pleasant moments together. I stopped myself and realized that life, love, and family was never easy, but without them, the true essence of life is lost.

I know that my relationship with my mother is a gift that will sustain me because my mother's love will not stop when the heavens choose to call Mom home; it will continue to grow in my heart each new day. What we had together will not die and be lost forever. I have realized that I am a reflection of her, with a great deal of her characteristics and values.

Although we were two separate and different people, in the end I found out that I was turning into a woman a lot like my mother. Many moms are custom to putting their needs last to their children's and my mother is one of them. The very day Mom received the news that she had Multiple Myeloma, a terminal blood cancer, she knew that she was not feeling well, but fought through it. Because she had high blood pressure, and was diabetic, her health issues were even more complicated. Mom did not feel sorry for herself; she turned the diagnosis into a stepping stone of life and made sure that it got her where she needed to be closer to her family.

Mom with her bright green eyes still shining, in spite of the medicines and cancer treatments, somehow she knew and believed that, "God is not done with me yet." Mom stayed positive through the pain while I cried my eyes out watching her bravely work through her suffering. It was in the fall of 2006, when Mom let the words that the doctor said, sink in a little, but it was not too long before Mom picked herself up and went on living under extremely difficult circumstances. I wanted to know everything that the doctors had told my mother. While Mom answered a few questions about her condition and what the doctors were doing about her illness, she would always change the subject to Christmas.

"Laurel, Marc's still has tea towels two for ninety nine cents. Maybe we can go out sometime and pick up a few. I need some more for Christmas."

"Sure, Mom. That sounds like fun," I said. But this seemed a little odd to me, that Mom would talk about tea towels after being diagnosed with cancer. But that was Mom!

"Are you really up for a ride to Marc's today?" I asked.

"Why not? Let's go," my mother answered in a bright optimistic tone. But I wished I could stop or change the sad news that she just heard about how bad her health really was. However, at the same time I was thinking maybe she needed to rest. My mother was thinking about Christmas on the very day she got word she was ill with cancer and may not recover. So, naturally I was very nervous about taking her shopping. I had visions of her collapsing in the store and the paramedics taking her back to the hospital. Fear really had its grip on me at that time.

"Mom, are you sure you are up for a ride to Marc's today?"

"Yes, I feel fine; let's go," Mom said impatiently. Mom's love of Christmas lasted all year.

It was her favorite time of the year. Mom would start shopping for her family in January and packed things away until December first.

Every year on this date is when all of the removal of all the boxes of all the gifts, from the attic were hauled downstairs and she reexamined and reminisced on whom she had bought each gift for. Mom would pull everything out and make a pile for each family member.

If one pile looked to have less, Mom would go out and find something at a secondhand shop, or K-mart and fill up the smaller pile. Mom put her heart into gift giving and tried to buy what she thought the family could use. So, if someone liked cats, Mom would find a coffee cup with a cat on it. Mom, being positive during that time in her life, helped me to stop worrying about her illness, and enjoy our time together. Mom realized that life is short; so she tried to live out the days that God had given to her as a gift. Mom and I had grown even closer together. Our love and our understanding for each other, over the years, evolved somehow that we understood each other's deepest feelings.

What I understood most of all was Mom's heart for giving; it brought her the most joy of all; seeing her happy put me at peace. Mom, like so many mothers out there when they go shopping, reach for the shopping cart and fill it up with love—love for a favorite meal or a puzzle for a grandchild that loved to build things or peanuts in the shell for a favorite son-in-law. Together, walking side by side with my mother in Marc's, I observed Mom's movements. She was looking down at her feet at each step that had slowed down quite a bit from a time when we both marched along these aisles some time back. Her movements were hesitant and labored. At this point even the slightest motion was an overpowering effort. It took a lot to simply get down the aisles. But Mom bravely trudged on because after all, it was Christmas and a "girl's gotta shop."

I noticed that Mom's hair was more gray and a different texture. It had lost its sheen from all the medications. I could see her weight loss and wished that I could share some of my extra weight with her. All the pain that comes with the tiring older years, and being bent over that cart hurt me to watch her bravely suffering in her pain. But her fragile hands were determined to hold onto the shopping cart and to keep filing it up with gifts for others.

I stopped and closed my eyes and was thankful that I had a mother with me in one of our favorite shopping stores. Mom's spirits were bright as I watched her face soften around her eyes whenever she found an item that she thought someone on her gift list would like. Mom had seen something in the aisles of merchandise at Marc's. She moved the shopping cart over and came to a stop picking up something and turning it over and then looked up at me.

"Do you think Veronica would like this beach towel? It's green and that is her favorite color."

A smile filled my face, "Mom, Veronica would love it." Mom placed it into her shopping cart and she continued to walk down the aisles looking for another item, for the next person on her endless shopping list.

The only person who had a Christmas gift list longer than Mom was Saint Nicholas himself. Mom stopped the shopping cart and walked over to the tools, "Laurel, can Billy use this hammer or do you think he has enough?

I laughed out loud. "Mom, with the way Billy works I'm sure he can use another hammer. Mom, you have gone out of your way by getting all these gifts for all of the people on your ever-growing Christmas gift list. What do you want?" I asked Mom.

Mom looked at me thinking over her words and said, "What do I want? That's easy, but you won't find what I want in any department store."

"I don't understand Mom? What do you really want for Christmas?"

"Well, Laurel, if Santa could bring me love, peace, and understanding for all of my children, it would be the best Christmas ever."

"Well, we might have a hard time finding all that in Marc's. We might have to go see Dr. Phil and Oprah for that one. But then again knowing my brothers and sisters we best go on the Jerry Springer show," I said teasingly.

We were a typical large blended family. We had arguments, misunderstandings and our share of love and support. Mom bumped me with the shopping card in a playful manner, "Laurel, you know that I mean."

"Yes, I do, Mom." For me when Mom's days came to an end and God called Mom home, I believed our good Lord would send Mom off from this world with all the joys of life. All of Mom's endless giving of herself, her love, her understanding, and endless worry for her children, hoping for the best for each of us, was something that she gave freely to all of her children and never ever expected anything in return. I believed that all of her children would be at a greater understanding because Mom's love was always there throughout all of our lives, even when we could not see clearly to appreciate it. While I was thinking these thoughts in my head, a little girl around eight years old, who was in front of us at the end of the aisle, asked her mother, "Mommy, can I please get this pink soft pillow for my room, please Mommy?"

"OK, you can get the pillow, but nothing else because I have to make sure I have all the groceries we need for the house."

"Thanks, Mommy."

I watched as the little girl put the pillow into the shopping cart and off the two off them went on shopping. I was happy and sad all at the same time. I was happy to see a daughter/mom relationship work, and it also reminded me of Mom and me when I was seven years old and Mom first started to take me on shopping trips. It was special. This shopping trip was even more special because I knew deep down inside that my time with Mom was coming to a close. This made me a little sad. But I knew I would have all these wonderful memories of that special closeness that Mom and I were blessed with, that would last me a lifetime.

It comforted me to know that my heart would warm up every time a memory of our shopping cart being filled with gifts and items I knew Mom could not afford on her meager social security pension, as we moved down the isles of grocery stores, secondhand stores, and discount department stores together, filling that shopping cart with love.

Together with my mother we went on to the produce lines and Mom said, "What a great buy on cantaloupe!"

"It sure is," I said and reached for a nice round ripe cantaloupe and placed it into the shopping cart. We love our Marc's like most folks in Northeastern Ohio because of the closeouts and the variety of brands available.

No shopping trip with Mom and I was complete without a meal out.

"Mom, are you up for going out to eat after we are finished with our shopping?"

"Sure, that sounds good. I'm getting really hungry."

I was grateful that Mom still had somewhat of an appetite even though it had declined a bit. A good meal, like so many other small seemingly insignificant moments, are what made our time together so special. That day may have started out rather gloomy when we heard the grim news of Mom's diagnosis, but she did not let it stop her from enjoying life and what it had to offer in her final days. Like so many other days we had shared in the past together, this one seemed somehow not so ordinary, but an event that played out as mother and a daughter together in a place we both loved to shop. We were just sharing and enjoying each other's closeness.

There was only the worry of time and how much time I had left with my mother. I whispered to myself and raised my eyes to the heavens and said, "Dear God, slow down the clocks and watches of the world, slow down the calendars, slow down Big Ben, please slow down Father Time." In Mom's final days, I prayed that I would be blessed with more time, and to this day I cherish those last days more than ever.

Chapter 39

The Reading

To watch Mom's health decline broke my heart wide open with different emotions that flooded my whole being. There were days I cried my eyes out until laughter from a happy memory that we shared together would take hold of me filling the room. It's funny how life and small moments can bring you to both laughter and tears at the same moment. I tried hard to get a hold of myself for a visit with my mother. She had been back in the hospital and I had finished the last few chapters of our book that is a tribute to her. I was anxious to read them to her because she not only knew about each chapter, Mom was hands on with this project and together we talked over each and every episode.

This project pulled us together as we remembered we laughed and cried, over the many events that helped to shape our lives and bond us together. While working on the stories, what I discovered and loved most was how it helped me find peace with my mother's failing health and a better understanding that life is truly a gift and we must utilize every moment we have with our loved ones while they are with us.

I looked at my face in the mirror and I looked a mess from crying until my head was pounding and seemed like it would not stop hurting. I was relieved that Nick was at work because he would suffer knowing I was suffering and he could not help me with my grief. I truly needed a good bawling to let out the pain.

You know the kind when you take air into your lungs, only to hear unrecognizable sounds that you never heard before come out of your soul. I sat on the bathroom floor crying when my two dogs, both slowly walked into our small bathroom, seeing me acting this way, and they tried to comfort me by putting their fuzzy Lab noses onto my lap. I got off the floor, feeling a little better just by crying and having both my Labs with me showing their faithful concern and love for me. The last chapters sat in my small office, waiting for me to read them to Mom. She had been asking how they were going, and I had been putting them aside not really wanting to read them, but today was the day to share them with her. These chapters were only tiny glimpses of our life and my love for my mom.

I only wished that I could stop what was soon to fall upon my mother and us. My two Labs were following me around the house and both seemed to offer sympathetic looks when I started to fill up again with tears. I told myself that was more than enough, and I needed to calm myself down and pull it together. I was truly aware and very grateful for what we had together as a mom and daughter, and that it was very special. I am proud to say she was my best friend. I realized life and time moves so swiftly, and I wished I had the power to stop time for a moment and for just one day sit with Mom again with her health restored and talk and maybe do a little shopping at one of our secondhand shops, but I already knew the day I would truly pick; Christmas Day—the day Mom looked forward to all year long. She had the true meaning of Christmas in her heart with her giving and sharing. Mom was the only person I knew that did Christmas shopping twelve months a year.

Her heart was all about giving every day, not just Christmas. What I believe and love the most about Mom was her unselfish and unconditional love that she gave freely, not caring if she was loved back or not, no matter what the time of day or night it was, or what a person's needs were, or how many times they hurt or disappointed her, she was there for all of us. Mom was just there to help and offer her love to all regardless of the circumstances or situation, and at times with the endless pain in her heart, knowing that one of her children were hurting.

It was a lovely day outside, even though it was a little humid. I went to the window to look out, and right under my feet were my dogs. I said the magic words. "Let's take a walk." With those words both Dolly and Cleo ran around in circles and barked frantically. Together we headed for the leashes hung on the basement door and ran out the backdoor. We took to the sidewalk and it was exactly what I needed to help change the sadness that had a hold on me. With both of my arms being pulled out of their sockets, they both came to an abrupt stop. I watched my dogs smell the fire hydrant to see which critter dared to take a bathroom break in front of our home. Even though it was only mid-morning, it was going to be a hot summer June day.

I looked up at the sky and my eyes hurt from looking right at the blazing sun. I felt perspiration on my forehead, and I already felt hot and wanted to turn back home and into the cool air-conditioned rooms waiting inside for us. That was not going to happen; with my dogs pulling me ahead we managed a short walk around the block.

"Well, Dolly and Cleo, we need to head back home," I said to my pups that had slowed down a bit from pulling me in a fast walking pace with their tongues hanging out and them panting fiercely. Walking into my home, I filled up the water bowl with water and looked at the clock. Time seemed to be getting away from me. I needed to shower and dress and I really needed to see my mother; I wanted to be near her and sit by her side but it was hard to see her this way lying in bed in pain.

I hated that my mom was back in the hospital and I felt a deep down helplessness on how to help her. Luckily, I found a parking space on a side street and walked to the hospital doors. I found the courage to get to her room and pulled up a chair next to her bed. I held my last few chapters in my hands and sat down next to Mom's bedside. I had a sad feeling, a lost feeling, and then a fear sank in and started to fill my mind. What can I do now with my grief? How could I ever manage the unbearable sorrow I was doomed to soon face?

I was scared knowing that soon the good Lord will need my mother back home with him. I guess that's the way life is. Unfortunately, we only spend a short time with the ones we love until their life ends here and they live on in the heavens. I felt helpless on how to help Mom. I wished there was some way I could take away her cancer, heart complications, and diabetes. I wish I could do something, anything, to help her. But that is the hardest part of it all. I could not do anything to help, but only sit next to her bedside and try to comfort her in her final days.

I realized while I sat next to my mom that she looked more beautiful to me with her green Irish eyes shining; however, her body was broken down and weak from her ailments to the point that she looked like a small child unable to move from her bed. The pain had a fierce grip on her and I could see that when I looked deeper into her patient eyes.

"Do you want anything for the pain, Mom? I can get the nurse," I said as I was getting out of the chair.

"No, Laurel, sit down, I am fine."

"Mom, how do you feel today?" I asked pulling up her cover around her ailing and frail body.

"Laurel, things could be a lot worse. I am feeling a little better today."

"Mom, I am sorry to see that you have to go through all this pain."

"We all will have a cross to carry one day, but I had a blessed life and God can't hold a good woman down," Mom said with soft laughter.

I laughed along with her and held back from crying. "Well, Mom, I am different from you on that one, you know that when I am sick, you know I make everyone around me miserable."

"Laurel, you are not that bad when you are sick."

I tried my best to smile at her and said, "Mom, you are too kind." Mom kept up a positive outlook to life each new day because she knew and understood that life is a precious gift with unfolding daily blessings. The nurse walked in to check on Mom's blood pressure and took her temperature. I moved away to let the nurse in. Mom spoke up and introduced me, "That is my daughter, Laurel."

I smiled and said "Hi."

"My daughter is writing a book about our lives together and she is getting ready to read the last few chapters to me."

The nurse looked at me and smiled and without hesitation said, "That's great! Every Mom and Daughter I know would love to have what you two have together. Do you have a title yet for the book?"

"Yes, I said, '*A Shopping Cart Filled with Love.*'"

"I love to read," the nurse said. "I'll look out for it when it is out. When do you hope to get it published?"

"In time. I am not putting a time limit on this project."

The nurse walked over to Mom's medical chart and wrote in it. She looked back at Mom and said, "Miss Wessel, I wished I had more patients like you. You make my job so easy."

"Well, your job does not look easy to me and I am a believer one needs to cooperate if things are going to get done."

The nurse walked out. I noticed Mom's skin color. She looked so pale and tired and she kept losing more weight each day. She looked half the woman she was a month ago. I took a deep breath to calm myself down and to try and hold back my grief. I did not want to cry in front of my mother, but knew if I did that would be fine, we both would cry together.

"Laurel, I am ready to hear what you have written." I reached for my bag and pulled out the chapters and sat back pushing my back straight into the chair.

I held the chapters in my hand and began reading out loud to my mother. That moment in time I will always hold dear to my heart; I got through the stories without breaking down into an emotional state. When I looked up at my mom, she had a tear that rolled down her cheek, followed by a soft warm smile. That is when a smile filled my face.

"Well, Mom, what do you think?"

"I loved it; I can't wait to read it in print, but really, Laurel, you don't have to publish a book about me. I'm a little self-conscious about this, and as I have been listening, I think you are giving me little too much credit. After all, your dad and your brothers and sisters too really helped to hold everything together in our bad times."

That was just like Mom, not wanting to take credit for all that she had done, and being modest to the very end.

"Mom, there really can be never enough pages or enough books to really tell how much you have done for everybody."

I had Mom's stamp of approval, and that is when I knew I wanted to share my mother's dear soul with others. At that moment I knew that there are other women out there like myself that loved their mothers and were proud to call them their best friends.

I looked into her face and saw the past years that we had together—the good times and bad. What I also saw was my mom lying sick in her bed. I saw a woman, like so many others, who were heroes in their own right, but, when they would be walking down a busy city street, no one may even take a second look at them. Right then I reaffirmed what I knew all along, what a special woman she really was.

She was like so many mothers who have passed on unnoticed for their untiring love, commitment, devotion, and unselfish care that they gave to their loved ones. My mom; My life; my friend always. I placed the chapters down on the chair and took a few steps around her room. Her roommate was released this morning. I was pleased to have time alone, and I was also thinking what I could do for my mother who was in need. Mom broke my train of thought and asked, "Laurel, do you mind helping me take out my bobby pins. I feel better when the doctor comes in if my hair is combed out." I got up standing over my mother. Her head was filled up with bobby pins and I started taking them out putting them into her dish that she always had them in. Mom reached up to help with the pins. I could see that it was hard for her to even raise her hands up to her head. These once strong hands that picked me up every time I fell, emotionally and physically, were now so frail and had diminished physical strength.

"No, Mom relax I'll get them." Mom laid her weak hands and arms back down onto the bed. I could see that she kept her eyes closed.

I was careful taking each one out of her hair. I began to comb out her hair when Mom said, "It always feels better when someone is doing your hair."

"Yes, Mom it sure dose feel nice. I like it too when someone is fixing my hair."

"Now I'll look pretty when the doctor comes in to see me."

"You do look pretty, Mom."

"For a sick old lady, I guess I'm not lookin too bad," Mom said with a playful smile.

"Mom, you can close your eyes and rest, I do not mind," I said.

"Do you want the TV on? It does not brother me if it's on."

"No, Mom I am fine. You look tired, you rest and I'll be right here. I brought a book with me to read."

Mom went to sleep and I sat next to her watching her sleep.

I did not read my book. I was comforted by simply being near her. I only watched her sleep and I prayed for her.

The next day I picked up Mom from the hospital because there was not much more they could do to help her.

Mom walked into our home and said almost relieved, "I am happy to be back at home and I hope no more hospital stays."

"Mom, I hope so too."

She looked smaller and very weak as she walked though her home and into the kitchen and drank a glass of water. It broke my heart to see how fast her health was declining and that the illnesses were taking control over her older body, but not her spirit for life. I helped Mom get settled back into her living room while she looked over her mail that had piled up over her stay at the hospital.

"Mom, do you want an Ensure?"

"Sounds good to me," Mom said in a tired, weary voice. I walked through the house and all the memories from our past came flooding back to me. It seemed like each room held their own stories of my mother. I thought about how when she was younger and was moving around the house with such graceful ease. As Mark Twain once said when he met an old friend on a train, "We steeped our souls in the reviving wine of the past." I walked past her bedroom, and there were medical bottles and prescriptions that filled the top of her dresser and her rosary that she prayed with each night. I walked into her room and picked up her rosary and looked around her bedroom and took in a deep long breath, laid on her bed for a fast minute, got up, and walked into the kitchen, and returned with the Ensure and sat next to Mom setting on the couch.

"Thank you for your help," Mom said and reached for the Ensure.

"I only wish I could do more, Mom."

"You have always done more than enough," Mom said and gently tapped my knee.

Then she looked around the living room. "I am so happy to be sitting here on my blue couch. What a relief and comfort it is to just be in your own home after being away for so long!"

"I know you are, Mom. I guess there really is no place like home."

"That's right, Laurel, not just my home, but this neighborhood in the Cleveland South Side. You know your dad always said that this is the best neighborhood in all of Cleveland."

"I remember, Mom. He never wanted to move. He was happy here," I said, looking over at my mother who reached for the Ensure and drank a little.

"Dad had a point. Why move? You have everything you need right here."

Mom took a drink, placed the Ensure on the table, and said, "No, Dad never wanted to move, this was his South Side, and I grew to love it as much as him," Mom said and a soft smile came across her face.

"Well, Mom you need some rest."

"I will not argue with you on that point, Laurel. Seems like anymore I'm always tired."

Mom started to get up a little too fast and lost her balance. I jumped up fast and was by her side helping her walk into her bedroom. Mom reached for her rosary, climbed into her bed, and she closed her eyes. And before I returned with her Ensure, I found her fast asleep.

I leaned against the dresser, moving her pill bottles aside, and took a last look at my sweet Mother. She seemed to be getting weaker by the day and by the hour. I thought, *"What do I do now?"*

I realized that I needed to pray for my mother. I prayed to God that he would take her home in a less painful manner and let her suffering stop. Or, do I become selfish and pray for her life to go on here for me because I just couldn't bear to let her go. Do I pray for life and not death? Seeing her like this was not easy; it tore me up in words that I cannot explain.

So I simply dropped my head and prayed for my mother that God's will would be done. In the next five short days, after my mother came home she passed away in her sleep in her own bedroom with her own comfortable surroundings—the home that she loved raising a family in. She ended her life in the place where we had every holiday dinner, every bit of enjoyment sitting together in the front room watching a movie, or watching our home town sports teams. In the house, I could feel every sacrifice Mom made so that we could have life a little easier.

We had all the good and bad times nestled in this old house.

Each and every memory and custom Mom valued was within these walls. That was Mom's world; her family and home that she had held dear to her heart.

I am thankful to the heavens that Mom passed in her home. I cannot think of a better place for my mother to pass this life and go on to the beauty of the heavens. This was the home that my father shared with his Miss America. I know that together up in heaven Dad and Mom are both taking turns holding my baby boy Nicholas and that thought makes this painful experience a little easier. I looked up to the heavens and said to myself in silent prayer, "Until we all meet again, all I can say is, thank you both for being my parents. I am thankful for all the compromises, sacrifices, and the commitment you both had to the ideal of family first, the rest of the world later. What a gift you both have given to me! I am especially grateful for the shopping cart that was always filled with love. Both of you will remain forever in my heart until we see each other again in the next life."

CPSIA information can be obtained at www.ICGtesting.com
Printed in the USA
BVOW080606190313

315823BV00001B/3/P